THE MEASURE OF MA

"Fascinating . . . A forensic psychologist reveals t.... motives that challenge our justice system and opens up the troubling workings of the human mind."
—**Robert K. Tanenbaum**, author of *Capture*

"Compelling . . . Dr. Cheryl Paradis offers a window into the world of a clinical psychologist who has made many assessments for the courts."
—**Katherine Ramsland,** author of *The Criminal Mind*

"Eloquent . . . Anyone concerned with the relationship between deviance and mental illness will find this excellent book to be of great value."
—**Simon Baatz,** author of *For the Thrill of It: Leopold, Loeb and the Murder That Shocked Chicago*

"Clearly written and comprehensive. . . . Dr. Paradis skillfully leads the reader through the labyrinth of the psychotic criminal mind and the maze of the judicial system."
—**Barbara Kirwin**, author of *The Mad, the Bad, and the Innocent*

"Insightful, remarkable . . . not to be missed if you want to understand the real-world dramas that underlie criminal justice."
—**Barbara Oakley,** author of *Evil Genes*

"Informative, discussion-provoking . . . a much needed, intriguing collection of personal reflections as well as fascinating cases."
—**Thomas M. O'Rourke,** director of forensic psychiatry, Kings County Hospital Center

"Riveting . . . Cheryl Paradis shows us a world rarely seen and one full of mystery."
—**John Coston,** author of *To Kill and Kill Again* and *Sleep My Child Forever*

THE MEASURE OF MADNESS

Inside the Disturbed and Disturbing Criminal Mind

CHERYL PARADIS

CITADEL PRESS
Kensington Publishing Corp.
www.kensingtonbooks.com

CITADEL PRESS BOOKS are published by

Kensington Publishing Corp.
119 West 40th Street
New York, NY 10018

All Kensington titles, imprints, and distributed lines are available at special quantity discounts for bulk purchases for sales promotions, premiums, fund-raising, educational, or institutional use. Special book excerpts or customized printings can also be created to fit specific needs. For details, write or phone the office of the Kensington special sales manager: Kensington Publishing Corp., 119 West 40th Street, New York, NY 10018, attn: Special Sales Department; phone 1-800-221-2647.

CITADEL PRESS and the Citadel logo are Reg. U.S. Pat. & TM Off.

First printing: July 2010

10 9 8 7 6 5 4 3 2 1

Printed in the United States of America

Library of Congress Control Number: 2010924994

ISBN-13: 978-0-8065-3105-2
ISBN-10: 0-8065-3105-3

I DEDICATE THIS BOOK TO MY FATHER,
HAROLD PARADIS,
FOR ALWAYS BELIEVING IN ME.

CONTENTS

FOREWORD

by Katherine Ramsland

Andrea Yates drowned her five children one morning before she called 911 and turned herself in. Despite a long and complex history of hallucinations, delusions, and suicidal depression, in the courtroom, months later, she seemed composed. A videotaped interview revealed that just after the quintuple homicide, she'd responded to questions without noticeable emotion, explaining why her children had to die. She looked exhausted and her words were forced, but she appeared oblivious to the enormity of what she had done. People around the world were stunned that anyone—even a killer—could be so seemingly blasé.

Serious mental illness can be camouflaged. Sufferers might dress well, respond to questions, and have a considered rationale for the murders, rapes, assaults, arsons, or thefts they have perpetrated. By the time they reach trial, they may seem even more normal because medication has restored their clarity. Thus, it can be difficult for ordinary people to accept psychological evaluations of offenders that "excuse" them. The media shows us that the psychotic are wild-eyed, slovenly, jabbering, and deranged—and sometimes they are. But not always. People with little background in psychology can be quite surprised by the diverse manifestations of serious mental

IX

illness. Therefore, an important task for a forensic psychologist offering expert testimony is to educate. But how do you persuade members of the TV-viewing public who sit on a jury that a composed, articulate person was too delusional during the commission of a crime to be criminally responsible?

This is one reason why the insanity defense is rarely used. Many jurors are suspicious of professionals who try to diminish the heinousness of an offender's harm to others. In addition, some are so attuned to media stereotypes that their preconceptions deflect what a psychologist says. But there's another factor as well, which is often ignored: mental health professionals must also deal with inaccurate stereotypes about their own role.

While a great deal of attention has been devoted to how the "*CSI* effect" has influenced the way laypeople understand forensic science, we've heard little mention of its impact on the perception of forensic psychology. Mental health professionals have shown up as characters on television shows such as *Law and Order, CSI, Bones*, and *Criminal Minds*. As a result, laypeople develop erroneous ideas. Whenever I say "forensic psychology" to nonprofessionals, I hear a range of impressions: Some people believe that forensic psychologists are investigators or that they deal primarily with serial killers. Others recall images of out-of-touch academics whom clever criminals can easily dupe, of greedy entrepreneurs promoting their own theories, or of "hired guns" saying whatever an attorney needs them to say to win a case. Only a few programs show how such professionals actually work. What, then, is a forensic psychologist? What does such a professional actually do?

Forensic psychology is the application of psychological concepts, practice, and research to the legal and investigative arena. While this covers a range of activities, the two most common for clinical psychologists are the assessment of competency to stand trial and the assessment of a defendant's mental state at the time of an offense (the "MSO"). Most people have heard of the latter, so let's focus on it for a moment.

The law recognizes that responsibility for committing a crime depends on two things: *actus reus*, or evidence that the accused could or did engage in the act, and *mens rea*, the mental state required to have intended to commit the act or foreseen its consequences. The legal system assumes that people are generally rational and can make decisions for which they are morally responsible. Mental health professionals, however, may discover psychological factors that erode an offender's culpability. Triers of fact (the judge or jury) must then consider excusing the behavior of those with diminished or absent *mens rea*. Although the defense of "not guilty by reason of insanity" is rarely used, poorly handled cases can draw the media spotlight.

Edmund Kemper, who'd killed his grandparents in 1964, when he was fifteen, was diagnosed with paranoid schizophrenia but released six years later from juvenile detention. He then picked up, murdered, and dismembered hitchhiking coeds in Santa Cruz, California. At the time of his post-release evaluation by a team of psychiatrists, who pronounced him cured, he had the head of one victim in the trunk of his car outside. Such stories sully the mental health profession, and people on juries remember them. So it's important to contrast the normal course of an evaluation and its consequences against these aberrant cases.

To be effective, forensic psychologists must know the operations and expectations of the court. As expert witnesses, they must be credible, confident, competent, and prepared. They should understand that the court prefers clear decisions, jargon-free evaluations, and objective information that directly address the issues at hand. While they must offer information that can assist those who will decide on guilt or innocence, they should refrain from making this decision themselves. They must also resist an attorney's attempt to persuade them about what to say.

In addition to competency and insanity evaluations, forensic psychologists appraise behaviors such as malingering (faking an illness), confessing, and threatening suicide. As consultants, psychologists may assist a forensic artist with behavioral factors for a facial reconstruction, or they may help an attorney select a jury. They might defuse a potentially violent situation with negotiation, offer a threat assessment, or assist a coroner with an ambiguous death determination. Some psychologists are employed at police departments to determine fitness for duty or perform trauma counseling. Many others work in prisons or hospitals for the criminally insane. Psychologists may also participate in forensic work outside the courtroom, including consulting for a cold-case team or a serial killer task force.

In this compelling collection of stories from a twenty-five year career, Dr. Cheryl Paradis offers a window into the world of a clinical psychologist who has made many assessments for the courts. Whether for the prosecution or defense, her job is to remain neutral as she offers the results of her interviews, assessment instruments, and observations of a range of disturbed people—and those who merely pretend they're disturbed. She's been hired to evaluate a person's present mental ability to stand trial, to waive rights, or to confess, and she's evaluated whether certain offenders appreciated the difference between right and wrong while committing their crimes. Her clients in the following chapters include an angry juvenile, a battered woman, a psychotic arsonist, a clever con man, a range of liars, and even an accused cannibal. What keeps you reading is that, while the issues from one case to another are similar, each case is also unique. Many are surprising.

In the end, forensic psychology is really about the defendants, and Dr. Paradis wisely recalls one of her earliest lessons: "Don't believe everything your patients tell you." In other words, listen with your third ear: Gather the facts as they know them, but be wise to their agendas and/or illnesses. This advice covers not just the delusional, but also connivers, psychopaths, and people with poor or distorted memories. While Dr. Paradis explains the steps of her clinical evaluations, the manifestations of mental illness (or its faux counterpart) take center stage, framed within important legal precedents. It's clear that these tales are not about therapy sessions and that the forensic psychologist is not a defendant's advocate. She's an essential player in a complex and difficult legal proceeding.

Psychologists who testify must be prepared for anything—aggressive attorneys, confused jurors, canceled sessions, and even uncooperative defendants. They do not make moral judgments or apportion blame. They simply make an assessment to the best of their ability and let the chips fall where they may. They may not know the outcome of a case unless they make an effort to find out. What makes these stories most compelling is Dr. Paradis's compassion. Once her part is over, she still wants to know what happened to the people she evaluated, so we get the end of the story. There's little doubt that this work is challenging, even risky at times, and it can be both depressing and satisfying. One thing is for sure: Each case offers something to make us ponder what it means to be human. Whether it's a demented mother with fatal religious delusions, a scheming psychopath hoping to slip his bonds, a person who cooks the flesh off his former friend, or a frightened victim acting out, each and every person's behavior teaches us about the human condition.

—Katherine Ramsland, Ph.D.
Chair, Department of Social Sciences at DeSales University
Associate professor of forensic psychology
Author of *The Criminal Mind: A Writers' Guide to
Forensic Psychology*

THE MEASURE
OF
MADNESS

INTRODUCTION

It was humid, I was sweating, and it was only eight o'clock in the morning. I realized how nervous I was walking past the old hospital buildings to find "the Annex," a dilapidated brick building housing the psychology department. It was July 1, 1985, the first day of my internship.

I sat down in the lobby with the other six interns and started filling out employment forms. We had to choose the department where we wanted to work for our first three-month clinical rotation. The only air-conditioned area in the old "G Building" of the psychiatric hospital was the jail ward. I quickly raised my hand to volunteer.

It wasn't that I was particularly interested in working with mentally ill defendants, but I hated the heat. To this day I am amazed that my entire career hinged on that minor decision. I became a forensic psychologist simply because it was hot that day.

Before my internship I had vague plans to develop a psychotherapy practice. That's what I thought most psychologists did. I expected I would spend the next forty years sitting in an office, treating patients—most, the "worried well"—one per hour.

That all changed after a few weeks on the psychiatric jail ward.

I recall one of my first patients was a withdrawn man charged with violating an order of protection against his neighbor. He did not seem especially interesting, until he started to describe how his neighbors installed listening devices in his apartment and "someone" was sending messages through his television. I can't remember what message was being sent to his television, but I know the one I got—"these forensic patients are much more interesting than anxious neurotics." Many were driven by hallucinations and delusions to hurt or kill people they loved. Their violent acts made me question my beliefs about free will, responsibility, and punishment.

It's been a long time since I completed my internship. Over the past twenty-five years I have evaluated thousands of disturbed and disturbing defendants. As a forensic psychologist my responsibilities are different than those of other psychologists. I must put away my "treatment" hat to think more like a detective. I often remember the advice of my first supervisor on the jail unit. He'd grin while warning me, "Don't believe everything your patients tell you."

Perhaps the most important lesson I have learned is not to accept a defendant's version of a crime. Instead I search for clues in their past—in court, school, and hospital records. I came to appreciate the advice of another supervisor who often said, "History is gold."

In the following chapters I include eighteen of my most intriguing, puzzling, and challenging cases. The first part includes cases of defendants raising a variety of psychiatric defenses at trial, such as insanity and extreme emotional disturbance. In the second part I describe a series of cases of defendants undergoing two types of evaluations: competency to stand trial and competency to waive Miranda rights. Competency to stand trial is the legal term indicating a defendant can work with his attorney and assist in his defense. Competency to waive Miranda rights refers to whether a defendant understands his legal protections against self-incrimination when he confesses to a crime. In the third part I include cases concerning juveniles and the justice system and the assessment of dangerousness and malingering or faking symptoms.

All cases are real and much of the dialogue is taken verbatim from my notes. Some of the dialogue and court testimony are based on my best recollections. At the beginning of each interview I inform each defendant that our conversations are not confidential. However, I still use pseudonyms and disguise most defendants' identities by changing or eliminating biographical or legal information.

I spend between ten to twenty hours with most defendants, and in this small window of time I try to see the world as they do. My job is not to pronounce guilt or innocence, but rather to understand what motivates them. Questions of responsibility and blame are not easy to answer when a defendant is mentally ill or suffers from brain damage. If a man obeys the voice of God instructing him to attack his mother, for example, is he really guilty and responsible for committing this crime? And should he be imprisoned or sent to a psychiatric hospital? These are the moral dilemmas I face every day in my work with mentally ill defendants. I hope these stories convey to you the excitement and challenges of my work as a forensic psychologist as I enter each defendant's world to measure the madness.

PART 1

*Evaluations of Mental State at the Time
of the Offense*

S ometimes, when I am retained to evaluate a defendant, there is no question about whether he or she is guilty of the crime. In all of the cases in the first part of this book, the defendants had already confessed and my job was to assess their mental state at the time of the crime.

It is the burden of the defense to prove that a defendant was insane or lacked criminal responsibility for his or her conduct. In other words, it must be proved that "at the time of such conduct, as a result of mental disease or defect, he lacked substantial capacity to know or appreciate either: (1) the nature and consequences of such conduct; or (2) that such conduct was wrong."[1]

The general public inaccurately believes that the insanity defense is widely used and is frequently successful. In actuality, this is not the case. The insanity defense is only raised in approximately one percent of cases and successful in approximately 20 percent of these cases.[2]

If a defendant is judged to be insane, he or she is legally not guilty of the offense. Typically, the individual is then sent to a forensic psychiatric hospital. By law, he would remain there until the presiding judge rules he is no longer dangerously mentally ill. At that point he would be transferred to a state psychiatric hospital and, if his condition continued to improve, after a period of time (usually measured in years), he could be released to the community.

The first part of *The Measure of Madness* deals with fourteen cases in which the legal question was the defendants' states of mind at the time they committed their crimes. Mr. Paulson confessed to killing his wife, but claimed he loved her. Mr. Abrams was also charged with the murder of his wife, but he insisted that he had no memory of it. In one chapter I discuss my work with Daniel Rakowitz who became headline news after his arrest for the killing of his roommate. It was rumored that he cooked her remains. Mr. Bailey was one of the most heartbreaking cases. He was only 22 years old when he aimed his gun at a group of police officers in an apparent "suicide by cop." In one chapter I review the cases of four bizarre and psychotic defendants who were charged with the murder or attempted murder of strangers. One claimed the victims were aliens and another insisted he was an undercover agent and the victim had "come back from the dead."

Yet another chapter in this part details the cases of two young women who raised a different psychiatric defense. Both claimed to be suffering from Battered Woman's Syndrome and raised the defense of extreme emotional disturbance. One was nine months pregnant when she stabbed her sleeping husband and then slit her own wrists. The other told me she was hearing voices at the time she killed her husband.

The defense for both these women hinged upon whether they acted "under the influence of extreme emotional disturbance for which there was a reasonable explanation or excuse, the reasonableness of which is to be determined from the viewpoint of a person in the defendant's situation under the circumstances as the defendant believed them to be."[3]

If these women were found to have acted under extreme emotional disturbance, they would still be convicted of a crime, but the degree of the crime would be lessened. Instead of being convicted of murder, the women would be convicted of manslaughter. In one of these cases I was hired by the defense attorney, in the other, by the prosecution. In both cases I needed to put myself in the position of these women to understand what drove them to kill.

Chapter 1

THE WIDOWER WALKS AWAY

Her body landed on the sidewalk. Did she jump or was she pushed? None of those crowded around could be sure. The police identified her as a resident of the apartment building. Minutes later, a man exited the building and began to stroll nonchalantly down the block. The neighbors identified him as the victim's husband, Mr. Paulson. The police asked him to take them up to his apartment. Signs of his futile attempts to clean up the apartment were more than enough to raise their suspicions. Within a few hours he confessed—he had strangled his wife, then thrown her body out the window to fake a suicide.

Mr. Paulson's attorney quickly realized that all the evidence pointed toward his client's guilt but that the act itself made no sense. How could Mr. Paulson kill his wife when he professed to love her? His client could not adequately explain his motive. All he said was that there had been an "argument."

Typically, when one spouse kills the other, there is a long history of severe marital difficulties, and substance abuse, or mental illness, or both. But Mr. Paulson had no history of emotional problems. He had never been arrested or behaved violently. Everyone involved in the case was confused.

It was necessary to bring in experts to search for psychiatric issues that could be raised as a defense to save Mr. Paulson from spending the rest of his life behind bars. His attorney called Dr. Daniel Schwartz who had years of experience as an expert witness. Dr. Schwartz, the director of Forensic Psychiatric Services at Kings County Hospital, was well known for his work on numerous high profile cases, including the Son of Sam, the Amityville Horror killer, and John Chapman, the man who shot John Lennon.

I was a newly licensed clinical psychologist and excited to be working on a forensic inpatient psychiatric unit. I had only been there a year when Dr. Schwartz asked for my help on this high profile case. I was surprised to learn that Dr. Schwartz had been unable to uncover any evidence of mental illness in Mr. Paulson.

"Cheryl, I examined him," Dr. Schwartz said, "I felt I was missing something. I don't know what was wrong with him."

"What do you mean?" I asked.

"He wasn't a violent man," Dr. Schwartz replied. "And the police knew it. When they took him to the precinct for questioning, they didn't handcuff him. In all my years in this field, I've never seen the police do that. They always handcuff suspects."

Dr. Schwartz asked me to administer some psychological tests. He was puzzled by the defendant's flat emotional state and hoped that the tests would help explain his uncharacteristic homicidal rage. Dr. Schwartz also asked me to conduct a neuropsychological evaluation of Mr. Paulson's perceptual motor skills, language functioning, problem solving, and complex reasoning abilities. There were much more experienced psychologists working on the forensic unit, but I was the only one trained to administer these specialized tests of brain function.

Before leaving for my appointment with Mr. Paulson, I asked for advice from a senior level neuropsychologist, Lucille Horn, Ph.D. We sat in her office and I told her what I knew about the case.

"And here's the strangest part," I said. "Dr. Schwartz told me the defendant had a 'neurological event' about forty years ago, but was never diagnosed with anything. He was hospitalized twice after he suddenly developed speech difficulties and weakness on the right side of his body. The symptoms resolved after a few months and he never relapsed."

As we talked, I began packing, doing my best.to take only those tests I would need. The tests were heavy and I was taking the subway.

"Well, you have to take the Purdue Pegboard," Dr. Horn said, gesturing at the large wooden board.[1]

"That?" I stared at it in dismay. It was 3-feet by 2-feet, easily the bulkiest of the tests in the room. But looking at her face, I knew better than to ignore her suggestion. She was the expert; I had to bring it. The Purdue Pegboard measures fine motor coordination and speed, and could reveal whether or not Mr. Paulson still suffered from brain dysfunction.

An hour later I arrived at my office. Usually the defendants I interview are incarcerated and too poor to make bail. I interview them in the forensic hospital, court holding areas, or at Riker's Island jail. I was meeting Mr. Paulson in my outpatient office, since he was out on bail.

I was somewhat taken aback when the elegantly dressed, 70-year-old man arrived at my office. While I knew the general facts about the case, I was unprepared for such a soft-spoken, polite defendant. With his gray hair, courtly manner, and easy smile, he actually reminded me of a favorite uncle. It was hard to remember that this reserved old man had strangled his wife and thrown her body out their twelfth floor apartment window.

I felt a rush of discomfort when Mr. Paulson walked into the room. He reached out to shake my hand and I experienced a sense of role reversal. His age and expensive suit made me feel like I was the one about to be evaluated. I wondered if he noticed the shabbiness of my office furniture.

Typically, I might be apprehensive to stay alone with a defendant charged with murder. However, Mr. Paulson's composure put me at ease. Later, I became more aware of how peculiar his equanimity was in such a situation. His calmness was out of place. Most individuals faced with such serious charges and the distinct possibility of spending the rest of their lives incarcerated would be extremely anxious or depressed. He denied any symptoms of mental illness and I observed none.

We took our seats. At least I was able to maintain enough equilibrium to sit on my side of the desk. I started the interview with the Mini Mental Status Exam (MMSE), a brief screening test of cognitive functioning that takes approximately ten minutes to administer.[2] It is widely used in medical and psychiatric settings to test for dementia. The test is composed of a series of questions to assess language skills, memory, and attention. Mr. Paulson passed easily.

Then I asked, as politely as possible, what had led to the killing. There are two big sources of conflict in any marriage: money and sex. Had Mr. Paulson or his wife been spending too much or hiding assets? Was one of them having an affair? He denied any serious financial or marital problems.

"What happened before you attacked her?" I asked.

"We had been arguing," Mr. Paulson readily admitted.

He then continued to explain dispassionately how, as with so many marital conflicts, theirs had begun as an argument about bills. He was an independent businessman, an importer, and business had been slow recently. While there was no objective reason to fear bankruptcy, he was feeling stressed. Mr. Paulson insisted that they cut their spending but his wife was resistant. They started to argue about a few recent purchases of hers that he considered excessive and unnecessary and then began to argue about the children.

I realized by this point that Mr. Paulson's typical pattern during their quarrels was to retreat and give in, saying, "O.K. honey, whatever you want." But this argument was different in important aspects. It escalated and became personal and bitter. He recalled how he tried to end the conflict by retreating; however, his wife blocked his exit, would not let him leave, and, as he pushed to get past her, she attacked him physically, scratching him on the face.

Although Mr. Paulson claimed that he could not recall everything that happened after she scratched him, he did admit that he had became enraged, angrier than he had ever been in his life. He remembered slapping her and, when she continued to scratch him, strangling her to death. He admitted feeling overwhelmed with panic afterwards and throwing her body out the window in a desperate attempt to stage a suicide.

After listening to his story about the argument and how he had strangled his wife, I refocused back to a less emotional part of the evaluation—the psychological testing. I continued with a typical battery of psychological tests, including the Wechsler Adult Intelligence Scale, the Rorschach or "inkblot test," and the House-Tree-Person drawings.[3]

In the Rorschach, an individual views ten inkblots and provides responses to the query "What might this be?" The individual's responses are thought to be important clues to underlying, unconscious thoughts and feelings. Frequently, psychotic individuals can respond with images which do not even conform to the blots. The House-Tree-Person drawings require a person to draw four pictures, one each of a house, a tree, a man, and a woman. Psychologists analyze both the content and the process—how the person completes the drawings, what the person includes (and leaves out), and what parts the person emphasizes. All provide important clues as to a person's mental state, feelings, and concerns.

Mr. Paulson's personality testing indicated that, while he had an extremely limited emotional range and a rigid, over-controlled manner, he was not depressed or psychotic. My jaw almost dropped, however, as I watched him draw the female—she was nude! What was even more unexpected was that this nude woman was wearing high-heeled boots.

While artists frequently draw nudes, it was a strange and puzzling drawing for someone of his background. While I did initially consider whether his drawing reflected some unconscious feelings about women, I instead concluded that he, at least during this task, showed poor judgment and self awareness—most intelligent defendants charged with murder would be careful to try to look as normal as possible and draw the female clothed.

Next, I administered the Wechsler Adult Intelligence Test.[4] Overall, Mr. Paulson had superior intellectual skills, but the tests revealed some subtle cognitive decline. He had trouble repeating back strings of numbers that I recited to him—a sign of attention problems. The more neuropsychological tests I administered, the more odd discrepancies I found. When I measured his verbal and visual memory skills, his verbal score was in the 45th percentile, but his visual score was in the 99th.

The Purdue Pegboard yielded the most striking results. I instructed Mr. Paulson to place pegs in the holes on the board as quickly as possible, first with his right hand and then with his left. He was right-handed, yet his left, nondominant hand was faster at placing the pegs. This was extremely unusual.

As I watched his right hand fumbling to insert the pegs, I remembered what Dr. Schwartz had said about the symptoms Mr. Paulson had exhibited decades earlier—weakness in the right side of his body and speech difficulties. The left cerebral cortex controls sensations and movement of the right side of the body and vice versa. His slower right hand indicated some dysfunction in the left hemisphere. The speech center is also located in the left hemisphere in most individuals. His history was more evidence of something wrong in his left cerebral hemisphere.

"Mr. Paulson, tell me about your hospitalizations forty years ago," I said. "What symptoms did you have?"

"It happened when I was twenty-four years old," he answered. "I started to have terrible headaches and trouble speaking." He told me he was admitted to a hospital twice but discharged each time after a few days when his symptoms disappeared. His hospitalizations occurred so long ago that sophisticated neurological tests were not yet in existence. There were no MRI (Magnetic Resonance Imagery) or PET (Positron Emission Tomography) scans to take.

Mr. Paulson recalled that the doctors performed a spinal tap. During a spinal tap a needle is placed into the spinal cavity to remove cerebral spinal fluid. The tap can find elevated protein levels, indicating an intracranial (within the brain) bleed. He recalled the doctors telling him he may have suffered some bleeding in his brain.

Mr. Paulson told me that he recovered within a few months with no lingering symptoms. Since he never experienced a recurrence, he paid little attention to what caused the two hospitalizations. Even when new, sophisticated brain scanning tests became available, he never considered going to a physician to investigate.

Looking at Mr. Paulson, I took a deep breath and folded my hands on the table. "Well, we're all done," I said. "The good news is you're not mentally ill. But I do want you to see a neurologist."

He accepted these results with the same bland expression he had been wearing all day. He shook my hand, thanked me for my time, and walked out. I never saw him again.

I called the defendant's attorney right away. "There's definitely something wrong in Mr. Paulson's brain. I think it's in his left cerebral hemisphere."

"What's the next step?"

"You should get him to a neurologist right away. He needs an MRI," I said.

After that, Mr. Paulson was referred to a prestigious hospital and evaluated by a team of the most well-respected neurologists and neuropsychologists in New York City. The attorney sent me a copy of their reports and the MRI scan. As I suspected, the MRI revealed an abnormality in his left cerebral cortex.

Mr. Paulson's MRI showed that an arachnoid cyst (a sack of fluid-filled tissue) had formed inside his skull but outside his brain. It developed in the protective lining, the arachnoid membrane, surrounding his brain, displacing his left temporal lobe, part of the frontal lobe, and the left middle cerebral artery. The cyst was huge, bigger than I had ever seen. I could not believe that he had lived all these years with the cyst slowly growing inside his skull without any obvious symptoms.

This kind of cyst is found in approximately 5 out of every 1,000 people. It can be present at birth or acquired later in life from an injury, and is usually asymptomatic. If the cyst grows large enough, however, it can cause a range of symptoms including cognitive problems, mood swings, headaches, dizziness, seizures, and psychosis, depending on the size and area of the brain affected.

Mr. Paulson was given an EEG (Electroencephalogram). Electrodes were placed on his scalp to measure brain electrical activity. He had a mild reduction of activity in the left hemisphere.

He was given a PET (Positron Emission Tomography) scan which produces a three-dimensional image of the brain. To create the image, the patient is given an intravenous injection of molecules such as glucose, to which small amounts of a radioactive material have been attached. The PET scanner detects the radioactive signal and generates an image of the tissues, possibly revealing abnormalities.

Mr. Paulson's PET scan showed that the cyst impaired function primarily in the regions in the left frontal lobe next to the cyst. The results were consistent with those of other tests. All the brain tests showed abnormal function in this brain area.

Dr. Schwartz and I discussed the significance of the medical tests. He would have to decide whether the results proved anything definitive about the defendant's mental state at the time of the offense. That was the million dollar question: was Mr. Paulson legally insane when he killed his wife?

"Have you ever heard of a psychiatric defense based on a brain cyst?" I asked.

"No, but clearly Mr. Paulson's cyst was affecting the functioning of the brain tissue around it," Dr. Schwartz said. "I'm convinced that his cyst played an important role in his impulsive attack."

We were silent for a moment. "I just wish someone had written down Mr. Paulson's statements when he was questioned by the police," Dr. Schwartz exclaimed suddenly. "It's strange that there are no police records of what he said when he was arrested." Typically detectives prepare reports of comments made by the defendant at the crime scene and during police interrogation. None seemed to exist in this case.

"What are you going to write in your report?" I asked.

"That Mr. Paulson was not responsible for the killing of his wife," he said.

I was not surprised by Dr. Schwartz's certainty. I believe he was as impressed as I was by the size of the defendant's cyst. A few days later, he gave me his report. It was short and to the point.

"It is this combination at the time of the present offense of dysfunctional frontal lobe pathways (due to the arachnoid cyst) and his wife's unusual, provocative behavior which in my professional opinion made it impossible for Mr. Paulson to appreciate the nature and consequences of his conduct or that it was wrong."[5]

Almost six months went by, and I got caught up in other cases. Dr. Schwartz called me one day to update me on a new turn of events. It turned out that Mr. Paulson's fate was riding on the admissibility of the PET scan at trial. The defense attorney was eager to use the PET scan results at the trial to convince the jury that his client's brain was so abnormal that he was not responsible for killing his wife.

The PET scan was a relatively new technology and the prosecution sought to exclude it from the trial, arguing that it was still an experimental test. The criteria for accepting scientific testimony is outlined by the 1923 Frye decision.[6] Scientific testimony is permitted if it is "generally accepted" in the scientific community.

Mr. Paulson's pretrial hearing, also known as a Frye Hearing, lasted several weeks. The presiding judge weighed testimony from many psychiatrists, neurologists, and experts in nuclear medicine. After hearing the scientific testimony, the judge ruled that the PET scan was widely accepted in the scientific community and could be presented during the trial itself.

I knew the prosecutor had offered Mr. Paulson a plea of murder in the second degree before the Frye hearing. On the day of jury selection, eleven days after the judge ruled that the PET scans were admissible, the prosecutor offered a much better plea—manslaughter. Mr. Paulson accepted and was sentenced to prison for seven to twenty-one years.

When I heard about Mr. Paulson's decision, I wondered what would have happened if he had gone to trial. Would the jury have believed that his cyst made him kill his wife? It would have been interesting to see how a jury would react to the psychiatric, neurological, and psychological testimony, but I understood his decision not to risk it. Perhaps he was afraid he would be convicted. Or he wanted to spare his children the trauma of a trial. Or he had run out of money to pay for his already quite expensive defense.

Years later, when Dr. Schwartz and I were discussing Mr. Paulson's case, he told me about a dramatic event that occurred the day before the trial was scheduled to begin. The prosecution "found" reports of Mr. Paulson's statements that he made to the police shortly after he killed his wife. For months before the trial, the defense attorney had been requesting all relevant records and had not been told of the existence of these transcripts.

Dr. Schwartz's usual cheerful and humorous tone of voice changed dramatically when he told me about the sudden appearance of these critical records.

"I read through those police notes for the first time right before the trial date," Dr. Schwartz said. "Mr. Paulson was incoherent at first. Only after hours of questioning did he start to make sense."

"What did you make of this?" I asked.

"Clearly, there was something wrong with him. If the prosecutor had turned over the statements when he should have, I would have realized immediately that Mr. Paulson had some kind of brain damage."

Dr. Schwartz's tone spoke volumes about his distaste for the prosecutor's tactics.

"I remember like it was yesterday when the police began video-taping defendants' interrogations," he said. "At the time I wondered why didn't they tape Mr. Paulson's confession?"

"What do you make of the whole thing?" I asked.

"I think they knew he wasn't in his right mind and they didn't want this captured on video!"

I am not sure what angered Dr. Schwartz more: the possibility that evidence had been unethically withheld, or that he had been unable to recognize Mr. Paulson's brain abnormality without the crucial police reports. I, on the other hand, was pleased that my neuropsychological testing detected the brain cyst. And, as a new-comer to the field, I was grateful to be given the extraordinary opportunity to play a part in a landmark case.

Not only was it the first case in which PET scan results were ruled admissible, it also became well-known by lawyers and forensic experts in the growing field of what is now called neurolaw. Neuroscience was beginning to transform the American legal system, and my Purdue Pegboard and I had been there at the beginning of it all. I can not thank Dr. Horn enough.

Chapter 2

A BOTCHED SUICIDE

It was 8:00 A.M. when the police officer finished his shift and signed out to go home. On his way out, he passed a thin, young man wearing a sweatshirt and sneakers. Something told him to look back. He turned around to get a better look, and at that moment the young man pulled out a gun. "I want to kill a cop," he said, and aimed at two other officers standing in front of the precinct. He pulled the trigger twice, and the gun misfired. The officers pulled out their guns and started shooting. The man fell to the ground, apparently wounded. When the commotion died down, it was discovered that not a single bullet had hit him.

Mr. Bailey was brought to the precinct in Queens, New York, where he signed a waiver of his Miranda rights. In a few scribbled paragraphs he explained that he had wanted to kill himself because he was infected with HIV. He had found a gun two weeks earlier and saw it as a sign from God. The night before the shooting he got on the subway and rode around in a loop for miles, thinking of ways to kill himself. When he got off the train near the precinct, he saw some policemen and thought, "I'll let them shoot me." He pointed the gun at the officers, aiming high so as not to hurt them, and yelled "Shoot me!" He heard gun shots, and, thinking he was hit, fell to the ground.

His confession concluded, "I didn't want anyone to die but me."

Mr. Bailey was taken to a psychiatric hospital immediately after his arrest. He told the staff that he was infected with AIDS and wanted to die, but could not bring himself to commit suicide. He was charged with six counts of attempted murder in the first degree, attempted assault, and criminal possession of a weapon.

Almost five months later I got a phone call from Mr. Bailey's defense attorney. He wanted me to assess his client for an insanity defense. After he filled me in on the details of the case, he told me a surprising fact—his client's HIV test was *negative*. The defendant had never been infected in the first place.

"Could this be a case of 'suicide by cop'?" he asked.

"It certainly seems so," I said.

"Suicide by cop" is a desperate act that is difficult for most people to understand. One of the earliest researchers of this phenomenon was Marvin Wolfgang. Of the 588 deaths he studied, he concluded that 26 percent could be classified as victim-precipitated suicide.[1] Daniel Kennedy and associates conducted a study in 1998 based on newspaper articles of 240 police shootings of which they determined nine were definitely suicide by police and another 28 could possibly be classified as such.[2]

Why commit suicide in this way? Some people want to go out in a blaze of glory, others lack the nerve to carry out the suicide act. Some want their families to collect on their insurance policy or even to create community unrest by provoking police violence. Many tell hostages they want to die, saying they prefer death over prison. Some even make religious references to resurrection.[3]

One of the earliest recorded examples of this behavior occurred in England in 1800, when James Hadfield entered the Haymarket Theater armed with a loaded pistol and shot at the king. One witness testified at the trial that Hadfield had told him, "I am a man tired of life; my plan is not to take away my own life, I sought therefore to get rid of it by other means; I did not mean to take away the life of the king, but I thought this attempt would answer my purpose as well." A judge later found that he was insane and ordered him confined to a psychiatric hospital.[4]

Mr. Bailey's attorney sent me a packet of legal and medical records to review. I picked up the grand jury minutes first. The grand jury is a group of people who hear evidence presented by the prosecution and vote whether there is enough evidence to indict the defendant for trial.

Five officers had testified in the grand jury. I read through their testimony and imagined how those officers must have felt when Mr. Bailey aimed a gun at them. One testified that the suspect "stopped about ten feet away from me and my partner, turned, pointed it at me and my partner, and pulled the trigger again. I heard the gun click . . . after I heard him pull the trigger, I heard another round go off on my side, which I assume was my partner's. I ducked for cover."[5]

His partner testified that he fired at the suspect and saw him fall. A third officer testified that he saw the suspect clench his stomach and collapse. A fourth recalled that he yelled, "Police, stop! Drop the gun!" He described the clicking sound of the suspect's gun. "At this time I thought he was shooting at me," the officer said. "I just let off a couple of rounds 'cause I thought he was going to kill another cop. I thought he was going to kill me . . . I had no choice but to try to neutralize the threat. . . . [I felt] scared, scared that I was going to get shot or killed."[6]

How did all the officers miss when they shot at Mr. Bailey? I wondered.

I tried to imagine how the policemen felt when they made that split-second decision to fire. I understood from personal experience how the police might have panicked and shot wildly. In 1981, my husband and I were held hostage in a bank's automatic teller lobby. It was early evening when we walked in. A man pointed a gun at us and told my husband to take out money from the cash machine. Looking around the small vestibule, I realized that there were a few other people being held hostage by a second gunman. The minutes seemed to pass unnaturally slow as more customers walked in, unaware of the robbery in progress. Each one looked horrified as soon as they realized what was going on.

Whether it was because I was young, naïve, or in shock, I did not understand the gravity of the situation. I felt strangely calm as the room filled with hostages. Eventually there were about fifteen of us crowded together. Fortunately, someone had a friend waiting outside who, after a long wait, became alarmed and called the police.

That's when the situation devolved into chaos. It seemed to me that almost fifty police officers were waiting outside as the gunmen started out the door, using two hostages as human shields. As soon as they opened the door, I heard dozens of gun shots being fired. We dropped to the floor as glass broke over our heads and bullets ricocheted off the walls. The shooting seemed to last forever, although in reality, it was just a few minutes. Luckily, one of the hostages was an off-duty police officer. He threw his badge out the open door and the barrage of bullets stopped. Miraculously, none of the hostages was injured. I heard the police whispering to each other afterwards, "Who started shooting?" they all asked.

My memory of this terrifying experience made me wonder if the police who shot wildly at Mr. Bailey were also in a panic. I heard from another attorney that they actually shot into a store behind the suspect, barely missing the owner.

The next day, I went to interview the defendant. When I arrived at the Supreme Court building, I took the elevator to the third floor and knocked on the door labeled "Corrections Department." The plate covering the small viewing window slid aside and the officer peered at me, then looked down at the I.D. badge I held up. The key turned and the heavy metal door opened. Once inside, I stopped to chat with the officers sitting behind the high desk in the front office, who invited me to help myself to some coffee. I grabbed a cup and headed toward the back where the cells and interview offices were located. I felt the familiar stab of guilt as I walked past the row of cells.

"Are you an attorney?" one defendant called out to me. "Do you know when I'm going to court?" I kept my head down, trying to avoid eye contact. The last thing I wanted was to be pulled into conversations with the desperate men waiting there.

I left my bags in a locker outside the offices, said a brief hello to the on-duty officer, and gulped down the rest of my coffee. Then I took a seat in the largest interview room available. I did not have to wait long.

I have given up any preconceptions about defendants' appearances, but when Mr. Bailey walked into the interview room, I was struck by how young and shy he was. He was 20 years old, and at 5-feet 5-inches tall, weighed only about 145 pounds. I would never have pegged him as a man charged with the attempted murder of police officers.

Mr. Bailey grew up in Jamaica. His parents were unmarried and both moved separately to the United States, leaving him to be raised by his maternal grandmother. His early life was unremarkable; he had no history of developmental delays, medical problems, or abuse. He told me that he never liked school and dropped out when he was 15 years old.

"What kind of grades did you get?"

"I was an average student, not perfect."

"And your reading?"

"I could read, just not as good as everyone," he admitted. He sounded defensive.

Mr. Bailey's hair was in dreadlocks and I was not surprised when he told me he became a "Rasta" (Rastafarian) at age sixteen. I knew only a little about the Rastafarian movement and Mr. Bailey willingly gave me a brief history. The movement emerged in Jamaica in the 1930s and currently 5–10 percent of the Jamaican population identify themselves as Rastas. They accept the former leader of Ethiopia, Haile Selassie, as the Messiah and God incarnate. They have prohibitions against cutting their hair and avoid eating meat, smoking tobacco, and drinking alcohol. The Rasta movement emphasizes the spiritual use of marijuana. Mr. Bailey told me he smoked marijuana every day and did not consider it a problem for him. I, of course, had a different opinion.

Mr. Bailey left home when he was nineteen and came to New York City to strike out on his own. He found a place to live with a few other young men from the Caribbean. He worked six days a week in a furniture store, yet he was barely able to support himself.

"Did you ask your family for help?" I asked. "No," he said, "I was too embarrassed."

Mr. Bailey was lonely and wanted a girlfriend, but was too shy to approach women. He turned to the Internet and arranged to meet a woman he contacted through a chat room.

"At the time, when I sleep with her, I didn't trust her and my condom break," he mumbled and looked down at the floor. "And I thought about it all the time."

"Thought about what?"

"I start thinking that she had some disease. I didn't trust her. That same night I start worrying. I heard on the radio that the Bronx has the most HIV. She was from the Bronx."

"Did you get tested?" I asked.

"No," he said. "I was too scared. Everything was building up in my mind. I start getting skinny. I got so depressed and I could feel my nerves jump all over my body."

Mr. Bailey told me he started having frequent and debilitating "attacks" a few weeks after this sexual encounter.

"The attacks come most times at night, when I'm alone," he said. "My heart be racing and I feel like I'm out of breath."

"How often did this happen?"

"It be like every night," he recalled. "I be afraid to stay by myself. I was afraid I'd take my life."

Mr. Bailey told me that a few months after the sexual encounter he became convinced he was infected and fell into a deep depression.

"Did you ever hear voices when no one was there?" I asked.

"Yes, sometimes."

"What did the voices say?"

"They be telling me I got the HIV."

"Did you believe the voices?" I asked

"Yes. I start having diarrhea a month before I was arrested. I be thinking I have AIDS," he said, now in tears. "I'd get muscle cramps, aches and pains, joint pains, I thought it had something to do with HIV. I didn't think it could be anything else."

It might be surprising in this day of "infomercials" and media that someone would know so little about HIV infection that he could reach such an erroneous conclusion. But Mr. Bailey relied on a strange mix of medical jargon and superstition to explain why he was convinced he was infected.

I noticed that Mr. Bailey paused before answering my questions and spoke in short, simple sentences. I began to wonder if he was mentally slow. I administered the Wechsler Adult Intelligence Test and Mr. Bailey scored a 72, placing him at the low end of the borderline intellectual range.[7] The average I.Q. score ranges from 90 to 110; a score of 69 or less typically indicates mental retardation. Mr. Bailey's low I.Q. explained his inaccurate understanding of HIV symptoms and was probably a factor in his inability to find any solution to his supposed illness. He thought suicide was his only way out.

I asked why he did not call his family for help. He started tearing up again. "I figured I couldn't tell them I had HIV."

"Why not?" I gently pressed.

"I was afraid they'd close the door in my face," he replied, his voice cracking. "I thought they would tell me I wouldn't amount to nothing. My grandmother be nice, but I don't know how she'd act in a situation like this."

"Did you try to tell her?"

"No," he admitted. "Every time I thought about it, I worried. I don't want to be around my little brother and sister, especially with a disease that strong. I was thinking I don't want to be around people if I got HIV."

"Why not?"

"I think it's a total sin. A Rasta shouldn't carry this disease. If you have HIV you can't have kids or family. You don't get to marry. If you got HIV no one want to marry you."

Mr. Bailey told me that he was afraid to kill himself. He said, "I always hear if you kill yourself, you go to hell. Sometimes I'd think I didn't want anyone to know what was happening to me. If I just pass, no one will know."

"What happened during the weeks before the shooting?" I asked.

"I found a gun in a trash can. I thought everything was matching up. I got the gun now. God was working on a way for me to go home."

"What do you mean?" I said.

"I was thinking God wanted me to go to heaven, that's why he put the gun in my hand. I was thinking everything was matching up. There was no need for me to stay here anymore."

I asked him how he spent the night before the shooting. He told me that he was riding the subway because he had no place to sleep. He dozed fitfully until the idea came to him, as if sent by God.

"All I could think of was dying," he remembered. "I didn't want to live. I realized that if the police saw me with a pistol, they'd try to kill me."

"What happened next?" I asked.

"It was very early in the morning." He spoke softly, as if lost in a dream state. "I get off the train and start walking. I saw the precinct and I knew I got the pistol. I start waving it. The cops see me. I knew they are going to shoot me. I was trying to get killed. I wasn't trying to hide. I was standing up to take the bullet."

He paused, and I waited for him to continue.

"One shot was very loud and I thought it hit me. I went down. Then they start to hit me. I tell them to kill me and just get it over with."

Mr. Bailey insisted that he never had any intention of shooting the police officers. He never loaded the gun and did not think the gun could fire. A police ballistics expert who later examined the gun found it loaded with eight bullets. It was a 9 mm Luger which held ten bullets. No one knew what had happened to the two missing bullets. It was never determined whether Mr. Bailey fired the gun or not.

After the second session with Mr. Bailey, I was nearly convinced that his was a case of "suicide by cop," but I needed to be sure that he was not lying or faking. Malingerers—those who exaggerate or fake mental illness—often have trouble keeping their stories straight. I needed to reexamine Mr. Bailey's police and medical records to see if the story he told me matched the story he told everyone else.

Mr. Bailey's stories were consistent. Two days after his arrest, he told a psychiatrist that he wanted to die but saw no way out. He also told hospital staff that he had been hearing voices before the shooting. They diagnosed him with major depressive disorder with psychotic features and marijuana abuse.

I called Mr. Bailey's grandmother to get a clearer picture of his childhood and mental state before his arrest. She seemed to be a caring, well-intentioned woman, and I felt tempted to console her when I heard the guilt and self-reproach in her voice. "His friends told me he messed around with a girl and he thought he had AIDS," she recalled. "They told me he was very depressed and talked about suicide a lot."

"Did you speak to him around the time of the shooting?" I asked.

"No, but later, a friend told me that the night before everything happened, my grandson was depressed and talked about suicide. He told them to give me all his music CDs after he died. He told them there has to be a better place, a place without pain. And said he wanted to go home."

It was clear that, for Mr. Bailey and his grandmother, home meant heaven.

Mr. Bailey was the only defendant I have ever evaluated who provoked the police this way. It was an unusual case because he lived to tell his story. There have been other cases, however, that have not ended so well. Suicidal shooters more often than not get their wish; they are killed by police.

Suicide in any form is a tragedy; suicide by cop is doubly so. The officers are forced to live with the knowledge that they were unwilling participants in what amounts to an assisted suicide. It made me doubly relieved that no one was hurt in the case of Mr. Bailey. What truly amazed me was that the police had shot at him and missed. I have always wondered, on some unconscious level, did they miss on purpose, somehow aware that he was mentally ill and not truly dangerous?

My evaluation was complete. All the clinical and legal information was consistent with the defendant's own story. I believed that Mr. Bailey was depressed and psychotic when he aimed his gun at the police officers.

I was convinced that Mr. Bailey was delusional and could not appreciate the nature and consequences of his actions or their wrongfulness. He felt trapped and believed that suicide would lead to "burning in hell forever." When he found a gun disposed in a trash can he psychotically concluded, "God had given me a way; he wanted me to do it." His only salvation was to provoke the police to kill him. His solution was to pretend to shoot at them.

I wrote and submitted a report explaining my conclusions.

Now the ball was in the prosecutor's court. Months passed while I waited to hear who the assistant district attorney would hire to assess Mr. Bailey. Would he choose a "hired gun," someone who was more likely to view the defendant as guilty? I was more than ready to testify about my opinion, but juries are unpredictable, and I knew it was likely they would find him guilty. There would be no need for a trial if the prosecution-retained expert also believed that Mr. Bailey was not responsible for the crime.

I was relieved to hear that the prosecution's psychiatrist agreed with my diagnosis and opinion. He, too, concluded that this was a classic case of suicide by cop. Since we both found Mr. Bailey not responsible, the case never went to trial. He was one of very few defendants found not guilty by reason of insanity. Assistant District Attorney David Kelly once told me that, since 1965, there have been only one hundred and thirty-three such cases in Brooklyn, a county with a population that would make it one of the largest cities in the United States.[8]

Insanity acquitees, the legal term for individuals in his situation, are regularly evaluated to determine whether they are still dangerous and need to remain in a secure forensic hospital. Many individuals found not responsible are kept in secure forensic hospitals because they remain psychotic, even when medicated. They often spend more time in a hospital than they would have served in prison if they had pleaded guilty.

I recently heard from Mr. Bailey's attorney. His client was stable in the forensic hospital and his depression had not returned. His treatment was successful but his future remained uncertain. We chatted a bit about whether he would be transferred to a less secure state hospital. Would he then be released to the community?

The last I heard, Mr. Bailey was still a patient in the forensic hospital, four years after he was admitted.

Chapter 3

THE BUTCHER
OF TOMPKINS SQUARE PARK

There was no physical evidence found at the scene of the crime; all the blood had been cleaned up. Police searched a Port Authority Bus Terminal locker and found a five-gallon bucket containing Ms. Beerle's skull and some bones. Someone had spent a good deal of time and effort removing the flesh from the bones, bleaching them clean, and packing them up. The bucket contained chlorophyll-scented cat litter to mask the smell.

Daniel Rakowitz, 28 years old and mentally ill, was the primary suspect, and Ms. Beerle, the victim, had been his roommate. Many were convinced that he had cooked Ms. Beerle's remains and fed them to the homeless. He became known as "The Butcher of Tompkins Square Park." The nickname reflected the public's fascination with the case, fueled by months of extensive media coverage.

Like most New Yorkers, I had been following this case closely in the news. The murder took place on the Lower East Side, a neighborhood in Manhattan that was once the destination of thousands of European immigrants. In 1989, gentrification had not yet taken

over the neighborhood, and the run-down blocks were widely per-
ceived as a wasteland of drugs and homelessness.

The killing occurred only a few blocks from where I had lived
a couple of years earlier. Then an unemployed graduate student, I
shared a tiny second-floor apartment on 2nd street off Avenue A
with some friends. My former roommates and I talked about the
Rakowitz case as a symbol of everything that was wrong with the
city during those years.

Mr. Rakowitz's defense attorney, Norman Reimer, retained Dr.
Schwartz to evaluate his client. At the time of this case, Dr. Schwartz
was about 60 years old and had been Director of Forensic Services at
Kings County Hospital for almost thirty years. He was a nationally re-
nowned psychiatrist who often got called in on high profile cases. The
psychiatric unit at Kings County was also famous in forensic circles
for having admitted a number of notorious criminals over the years.

Dr. Schwartz ran the department democratically and made a
habit of inviting junior staff members to work on cases with him.
One morning, he called me into his office, "I'm evaluating Rakowitz
for an insanity defense," he said cheerfully. "Would you like to work
on this case?"

I was a newly licensed psychologist, having graduated only four
years earlier from my doctoral program in clinical psychology. I had
some experience taking the stand in more routine cases, but this
was the first time I would be testifying at a trial with so much media
attention.

"Yes!" I said. "I'd love to." Privately, though, I thought: I hope I
don't say anything really stupid at the trial.

All my pressing hospital work was put aside as Dr. Schwartz took
me through the complex story of Beerle's murder and Rakowitz's
arrest. I sat transfixed in his office for what seemed like hours.
Dr. Schwartz loved to tell stories, and he was in no rush.

His enthusiasm for bizarre crimes and difficult cases was evident, but his ebullience was a little at odds with the gory details of

this particular case. As we talked, I looked around at his diplomas and crime memorabilia, the bust of Freud on his desk, and the framed newspaper articles featuring him as the expert witness in famous cases. Then I looked back over at him. Dr. Schwartz was a short man—a fact accentuated by the large wooden desk he sat behind—yet his height never seemed to affect his confidence.

"I was hired to examine Rakowitz for competency to stand trial," he told me. It was a complicated hearing with three doctors testifying for the defense and two for the prosecution. Mr. Rakowitz was eager to be found competent and insisted on testifying at the hearing as well.

Dr. Schwartz leaned over his desk and handed me the judge's ruling. "Rakowitz's testimony was quite a spectacle. Three of us thought that Rakowitz was not competent but the judge ruled that he was able to stand trial." There was no hint of annoyance or wounded pride in his voice. Dr. Schwartz had testified in hundreds of cases and I assumed he was accustomed to having judges and juries disagree with his opinion.

Dr. Schwartz, always busy with hospital business, answered a few phone calls while I finished reading the judge's ruling. Then he went on. The murder allegedly occurred in August, but the police did not begin their investigation until September. During the weeks before his arrest, rumors spread through the community that Mr. Rakowitz had killed Ms. Beerle and cooked her remains to serve in soup.

Initially the police did not believe the defendant could commit such a violent crime. "Rakowitz was a colorful character," Dr. Schwartz said, "and the police thought he was harmless." Rakowitz must have appeared to them as one of the many drug addicted, mentally ill homeless people living around Tompkins Square Park.

"No blood evidence was found in the apartment," Dr. Schwartz continued, "but Rakowitz led the police to the Port Authority locker and confessed. He doesn't stand a chance to be found factually not guilty at trial."

Dr. Schwartz gave me a file of newspaper clippings to review.

In sensationalized cases like this one, the criminal always seems to steal the spotlight. I skimmed through the articles, trying to get a sense of who the victim was.

Monika Beerle was a 26 year old year old Swiss student. She was studying at the Martha Graham Center of Contemporary Dance and working as an exotic dancer. There was little objective information about the sequence of events that led to her murder, but it was believed that Mr. Rakowitz invited her to move in with him a few weeks before her disappearance. He had recently moved in to the inexpensive walk-up on East 9th Street, and the lease was held under the name of a few acquaintances. Soon after moving in, Ms. Beerle changed the lease to her name and demanded that Mr. Rakowitz move out.

The articles described Mr. Rakowitz as a strange character, even by New York standards. Originally from Texas, he had been living in New York City since 1985, eking out a meager living by selling marijuana. Frequently homeless, he was often seen carrying a chicken under his arm and proselytizing about the magical powers of marijuana. He referred to himself as the "God of Marijuana."

A photo showed a bizarre-looking man with blond hair, a scraggly unkempt beard, and piercing blue eyes. He was rail thin and bore an uncanny resemblance to the popular image of Jesus.

I took the subway to downtown Manhattan to meet with Mr. Rakowitz's lawyer. Mr. Reimer told me that his client had rejected a psychiatric defense. Mr. Rakowitz was deemed competent to stand trial so the law stipulated that he was also competent to refuse the insanity defense. Therefore, I was to limit my report to a description of his history and my opinion as to his psychiatric diagnosis.

Mr. Reimer handed me a packet of his client's legal and psychiatric records. He also gave me Mr. Rakowitz's videotaped confession. I couldn't wait to get home to watch it.

I felt a sense of anticipation as I pushed the tape into the VCR. Finally, I would be seeing Mr. Rakowitz in action. I was again struck by his resemblance to Jesus. I wondered if he cultivated that image, or if his physical appearance naturally fed into his delusions of divinity.

Mr. Rakowitz appeared fairly normal to me at the beginning of the tape. He was dressed neatly enough in a shiny thin jacket. He was friendly with the detectives and assistant district attorney. He chuckled and seemed oddly relaxed, considering how much trouble he was in.

Mr. Rakowitz began talking about the events leading up to Ms. Beerle's murder. He explained how he invited her to live with him. Their relationship quickly deteriorated when, within a few days of her moving in, his cat was killed by a pitbull when Ms. Beerle let the cat out of the apartment. There were also misunderstandings about his rent payments. He said she threatened to have him "beaten up" if he did not pay rent. She tried to kick him once.

Mr. Rakowitz then described their last confrontation. Soon after Ms. Beerle changed the lease to her name, she attacked him with a knife. He punched her once in the throat and she fell to the floor. He told the prosecutor that he never meant to seriously harm her. He had been angry, but he was acting in self-defense.

Incredibly, Mr. Rakowitz insisted that he thought she was "faking it" when she lay motionless on the floor, gurgling sounds coming from her throat. He stated that she did not *seem* to be breathing but he could hear her heart beating. He smoked a joint and left the apartment. When he returned, he found her body cold. Only then did he realize she was dead.

Mr. Rakowitz was afraid he would be arrested, so he decided to hide the evidence of her death. Over the next ten days, he dismembered her body in the bathtub and cooked the flesh. He claimed that other individuals came to the apartment in those weeks and saw the macabre scene.

I almost felt nauseated listening to Mr. Rakowitz's confession. He described the killing and dismembering in a strangely calm manner, as if it were no more than an unpleasant job assignment. I watched the video over and over and never saw a hint of remorse in his face or voice. He seemed rather to be appealing to the assistant district attorney for sympathy. He explained how "difficult" he found the job. He even went so far as to complain that he had trouble eating during those days.

If the confession was not strange enough, Mr. Rakowitz's beeper went off several times during the interrogation. I had never seen anything like it in a videotaped statement. He was being paged while confessing, presumably by individuals who wanted to buy marijuana from him.

Mr. Rakowitz smiled sheepishly when his beeper sounded, as if caught with his hand in the proverbial cookie jar. He even asked for a piece of paper to write the numbers down. He seemed to assume that he would be released later that day to make deliveries. Up until that point, the prosecutor and detectives had remained polite and businesslike, but after the beeper sounded for a third time, the impatience in their voices was notable. They commanded him to turn it off.

Mr. Rakowitz's psychosis leaked out approximately thirty minutes into the interview. He told the assistant district attorney that he tried to enlist in the FBI the year before to help prosecute satanic cult members. He had learned about the cults as an adolescent, he said, and knew that cult members used infants as human sacrifices.

Mr. Rakowitz implored the assistant district attorney to let him make amends for killing Ms. Beerle by working undercover to expose members of these satanic cults. He said that his arrest would give him the "street cred" necessary to gain control over the cult members and bring them to justice.

At this point in the interview I heard mumbling in the background. I figured that the prosecutor and the detectives were conferring about what to do next. I felt oddly amused by this. I could imagine their panic, now that the interview was spinning out of control and right into the hands of a defense attorney looking to plead insanity. Mr. Rakowitz was beginning to look less like a cold-blooded killer and more like a deranged lunatic.

The assistant district attorney abruptly interrupted Mr. Rakowitz's ramblings about satanic cults, announcing that they had talked long enough. I could not help smiling. I knew she did not want any more of Mr. Rakowitz's craziness to show up on the tape.

I bet the assistant district attorney wished she had stopped the interview earlier. I wondered how the case would have played out if she had ended the interview right after Mr. Rakowitz confessed to killing and dismembering Ms. Beerle. If the tape had stopped there, Mr. Rakowitz would have come across as a rational, but strange, individual. Yet she allowed him to keep talking.

It was an extraordinary confession. I was astonished to see that Mr. Rakowitz seemed to enjoy the interview, as if he did not realize that he was going to be charged with murder. I put the video away. It was time to see him in person.

When the corrections officer escorted Mr. Rakowitz to the drab interview room, I immediately noticed the drastic change in his appearance. He still had the long blond hair and beard, as well the cheerful grin, but now he had a definite paunch and full cheeks. He had gained a considerable amount of weight during his incarceration.

He reached out to shake my hand. He seemed eager to meet me and happy to be back in the spotlight. I could not decide if he did not understand the trouble he was in, or if he was just unrealistically confident about his chances at trial.

It was a challenging series of interviews. Mr. Rakowitz was clearly manic. I tried to write down his words verbatim, but he spoke too quickly for me to keep up. His thinking was so disorganized that he was impossible to follow at times and he often broke out into uncontrollable laughter.

Mr. Rakowitz frequently interrupted the testing with bizarre comments. He told me that very special things were going to happen to him in 1996. He might be elected sheriff, President of the United States, or the leader of a satanic cult whose members he would turn from bad to good. He told me his dreams could foretell the future.

I was struck by the sophisticated words he used. One of the best ways to estimate a person's I.Q. is by his or her vocabulary. I gave Mr. Rakowitz an I.Q. test and he only scored within the average range, but many of his scores on the individual subtests comprising the test were above average or superior. On the math subtest, for example, he answered every question correctly.

I administered several other tests referred to as projective or unstructured personality tests. I gave him the House-Tree-Person drawings, the Rorschach (Inkblot Test) and the Thematic Apperception Test.[1] Many individuals who appear psychologically healthy on the highly-structured I.Q. test reveal their psychotic thinking through these more ambiguous and unstructured tests.

Mr. Rakowitz's drawings were weird and disturbing. He drew a tree floating in space. It was as if he literally was not grounded. He drew a frenzy of leaves representing his disorganized, chaotic thoughts. Normal people draw a house with a door and windows. He drew a greenhouse with a marijuana plant in it. "You have to draw something people live in," I told him. He added a little line at the bottom and said, "Those are the steps to the basement." It was as if he created an invisible basement where no one could find him or even see him. He was totally alone with his marijuana.

After we finished with the tests, I asked Mr. Rakowitz about his case. To my surprise, he referred to the victim as "some woman" that his ex-roommates had killed. I confronted him with the medical expert's autopsy report but he told me he was not convinced that the body found by the police was actually Monika Beerle's.

I then asked Mr. Rakowitz why he confessed. He told me that he made the tape under duress, that the officers had threatened to kill him if he refused. He said he planted hidden, yet obvious, errors in the confession to alert viewers to its falseness. He described specific instances of this, but his explanations made no sense to me.

I returned home and carefully watched the tape over and over, looking for these "errors." I could not find any.

During the next session, Mr. Rakowitz told me that various people in the community were plotting against him. He was convinced that these people resented his divinity and his drug business. He said that both he and Monika Beerle had been placed in that apartment as part of a year-long plot to incriminate him.

Mr. Rakowitz described many other grandiose delusions. When I asked him to show me proof of his divinity, he said he did not have real physical proof until a few years ago when he looked at a certain picture. He recalled that, through divine intervention, he saw his own image emerge from the picture. The picture then morphed again into the image of a dog.

The next week, Dr. Schwartz and I sat down to discuss the case. We were both struck by Mr. Rakowitz's illogical insistence on his innocence. All the physical evidence, including the self-incriminating video confession, pointed to his guilt. Yet, he maintained to both of us that the murder was committed by unidentified others.

"I think he did it," Dr. Schwartz said, "but Rakowitz insisted he was innocent. He told me that Ms. Beerle's murder was part of an orchestrated scheme to prevent him from forming the 'Freedom Party' and becoming President."

Dr. Schwartz continued, "Rakowitz believes he was visited by angels. He told me that he is the Lord and was sent to help the homeless. And he uses strange numerological equations. He told me that 1996 is the year he's meant to become President because the numbers in his date of birth somehow add up to that year."

Mr. Rakowitz's birthday was 12/24/60. I took out a piece of paper to add up the numbers, but could find no way that they added up to 1996.

"I've heard a lot of grandiose delusions," Dr. Schwartz said. "But his might be the strangest."

I concluded that Mr. Rakowitz was a paranoid schizophrenic who was psychotic, not only when I met with him, but also at the time Ms. Beerle was killed. I completed my report and sent it to the defense attorney. It was time for the prosecutor to hire his own experts. Months passed, and I became busy with other cases.

The trial finally took place in the State Supreme Court building in Manhattan in February of 1991. Mr. Rakowitz's defense was that someone else had killed Ms. Beerle. Initially, he refused to permit his attorney to enter an insanity defense. He changed his mind the day before I was scheduled to testify. Then he allowed his attorney to put forth two diametrically opposed defense strategies: one, that he was factually innocent and had not killed Ms. Beerle and two, that if he *had* killed her, he was insane at the time.

Mr. Reimer called me that night to let me know of the abrupt change in defense strategy. I hung up the phone in shock. I had only a few hours to prepare for what turned out to be some of the toughest questions I would ever be asked on the stand.

The next morning, I got off the elevator and headed to the courtroom. The press was already there setting up their equipment. I sat on the wooden bench outside, nervously reviewing my notes and waiting to be called. Finally, a court officer came for me. I walked through the crowded courtroom to the witness stand and glanced over at the defendant. He was dressed neatly with his long blond hair neatly combed, but he still looked other-worldly. He grinned broadly at me, seemingly amused by the proceedings.

After I was sworn in, Mr. Reimer began the direct examination. Direct examination is when a witness is questioned by the attorney calling him or her as a witness. His questions about Mr. Rakowitz's psychiatric treatment laid the groundwork for an insanity defense.

I explained to the jury that Mr. Rakowitz had been diagnosed with paranoid schizophrenia years before his arrest. He had confided to the hospital staff that he could kill people with prayer. During his two previous psychiatric hospitalizations in Texas, he told staff that he had heard the voice of God.

I testified that the psychiatrist who treated him at Riker's Island jail after his arrest also diagnosed Mr. Rakowitz with paranoid schizophrenia and had prescribed Thorazine, an anti-psychotic medication.

When Mr. Reimer asked me about Ms. Beerle's psychiatric history, the atmosphere in the courtroom became charged.

"These are psychiatric records for Monica Beerle at Saint Vincent's Hospital," Mr. Reimer said, holding up the documents. "In attempting to come to your conclusion concerning the events in question in this case, did you in any way rely upon information that was contained in those documents?"

"Objection!" Assistant District Attorney (ADA) Mathis exclaimed.

"She can tell us what she relied upon and then you'll have an opportunity to cross-examine her if I permit it," the judge ruled.

"Can you tell us, specifically, what information [in her records] was germane to your evaluation here?" Mr. Reimer then asked.

Before I could answer, the prosecutor interrupted again. "Objection," he said.[2]

The judge ruled that I could answer. I had mixed feelings about describing Ms. Beerle's psychiatric records. I did not want to give the impression that I was blaming the victim for her own death, but her psychiatric records were valid sources of information for the jury to consider.

"She was suffering from a serious psychiatric illness," I said. "She was hospitalized at least twice here in New York. And during these episodes she also became psychotic and behaved irrationally. She was prescribed Lithium—"

The prosecutor again interrupted. "Objection, your honor."

"No, I'll permit it," the judge ruled.[3]

"She was found walking, I believe," I continued, "on the Verra-zano Bridge, and even in the hospital she had to be kept in seclu-sion . . ."[4]

Ms. Beerle's psychiatric records put things in a new light. I glanced over at the jury and could see them considering the idea of two mentally ill people living together in the small apartment. It did not take a clinical psychologist to tell that it was a recipe for disaster.

Mr. Reimer then focused his questions on his client's psychotic illness. I testified that Mr. Rakowitz referred to himself as the "New Christ."

"What he sees as reality is not what we see as reality. It's part of [his] psychosis," I said. "The belief that people can influence your mind, [that] they put thoughts into your mind or make you have vi-sions is a very definite symptom of schizophrenia. And [Rakowitz] appears to have had it for many years."[5]

As I spoke, I watched the defendant to gauge his response to my testimony. I felt somewhat awkward talking about his mental ill-ness in front of him. But he continued to smile, serenely, even as I called him delusional and psychotic. It was surreal. I wondered what the jury made of this man who seemed to enjoy standing trial for murder.

After that, Mr. Reimer began asking questions about the murder itself. I testified that Mr. Rakowitz had told me he was innocent. I mentioned the hidden messages in the videotaped statement, add-ing that I was unable to find them.

Finally, Mr. Reimer asked me the most important question, whether the defendant fulfilled criteria for an insanity defense which in New York State is called a "not responsible" defense. I re-plied that, in my opinion, *if* Rakowitz had killed Ms. Beerle, he was not responsible at the time. If he had killed Ms. Beerle, he was un-able to know or appreciate the wrongfulness of his actions.

The first part of my testimony, the direct examination, was now complete. The court broke for lunch. Since my testimony was interrupted by the recess, I was still technically on the witness stand and was, therefore, not permitted to discuss the case with the attorneys. I ate alone to avoid any image of impropriety.

We would not reconvene until 2:15, leaving me with over an hour to eat. I would return to the witness stand after lunch for the cross-examination, the questioning by the other side, in this case, the prosecution.

I headed uptown toward Chinatown for lunch. The walk gave me the chance to stretch my legs and relax for the first time in hours. At one of my favorite restaurants, I took a seat and pulled out a crossword puzzle. I needed to clear my mind of the repetitive, nagging thoughts about what I should or could have said differently.

At 2:30 I again took the stand. It was time for the prosecutor to question me. He began by talking about Mr. Rakowitz's intelligence.

"Isn't it a fact the defendant has the intelligence to mislead an examiner if he chooses?" ADA Mathis asked.

"Sure," I said.[6] I knew that any defendant can lie and that Mr. Rakowitz was much smarter than many other defendants I had evaluated. The prosecutor then returned to the question of Ms. Beerle's psychiatric illness.

"So you don't have an opinion with a reasonable degree of medical certainty how Monica Beerle acted on August 19th?" he asked.

"Of course not."

"Your Honor, I move to strike all of the opinions about how Monica Beerle may have acted on August 29th given the doctor's testimony."

"Overruled," said the judge.[7]

I had barely caught my breath from this surprise motion when the prosecutor asked the judge to throw out *all* of my testimony.

"I note she has given an awful lot of opinions that aren't in her report," the prosecutor said, "and I understand the law; a report that doesn't give the opinions that the expert is going to testify to, the psychiatric expert fails to give notice, and on that basis, Your Honor, I am going to move her testimony be stricken."[8]

Judge Haft denied the motion to strike my testimony. He told the jurors that the defendant's authorization to interpose the insanity defense was not given to his attorney until the previous day. The judge explained that he had already given permission for me to testify about conclusions that I had not included in my report.

I was relieved. I knew I had not done anything wrong in the preparation of my report, but when the prosecutor asked that my testimony be stricken, I felt like I was being accused of incompetence.

I was excused from the witness stand a few minutes later. With a deep sigh, I stepped down from the witness stand. It had been a long day.

The trial continued. Dr. Schwartz also testified that the defendant was not guilty by reason of insanity. Perhaps the highlight of the trial came when Mr. Rakowitz testified in his own defense and told the jury that he did not kill Ms. Beerle. I was not present in the courtroom for his testimony but I was told that it was quite an outlandish presentation.

After nine days of deliberations, the Manhattan jury concluded that Mr. Rakowitz was not guilty by reason of insanity. I wondered how much weight the jury placed on my testimony. I suspected that the most powerful piece of evidence was the defendant himself. The jurors watched him testify. They looked across the courtroom and saw him smiling bizarrely, day after day, week after week. I am sure they recognized how profoundly disturbed he was, even though no clear psychotic motive was ever presented at the trial.

When the verdict was read, Mr. Rakowitz gave the jury a bizarre farewell address.

> "I hope someday we can smoke a joint together . . . I won't fault you for your verdict . . . the prosecution had an overwhelming case against me. But I'll be getting out soon and I'll sell a lot of marijuana so I can bring to justice the people who actually committed this crime."[9]

Mr. Rakowitz's prediction that he would be quickly released did not come to pass. He remains in a forensic hospital to this day. He has the right to periodic reviews to determine whether he remains mentally ill and dangerous. If a judge determines that he is not dangerous, he could be transferred to a state psychiatric hospital. In time, he might even be released. So far, he has twice requested hearings, first in 1995 and then in 2004. He was turned down both times.

Chapter 4

THE ALIEN INVASION AND
OTHER DELUSIONS

The following four defendants came from very different back-grounds but were all charged with violent crimes. All killed or attempted to kill complete strangers. None had a rational motive. All had been hospitalized for psychiatric treatment at some point before they were arrested.

The Alien Invasion
A man shot wildly into the group of sanitation workers, wounding two of them. Witnesses alerted two police officers who were sitting in a parked police car nearby. One of the officers shot Mr. Wilson as he fled the scene. As he lay there, waiting for the ambulance to arrive, he warned the police to watch out for "the aliens." He was rushed to the hospital. The next day he was charged with attempted murder in the second degree.

Mr. Wilson's attorney contacted me to assess his client's mental state at the time of the shooting. He told me that the defendant, who was 29 years old, had never been in any sort of trouble before. "Well, not *legal* trouble," the attorney amended. Mr. Wilson had twice been admitted to psychiatric hospitals and diagnosed with paranoid schizophrenia.

I reviewed the box of psychiatric records the attorney mailed to me. The papers detailed the sad downward spiral of a young man who, after showing much academic promise early in life, had suffered the devastating effects of schizophrenia.

Mr. Wilson's early years were for the most part unremarkable, but as an adult, he was never able to "make it" in the real world. He could not hold a job for more than a few months and relied almost entirely on family support and monthly Social Security checks. At the time of the arrest he lived with his parents, still sleeping in his childhood bedroom. Their house was located on a quiet street off a busy avenue in a residential Brooklyn neighborhood.

Several months before the shooting, Mr. Wilson was admitted to a psychiatric hospital where he told the psychiatric staff that an alien invasion was imminent. He was prescribed antipsychotic medication and eventually stopped talking about the aliens. After two months, he was discharged with a few days' worth of antipsychotic medication and an appointment for outpatient treatment. No one followed up to make sure he kept the appointment or stayed on medication.

When I finished reading through Mr. Wilson's records, I called the jail medical unit of the hospital to schedule a visit. The defendant had been there a few weeks, recovering from his gunshot wounds.

I walked into the hospital room the next day and introduced myself to the thin young white man lying in bed, dressed in blue institutional pajamas. Typical of a long-stay hospital patient, his complexion was pallid and his body frail. He smiled politely when I introduced myself and I was struck with his tranquility. He seemed safe enough so I did not bother to wake the corrections officer when he started napping a few minutes later.

The officer had closed his eyes and leaned back in his chair in the corner of the hospital room. His bulletproof vest was unzipped for comfort. Only after an hour, when I leaned over Mr. Wilson to say, "Tell me about those aliens," did the officer's eyes open in shock and he quickly zipped up his vest. I stifled a chuckle as I watched him almost snap to attention and resume his guard duties, despite the fact that I had essentially been alone with the defendant for the entirety of the interview so far.

"Tell me about those aliens," I said.

"I knew the aliens were communicating with me," Mr. Wilson said.

"What did they say?"

"They threatened me," he replied. "They said things like 'We're going to kill you' and 'We're watching you.'"

"Did you ever see any unusual things?"

"Well, three months before the shooting, I saw a UFO," he said in an offhand way.

"Tell me more about this UFO," I encouraged, scribbling in my notepad. I did not want to miss a word.

"I saw one close up, in Pennsylvania. I was on a bus and it was right alongside of the bus. It had big red lights."

I was silent for a minute, writing, and Mr. Wilson continued, "I thought aliens could control my mind."

"How did they do that?"

"They inserted thoughts into my mind," he said slowly, as if trying to explain a difficult concept in simple terms. "My mind was taken over. Aliens could control time, space, and humans. I thought they could speak to us telepathically. I've heard about people abducted, cows taken, and women who have been impregnated by aliens."

"Did you think you were abducted?"

"I wasn't sure," he replied in a concerned tone. "I was convinced that the aliens were watching me through the TV. I made my family unplug all of the television sets."

We had been talking for two hours, and that was enough for one day. I realized I needed to talk with his family to get a nonpsychotic version of the events leading up to the shooting. But before leaving the medical unit, I stopped by the nurse's station. I showed the head nurse the judge's order granting me access to Mr. Wilson's medical records and she pulled out his chart.

One note in particular caught my attention. After his arrest, blood tests had detected alcohol, cannabis and phencyclidine (PCP or angel dust) in his system. Angel dust is a hallucinogen and its effects include confusion, delirium, paranoia, and hallucinations. From my clinical experience, I knew that people on angel dust often behave extremely bizarrely or violently. There are reports of users taking off their clothes, killing themselves, and attacking others.[1]

Traveling home that evening, I considered whether Mr. Wilson's attack on the sanitation workers could have resulted from his drug use. It was likely that the drugs triggered psychotic symptoms but I did not believe that the drugs alone could explain the shooting. And his past drug use certainly could not explain why, when I visited him weeks after the shooting, he was still acting psychotic.

I called his family a few days after the first interview. His sister answered the phone and we talked for a half hour or so. "He told us to watch out, to be careful," she said. "My brother said people were watching him through the TV and made us unplug it. And he warned us to move out of New York City."

Next, I talked to Mr. Wilson's mother. It was a difficult conversation. "We rarely saw him," she said, the pain evident in her voice. She told me he spent most of his time upstairs in his bedroom. She and her husband had not realized that their son had stopped taking his psychiatric medications and were unaware of the extent of his marijuana and alcohol use.

*   *   *

I started the second session with Mr. Wilson by asking him about his drug use. "Oh, I've been smoking pot for years," he said. In the months before the shooting, he was smoking a nickel bag and drinking a pint of alcohol each day. He explained that smoking and drinking "relaxed" him.

I confronted Mr. Wilson with his testing positive for angel dust. He repeatedly denied smoking angel dust. I considered whether it was possible that the marijuana he smoked was laced with it.

I decided to lay that issue aside for the moment. "Tell me what happened the night before your arrest," I said. Mr. Wilson told me that he lay awake most of the night, watching the cars pass outside his window. The license plate messages he deciphered that night confirmed his worst suspicions: the aliens had landed. He heard a voice announcing, "We are here." He fell into an uneasy sleep.

The next morning Mr. Wilson awoke and smoked a joint to relax, but he could not calm down. Feeling anxious, he decided to bring his gun when he left his house. He glanced down the block and noticed four men standing and talking at a construction site. He was convinced that they were aliens, that their uniforms were disguises, and that they were about to attack him. Terrified, he shot wildly into the group, wounding two of the workers.

Mr. Wilson saw two of the "aliens" collapse and fled in panic. The next thing he remembered was the pain of the bullets. Lying on the ground, waiting for the ambulance, he gasped out a warning to the police about the alien invasion.

Mr. Wilson began taking antipsychotic medications after he was arrested and his psychosis gradually remitted. By the time I finished my interviews with him, he already doubted that the workers were aliens and that he had ever been in real danger. His attorney recommended an insanity defense and Mr. Wilson agreed.

I concluded that the defendant was exactly the type of defendant the insanity defense was intended for. As far-fetched as it seemed,

Mr. Wilson actually believed the victims were aliens in disguise. He was terrified that they were going to capture or kill him and he fired in self-defense. He truly did not appreciate that what he was doing was wrong. I completed my evaluation and diagnosed him with schizophrenia and polysubstance abuse.

Three other forensic clinicians examined Mr. Wilson. In addition to my services, the defense retained a psychiatrist and the prosecution hired both a psychiatrist and psychologist. All four of us agreed that the defendant was psychotic and delusional at the time he shot at the sanitation workers. All concluded that his drug use contributed to, but did not cause, his psychosis.

The assistant district attorney decided to offer an insanity plea. Mr. Wilson quickly accepted it and never went to trial. If the prosecution-retained experts had concluded that the defendant's violent act was primarily drug-induced, the prosecutor would never have offered the plea.

Mr. Wilson was one of very few defendants to be offered an insanity plea. He was transferred to a forensic hospital where he continued to take antipsychotic medication and improved dramatically. His hallucinations and delusions ceased. Treatment then focused on helping him understand the importance of remaining on psychiatric medications and avoiding all use of drugs and alcohol. Within a few years, the psychiatric staff concluded that he was psychiatrically stable and that his mental illness was in full remission.

After seven years, the presiding judge ruled that Mr. Wilson was still mentally ill but no longer dangerous and ordered him transferred to a state psychiatric hospital. He was granted more freedom. First, he was permitted unescorted ground privileges which allowed him to walk around the hospital grounds, socialize with other patients, and attend the treatment and vocational programs offered in different hospital buildings. Later, he was granted escorted home visits. A psychiatric aide went with him to make sure he returned.

Today, almost twelve years after the shooting, Mr. Wilson remains in this hospital but is allowed unescorted furloughs off grounds. He spends almost every weekend with his family. I expect that he will be discharged within the next few years. His parents eagerly await the day he will return to live with them.

"He Said He Was Going to Kill Me (in Chinese)"

For no discernible reason, Mr. Lao, a 29-year-old Chinese American man, stabbed his apartment superintendent, then ran out into the street, hailed a passing car, and asked the driver to call the police. When the officers arrived, they found Mr. Lao standing outside the building, his shirt and hands covered in blood. "I killed the super," he confessed, handing the officer a knife.

In reality, the victim was not seriously injured. The attack was sudden and unprovoked. There was no evidence that the two men had been arguing before or during the attack; they had not even been talking. Mr. Lao was charged with attempted murder.

Mr. Lao made many peculiar comments after his arrest. He told the police that the Puerto Rican super had been cursing and threatening him in Chinese. Mr. Lao's statements, in the context of his documented history of mental illness, prompted his attorney to request a competency to stand trial evaluation.

The court-appointed competency doctors noticed that Mr. Lao appeared strangely distracted and was apparently hearing voices. They diagnosed him with paranoid schizophrenia and concluded that he was not competent. The judge ordered Mr. Lao committed to a forensic hospital for treatment. The goal was to restore him to competency so that he could return to court and face his charges.

Mr. Lao remained in the secure forensic hospital for almost three years. The voices disappeared with the help of antipsychotic medications, but he never became symptom-free. He continued to believe that the victim had threatened him.

Eventually, Mr. Lao appeared willing and able to cooperate with his attorney. He was still undoubtedly mentally ill, but his condition had improved to the extent that the judge ruled him competent. He was returned to Riker's Island jail.

Mr. Lao's attorney contacted me soon afterward. He told me he was convinced his client was psychotic when he stabbed the victim. "My client had to be hallucinating," the attorney said. "The super doesn't speak Chinese. Can you evaluate him for an insanity defense?"

I spoke with Mr. Lao several times through a Mandarin interpreter. Even with the interpreter I found him difficult to understand. At times during my interviews his thinking was so disorganized that I could not be sure of what he meant. At other times he actually started giggling for no reason I could fathom. I'm sure he was laughing at something, but he wouldn't—or couldn't—tell me what struck him as so funny.

Mr. Lao was on a regimen of psychiatric medications but remained quite ill. To say he was a man of few words would be an understatement; he was very withdrawn and never spoke spontaneously.

During the first session I reviewed his upbringing and history. He told me that his early years in China were uneventful; he graduated high school and studied for one year at Zhejiang University in Hangzhou province, near Shanghai. It was at this time in his life that he began to withdraw from people.

He abruptly left the university and never returned to finish his degree. Although he was vague and unable to adequately explain his reasons for dropping out, it was likely that he was in the earliest stage of schizophrenia, what is termed in psychiatry as the "prodromal" stage. The prodromal stage can last from weeks to years. It begins with the first observable changes in behavior and lasts until the most obvious symptoms of psychosis emerge.

Mr. Lao recounted how he and his family immigrated to the United States when he was 20 years old. They settled in Queens, New York, in a thriving, busy neighborhood popular with new immigrants. The next few years were unproductive; he lived with his parents and younger sister, never worked and had no friends. He described a solitary life, his days spent alone in his apartment.

Mr. Lao told me how he frequently argued with his parents. At one point, an argument over his excessive smoking escalated and he attacked his father. His mother called 911; he was arrested and charged with assault. He accepted a plea of time served with six months probation and was released from custody.

I called his family after the first session and arranged to meet with Mr. Lao's sister who was fluent in English. She described what occurred after her brother was released from jail. Her parents wisely decided it was time for their son to live elsewhere. Accepting the fact that he was unable to care for himself, they rented him a small apartment down the hall from theirs. They continued to buy his clothing and cook his meals. Her brother's extremely solitary life never improved; he only minimally interacted with his parents and sister. Mr. Lao's parents never took him for psychiatric treatment, but they were painfully aware of his peculiar thoughts and behaviors.

"What was he like?" I asked his sister.

Staring at a place on the floor and avoiding eye contact, she told me, "He doesn't like noisy things, that's why he puts a box on his head."

"Tell me more about this box."

"He made a hole in it to see out of. He sat in a large box and put a lamp inside to read."

"Do you know why he did this?" I gently asked.

"He sits in the box because he doesn't like noise. He's afraid for no reason. He told me that the Chinese FBI is following him."

Parents are often at a loss about how to best help their severely mentally ill child. I have noticed this to be an especially common reaction in many immigrant families. Some are in denial about their loved one's severe mental illness. Others are unaware of the treatment resources available to them here in their adopted country. Many mistakenly hide their relative's mental problems from the community because of the stigma associated with mental illness. Research in the field of help-seeking behavior has shown that many Asian immigrants rely on traditional medicine rather than utilize mainstream medical services.[2]

During the second interview with Mr. Lao I asked about the Chinese FBI. His explanations made little sense. He told me that he was uneasy walking outside on the streets. He was convinced that he was under surveillance and carried a small pocket knife for protection when he left his apartment.

"What made you think you were being watched?" I asked.

"Lots of cars are following me because they are trying to investigate me," he replied.

"Did this have anything to do with the super?" I asked.

Mr. Lao described the super as "The Supreme Power" who was above the law and permitted to do anything he wanted. He told me that he knew the super carried a knife and was planning to stab and kill him. During the days before the stabbing, according to Mr. Lao, the super repeatedly threatened him, always speaking in Chinese so that others in the building would not understand.

Mr. Lao was also convinced that the super had made sexually provocative comments, saying that he, the defendant, ran a prostitution ring. It was obvious to me that he was tormented by persecutory delusions; there was no evidence that the super was in any way threatening or disparaging.

Mr. Lao started giggling anxiously as he told me about his thoughts just prior to his pulling out the knife. He believed that the super had been inside his sister's bedroom earlier that evening.

"Why did you think he was in her bedroom?" I asked

"I felt he was in my sister's room and this was not normal," he replied. "This made me angry. I felt he was threatening my sister."

"Did you talk to him before you stabbed him?" I asked.

"The super said if I ignore him, he would kill me savagely," he replied in an angry tone. It was as if he were reliving the imagined threat.

"How did you feel before you stabbed him?"

"I felt that he was acting like a man in a lawless country," he answered. "So that made me angry, but afterwards I regret what I had done."

I was struck by Mr. Lao's delusion that the super was in his sister's bedroom. I considered the possibility that he had sexual feelings toward his sister, which he projected onto the super. Projection is one of the psychological defense mechanisms identified by Freud. It occurs when individuals experience unacceptable thoughts or feelings. They deny and repress the feelings, then assign or "project" them onto other people.

Perhaps Mr. Lao's unacknowledged sexual urges were one source of his intense violent emotions. Of course, he was totally unaware of any inappropriate sexual feelings toward his sister. When I gently raised the possibility, he looked outraged. He insisted, "It was the *super* who was in her bedroom!"

I concluded that Mr. Lao was psychotic at the time he stabbed the super. He was hearing threats that were never uttered and was plagued with paranoid delusions. I prepared a report in which I concluded that he was not responsible at the time he stabbed the super.

The prosecution hired a psychiatrist who reached a different conclusion. While he agreed with me that Mr. Lao suffered from paranoid delusions and was psychotic at the time of the offense, the psychiatrist believed that the defendant understood that stabbing the super was "wrong" and against the law.

* * *

When the case was ready for trial, the defense attorney decided on a bench trial. A bench trial is the legal term for a trial in front of a judge rather than a jury. I remember the trial was fairly low key and the prosecutor was polite and easygoing. Unlike other trials where I had testified, the atmosphere was businesslike and I did not feel "attacked" or belittled on the stand.

Three experts testified, me and a psychiatrist for the defense, plus one psychiatrist for the prosecution. After the trial, the defense attorney called to tell me of the verdict.

"Mr. Lao was practically comatose during the trial," he said. "My client never said a word. He never took the stand."

"And the decision?"

"The judge ruled that my client was not guilty by reason of insanity. The judge came back pretty quickly with his verdict." We both agreed that Mr. Lao's illness was as apparent to the judge as it was to us.

I felt relieved. Now Mr. Lao would receive the psychiatric treatment he needed and would not be a threat to the community. Today, eight years later, Mr. Lao remains in the forensic hospital. His condition has not improved and he is still convinced that he has no mental problems. He continues to believe the super had threatened him and his family and expresses little remorse for his violent attack.

Considering his total lack of insight about his psychiatric illness, I am sure the psychiatric staff is leery about recommending his transfer to a less secure facility. His case illustrates the fallacy of the public's beliefs about the insanity defense, that those found not guilty by reason of insanity are quickly released. Mr. Lao will probably spend more time in the forensic hospital than if he had pleaded guilty to the charge and served time in prison.

My Badge Is in the Mail

The landlord found the body of his 68-year-old African American ten-
ant, Mr. Griffith, on the floor beside the bed in his rented room. He
had been stabbed twice and died of blood loss. Even though the room
was barely large enough for a bed, dresser and chair, there was no sign
of a struggle or a robbery. The police questioned the other men living
in the single room occupancy (SRO) apartment building on the Upper
West Side of Manhattan. They all mentioned the strange man living
down the hall.

When the police knocked on his door, Mr. Rodriguez, a 30-year-
old Hispanic man, answered. Without any prodding whatsoever,
he confessed that he had stabbed and killed his neighbor. At the
precinct, he gave both a written and videotaped statement and was
promptly arrested. The defense attorney met with him and requested
his client be evaluated for competency to stand trial.

During the competency interviews, Mr. Rodriguez candidly, and
in great detail, told the court-appointed doctors about his many peculiar and grandiose delusions. He told them that he was the "Creator"
and a genius. He was a "Supreme Being" with extraordinary powers,
which were recognized during childhood by a pyramidal mark on his
penis. He told them he had earned Ph.D.s in chemistry, physics and
medicine.

Mr. Rodriguez's delusions of grandeur were unmistakable and the
doctors diagnosed him with schizophrenia. They concluded that he
was not competent. The judge agreed and ordered him transferred
to a forensic hospital.

Mr. Rodriguez was not, as is said in the forensic field, "restored
to competency" quickly after his arrest. Treatment at the forensic
hospital was only minimally successful and he remained hospitalized for four years. Eventually, he told the staff that he wanted to
work with his attorney to resolve his case and would agree with his
attorney's advice to enter an insanity defense. The hospital psychia-

trists believed Mr. Rodriguez had improved sufficiently enough to be returned to court to face his charges. Even though still delusional, the judge ruled he was finally competent to stand trial.

Mr. Rodriguez's attorney then hired me to assess his client for an insanity defense. He sent boxes of psychiatric records, crime scene photos, police records, and most importantly, his client's videotaped confession. I had a lot of work to do before even seeing the defendant.

First, I read through all the competency reports. The evaluating doctors spoke with Mr. Rodriguez's parents and learned that they took their son to a psychiatric hospital on two occasions when he was talking to himself and seemed to be hearing voices. Each time he was admitted, prescribed antipsychotic medications, and discharged after a few weeks. Both times he promptly stopped taking his antipsychotic medication after being released.

I then looked through the police reports. One neighbor described the defendant as a man who "laughs out loud and talks to himself." Another told the police officer that the defendant made him feel "uneasy." This neighbor explained how the defendant "talks to himself, answers himself, and talks to people who aren't there."

Finally, it was time for me to watch Mr. Rodriguez's confession. His video was the strangest one I had ever watched. He matter-of-factly told the detective about how and why he killed the victim. The weirdest aspect of the entire tape, however, was that he did not act like a suspect. He spoke calmly, as if he were not confessing to a crime. He behaved as if he were giving an end of the day work report, reporting to his superiors about successfully completing his job assignments.

In the video, Mr. Rodriguez told the detective that he was on a job assignment, working for the CIA, FBI *and* DEA (Drug Enforcement Agency). No mere tenant, he had instead been "placed" in his apartment in order to conduct "field work" and compile "surveillance" on an international drug cartel run by the victim. He never mentioned the fact that the mastermind criminal he was watching was almost 70 years old.

I watched the interviewing detective's behavior and was awed with how he remained relaxed during the lengthy interview. His voice remained calm and measured. This was even more impressive considering the back story involved. I was sure Mr. Rodriguez was the most psychotic, severely mentally ill suspect he had ever questioned. Yet few signs of anxiety were evident in his voice or posture. He sat comfortably, asking questions about the defendant's delusions without ever indicating that he knew the suspect was psychotic. He maintained a friendly, not accusatory, "we're just chatting" style. Testament, once again, to the skill of a natural or experienced interrogator.

Watching the video, I noticed that the defendant seemed equally relaxed while describing his bizarre paranoid and grandiose beliefs. He certainly was comfortable with his imaginary world and had no inkling that others would find it extraordinary or frightening. The only time he seemed at all on edge was when the detective politely asked for proof of his government affiliation. Mr. Rodriguez somewhat nervously admitted that, for reasons he could not understand, his badge and gun were "lost in the mail."

In the video Mr. Rodriguez described his year-long mission spying on the victim and his drug smuggling colleagues. He told the detective that other members of the drug cartel lived in the SRO hotel and had tried to murder him in the past. In self-defense, he had killed them, but they had "come back from the dead." Since these criminals had special powers of resurrection, he explained, they posed a serious threat to his life.

The only time I heard any signs of stress in the detective's voice was when he interrupted one of Mr. Rodriguez's longwinded answers to ask, "Have you killed anyone who has *not* come back from the dead?" I assumed this slight break in his characteristic composed manner meant that he was genuinely alarmed by the possibility that there might be a few bodies buried somewhere. Fortunately, Mr. Rodriguez replied, "No, everyone I've killed has been resurrected."

After watching this extraordinary video a few times and reviewing the boxes of materials the defense counsel had sent me, it was time to see the defendant. I walked into the tiny interview room and took a seat with my back to the wall, waiting for the corrections officer to bring in the defendant.

Walking next to the officer, with his hands cuffed in front, Mr. Rodriguez looked even shorter and more skeletal than he seemed on the videotape. He was, upon closer inspection, particularly waif-like. He was disheveled, his clothing stained, and wore a not-so-faint scent. Evidently, he had not been washing, a common symptom of schizophrenia.

I found Mr. Rodriguez talkative but remarkably easy to question. He would go off on tangents and I needed to interrupt in order to bring him back to the topic. In psychiatry, this is referred to as tangential thinking. Unlike many defendants who need time to feel comfortable and open up with me, he launched right into confiding his beliefs and experiences. He told me all about his advanced degrees in chemistry, physics, and medicine from Harvard and Yale. He explained that it was his advanced knowledge that first interested the government.

"When did you start working for the CIA?" I asked.

"It started in the 1970's," he cheerfully answered. "They contacted me. I met with a gentleman, he was a chemist. We talked about science and the stars. I met with other scientists. I had a project in mind, dealing with the planets. I was involved in metaphysical sciences. I was designing a new space station. The government and me, we're working together on a secret project. The government wants to keep hush-hush about a cult of people that are trying to ruin this country by bringing in drugs."

He continued recounting his work on high security and secret government projects. There was no question about it—even after years of being on antipsychotic medications, his intricate, grandiose delusions remained. In psychiatry such delusions are classified as fixed, or unchangeable, and systematized, or intricately developed.

"How did you decide to rent your room?" I somewhat rudely interrupted, sensing he could go on for hours about his special abilities and imaginary jobs.

"I was told by the CIA to watch them, the men living there, and to investigate who they know, watch their daily routines and take photographs."

"Tell me about your interactions with the other people in your building," I suggested.

He replied, "I've had a few incidences in which people have tried to kill me. Machine guns were pointed at me. I was almost stabbed. Mr. Griffith and the people living in the house, they can come back from the dead. I've also been killed before and I came back."

"Tell me about that."

"It was around 1984," he recalled. "I was killed by a gun shot to the head. Then, a few months ago, Mr. Griffith tried to shoot me with a revolver. He said he was going to kill me and hurt others that I love. Once, the other men in the cartel put something in a rag and put it to my mouth. I passed out and when I woke up, everything was stolen from my room. My whole room was turned upside down. There were needle marks in my arms. For months, I couldn't remember things and had headaches and dizzy spells. I think they used a memory penetration drug to stop me from knowing what was going on and to infiltrate me somehow, to get me to do what they wanted."

"What did you do about this?" I asked.

"I called 911," he recalled. "They sent one cop in a blue and white, he told me not to go back to the building, he told me to move out."

"What about your interactions with Mr. Griffith?"

"A few weeks ago he grabbed me when I came into the building,"

Mr. Rodriguez replied. "He put a knife to my throat and I pushed him away and ran out of the building. He threatened me three other times. I stayed away for a while and slept in Central Park. I had to make believe I was homeless."

After listening to his outlandish delusions I questioned whether he was actually competent to stand trial. I asked whether he understood his charges and his defense options. He apparently understood that he might be convicted at a trial and would then serve a long prison sentence. He acknowledged, "I could go away for life."

"Do you want to plead insanity?"

"Yes," he said. "I wasn't feeling well when I stabbed him. I was under stress. I was sick."

"And what happens if you are found not guilty by reason of insanity?" I asked.

"I know I'd be put in a psychiatric hospital for a time," he replied. "And I'd be given medication. The medication keeps me from feeling a little paranoid; it takes the edge off thinking about these people."

"And your attorney?" I continued. "Do you think he's helping you?"

"Yes, I think he's doing a good job."

I still had some reservations, but agreed with the court-appointed competency doctors. Mr. Rodriguez was delusional, but trusted his attorney and wanted to resolve his case. He seemed to fulfill the basic criteria for competency.

I then asked Mr. Rodriguez about the stabbing. In his now familiar, rambling style, he told me:

"I started sneaking into the building. I'd see if Mr. Griffith was there first, then quickly I'd go to my room and put a chair under the knob to lock it. On the day it happened, I wanted to go out for food. I put my ear to his door and didn't hear him, so I went down the hall to the stairs. Then he came out of his room, he started whacking me in the head with a pot, seven or eight times, I was dizzy. Then he took out a knife and tried to slash me in the throat. I had to get him from attacking me so I grabbed the knife and we struggled and fell onto the floor. He slipped right on top of me and the knife went inside of him. He was trying to strangle me. I couldn't breathe, so I struck him in the neck with the knife. He slowly let go of my neck."

Mr. Rodriguez then explained how he concealed the killing. First, he dragged Mr. Griffith's body back to his room. Then, he mopped up the blood from the hall floor. Finally, he left the building to throw the knife in a dumpster and returned to his room.

Listening to this detailed, matter-of-fact description of a brutal crime, I watched Mr. Rodriguez's face, searching for some sign of guilt. I saw none. The only time he appeared at all remorseful was when he explained why he left the victim on the floor. He told me that he was feeling weak after the struggle and was not strong enough to lift Mr. Griffith's body onto the bed.

"And what about Mr. Griffith?" I obliquely asked, as if I too believed he could still be alive.

"I think he is in hiding," Mr. Rodriguez calmly explained. "I'm using remote viewing and can see into the future. I believe he's living with his cousin in Brooklyn. It's just like many years ago when he got hit by a truck and died. He was resurrected."

He was chillingly emotionless and I briefly considered whether Mr. Rodriguez was a psychopath. Then I realized that he did not feel guilty because, from his delusional perspective, he had not done anything wrong. And, even more importantly, the victim was not really dead.

I concluded that Mr. Rodriguez was insane when he stabbed the victim. His paranoid and grandiose delusions were so all-encompassing that he was totally out of touch with reality. He was unable to appreciate the fact that what he was doing was wrong. The psychologist retained by the prosecutor agreed with me. The assistant district attorney then offered a not responsible plea and Mr. Rodriguez accepted.

As an insanity acquittee, Mr. Rodriguez was transferred to a forensic hospital. Years passed. I recently spoke to the assistant district attorney monitoring all the insanity acquittees in the county. He told me that Mr. Rodriguez has remained in the same secure forensic hospital for the past six years. From the time of his arrest, he had been institutionalized for approximately ten years. The antipsychotic medications had not eliminated his symptoms.

I doubt whether Mr. Rodriguez's grandiose and paranoid delusions will ever disappear. I do not expect him to be released for many years. If ever.

A Subway Pusher

At 8:30 A.M. on a crowded subway platform in Queens, New York, a middle-aged man pushed a young woman onto the tracks. To the horror of the onlookers, she was dragged under an oncoming train. One bystander grabbed the man as he tried to leave the station, and held him for the police. Mr. Bolton was arrested and charged with the murder of Ms. Grant.

Mr. Bolton was admitted to the forensic unit of a psychiatric hospital shortly after his arrest. His defense attorney contacted me to conduct a psychological assessment of his client. He mailed me Mr. Bolton's videotaped statement, his psychiatric hospital records, and the reports from a previous arrest.

I had never before interviewed a person who pushed someone onto the subway tracks. Before I began reading through the psychiatric records, I searched the Internet for information on subway homicides. More items popped up than I expected. I found a retrospective study of 36 individuals who pushed or tried to push strangers onto subway tracks between the years of 1975 and 1991. The researchers examined data from twenty offenders who were referred for psychiatric assessment. At the time of the crimes, sixty-five percent were homeless and 95 percent were psychotic. Most had long histories of criminal behavior and psychiatric treatment. All the victims were strangers.[3]

I turned the computer off and picked up the pile of psychiatric records. Mr. Bolton shared many characteristics with the subway pushers described in the study. Diagnosed with schizophrenia and polysubstance dependence, he had a long history of treatment. In the past eighteen years he had been admitted to psychiatric hospitals twelve times. He once confessed to a psychiatrist that he was hearing voices commanding him to hurt people. Years earlier he had been arrested after striking a woman on the head so hard that she suffered a concussion. He was also arrested for slashing a panhandler in the face.

Mr. Bolton left the state psychiatric hospital without permission two weeks before he killed Ms. Grant. He had been granted grounds privileges on the 122-acre hospital campus. I could not understand why he had been given freedom to roam the hospital property in the first place. This was not the first time he had run away from a mental institution; in fact, it was not the first time that he had escaped from that particular hospital. He had, in hospital jargon, eloped from there no fewer than four times earlier that year. No one knew for sure what the defendant did in the days before he killed Ms. Grant. There were reports that he slept on the subway and it was suspected that he used drugs.

I spent hours reading through all of Mr. Bolton's records, and then moved to the couch to watch his videotaped confession. He was a middle-aged white man. His physical appearance was striking: he was disheveled, his straight brown hair uncombed, his nails long and dirty. He spoke strangely, often referring to himself in the third person. When the assistant district attorney asked if he was aware that the train was entering the station as he pushed Ms. Grant, he answered, "Yes." The assistant district attorney asked if he knew she would be killed. Mr. Bolton replied, "Exactly."

Then he abruptly turned his head to the side and muttered excitedly. He seemed to be having a conversation with an invisible person in the corner of the room.

I watched the video a few times just to be sure. I was amazed: this was the best evidence of psychosis I had ever seen. I have never seen a suspect hallucinating while being questioned on videotape.

I interviewed Mr. Bolton on four occasions and administered a battery of psychological tests. First I gave him an I.Q. test. Then, I gave him a few projective tests. Projective tests use ambiguous stimuli to assess personality and psychological functioning. The test taker responds to these stimuli and the psychologist analyzes the content and quality of the responses to gain insight into the test taker's inner life.

I showed Mr. Bolton a series of pictures and instructed him to make up stories about the characters depicted. This was the Thematic Apperception Test.[4] A test taker's stories are actually not truly about the characters in the pictures. Instead, their stories reveal much about their own inner life.

Mr. Bolton's stories were quite peculiar. He responded very strangely to a picture of a small boy with a dejected expression sitting in front of an old, broken-down house. The image typically elicits stories about loneliness or abandonment, since normal test takers identify with the boy. But he identified with the house.

This was his brief story: "A house isn't anything to consistently keep in worry. Houses help protect people from the weather and help them rest their heads after a day of excitement."

"What about the boy? What is the boy thinking?" I prompted.

"The little boy is worrying why there is no door in the house. He's worried that nobody can walk inside his house."

There was, in fact, a door in the picture; the boy was sitting in front of it. Through the tunnel vision of his psychosis, Mr. Bolton completely missed the obvious. His inability to see the door revealed how he was disconnected from reality.

Mr. Bolton's psychosis was also evident in the drawings I asked him to make. He drew pictures of a house, a tree, a man and a woman. These pictures illustrated aspects of his inner feelings and personality make-up. He drew a house that was floating in space, ungrounded, just like him. The front door had no door knob. This would keep people out. This omission indicated that he was totally closed off from others.

Mr. Bolton added three extra large windows over the door and an extra, elaborate, circular window on the roof. People rarely draw windows in the attic. I interpreted his windows as representing his paranoid need to watch for intruders and threats.

Mr. Bolton's drawing of a tree was equally peculiar. The tree was drawn without a ground to support it. It appeared to be floating. The root system was so extensive that it was cut off at the edge of the page, its long roots trailing over the ground like grasping tentacles. His break with reality was obvious, since roots do not usually grow on top of the ground.

After he completed the psychological tests I started to ask him questions about the crime. I asked him several times why he pushed the victim to her death, and he never gave me a coherent story. His account changed dramatically with each retelling. He did not even recognize the inconsistencies in his story from session to session.

One time he told me it was an accident caused by the crowd on the platform. The next time I saw him, he said, "I was trying to save her from falling." During the third session he told me:

"I got off the subway to try to get some work. My old boss works in the 34th Street area. I was making a cross out of a straw. To see if I believed in Christ or not."

"What did the straw mean?" I asked, trying not to sound as confused as I felt.

"If it was hard for me to make the cross, it would mean I didn't believe in Christ."

"What does this have to do with pushing Ms. Grant?"

"It means I don't have faith. The devil was more believable to me. It was upsetting."

"And the woman on the subway platform?" I persisted.

"I put the cross in my pocket. The lady was in front of me. I moved by her fast."

"Then?"

"I went outside to the escalator."

"Before that?"

"I bumped her and she fell on the tracks."

Eventually I gave up. I was never going to get a coherent story from him. Instead, I looked for answers in the records and witness reports and arranged interviews with his family and doctor.

Mr. Bolton visited his mother after he ran away from the hospital just a few days before he killed Ms. Grant. His mother told me that her son "was in another world, he wasn't rational." She recalled that he was laughing to himself and that "his talk didn't make sense."

I spoke with the psychiatrist who treated Mr. Bolton in the weeks prior to his arrest. The doctor told me that his patient was hearing voices telling him to hurt people. Perhaps the best evidence of his psychotic state was the record from the hospital where he was taken immediately after his arrest. The hospital staff noted that he was delusional and hallucinating and that he "talked to unseen objects or persons." He was acutely paranoid and, at one point, accused the staff of spying on him. He was diagnosed with paranoid schizophrenia.

I was convinced that Mr. Bolton was psychotic at the time that he killed Ms. Grant and lacked criminal responsibility for his actions. I submitted my report. Now it was up to the assistant district attorney to hire a forensic expert.

Weeks passed before I heard that the assistant district attorney would not offer an insanity plea. I was not surprised. The assistant district attorney probably wanted this high profile case resolved by trial.

Mr. Bolton's trial began a few months later. When the defendant's videotaped statement was played at the trial it had a powerful effect on the jurors. They saw what Mr. Bolton looked like on the day he was arrested. I was sure it was evident to them that he was hearing voices and responding to them while giving his confession. Jurors rarely find a defendant not responsible, but they did in this case. Mr. Bolton was transferred to a forensic hospital, where he remains a patient to this day.

Most defendants who go to trial pleading not guilty by reason of insanity are found guilty. In a recent conversation I had with assistant district attorney (ADA) David Kelly, he said, "The last time a Brooklyn defendant was found not responsible *at trial* was in 1996."[5]

ADA Kelly then told me about another subway pusher. In 2003, a 25-year-old man stabbed his grandmother to death in Clinton Hill, a small neighborhood in Brooklyn. The next day, he was arrested on the platform of the subway in Manhattan after attacking two men and pushing one off the subway platform. Fortunately, a train was not coming, and the man was not seriously injured.

In this case, the Manhattan and Brooklyn District Attorneys' offices and defense counsel all agreed to an insanity plea. There was no trial. The defendant was so obviously psychotic that no one involved in the case suspected malingering. He was convinced that he was God and a feeding tube had to be surgically placed in his chest because he was not eating. He believed that God did not need to eat.[6]

A few years earlier another tragedy occurred in a New York City subway station. On January 3, 1999, Andrew Goldstein pushed Kendra Webdale to her death from the 23rd Street subway platform in Manhattan. Goldstein's schizophrenic illness began to manifest itself after he graduated from the prestigious Bronx High School of Science. He had been hospitalized thirteen times in the two years before he killed Ms. Webdale. In that same time period, he attacked thirteen people, including doctors and nurses on the psychiatric units.

Passengers are very rarely pushed onto the subway tracks, yet it is a crime that is widely publicized and terrifying for many New Yorkers. In 1999, the New York State Legislature passed Kendra's Law mandating assisted outpatient treatment for mentally ill individuals with a history of multiple psychiatric admissions, noncompliance with medication, and violent behavior.[7] When a judge determines that a patient qualifies under Kendra's Law, he or she is referred to mental health treatment in the community. If the individual does not comply, he or she can be forcibly returned to a psychiatric hospital.

Perhaps Kendra's Law will be effective in preventing further tragedies from occurring on the subway, but I am not very optimistic. Most days, as I wait on the subway platform, I stand far back from the edge.

Chapter 5

THE WOMEN WHO WEPT

Both of the women described in this chapter killed their husbands after what they claimed were years of emotional and physical abuse. The abuse could never be proven, but I evaluated both of them to determine whether they were driven to kill because of Battered Woman Syndrome (BWS).

BWS is not listed as a psychiatric illness in the Diagnostic and Statistical Manual IV.[1] It is considered a syndrome or a cluster of anxiety and depressive symptoms resulting from exposure to severe and ongoing abuse by a spouse or partner. Women with BWS often experience distorted thinking and may believe the abuse is their fault or that the abuser is all powerful and all knowing. They typically feel helpless to escape.

BWS is closely related in cause and effect to post-traumatic stress disorder. Individuals suffering from post-traumatic stress disorder typically experience depression, fear, anger, flashbacks, and sleep problems. Their self-esteem plummets and many become "frozen" and unable to plan or carry out a successful escape plan. They frequently experience what Martin Seligman, a famous social psychologist researcher, termed "learned helplessness."[2]

Domestic violence is a huge problem in our society. In her landmark North London study, Jane Mooney found that one in three women report violence in an intimate relationship.[3] In that sub-group, one in thirty fear being killed at some point in their lives. Statistics from the U.S. Department of Justice show that approximately one third of all female murder victims were killed by a domestic partner, compared with only 3 percent of male victims.[4]

Fortunately, the majority of battered women are not killed. Many successfully escape their abusers, some fight back, and a few kill their partners. Jurors tend to be more sympathetic to women who kill their abusive partners in self-defense compared with those who attack while their abusers are asleep or unarmed. "Why didn't she just leave?" jurors ask. "Why did she kill him when she wasn't being threatened?"

These complex legal questions have been at the forefront of public discourse for decades. The desperate situation of battered women was vividly illustrated in the 1984 television movie *The Burning Bed*, starring Farah Fawcett.[5] This movie was based on the real case of Francine Hughes who was found not guilty, by reason of temporary insanity, of killing her husband by lighting his bed on fire, as the title graphically conveys.

Mrs. Hughes was one of the few lucky defendants actually found not guilty. In the past, most abused women charged with murdering their husbands were convicted, since the courts did not recognize their actions as a form of self-defense. Public sentiment drastically changed when psychologist Lenore Walker began publishing research on the psychological effects of domestic violence, which she termed "Battered Women's Syndrome."

Dr. Walker became a nationally recognized expert on BWS with her now-classic work, *The Battered Woman* (1979).[6] She testified in many well-known BWS cases on behalf of the defendants, who, she explained, saw killing as their only means of self-preservation—the essence of legally sanctioned self-defense.

The famous criminal attorney Alan Dershowitz has been critical of the BWS defense, and many consider it a "get out of jail free card."[7] In reality, the defense is rarely successful. The defendant is more likely to succeed in getting a plea bargain than an acquittal. In a large study of 200 women who killed their partners, only forty-six were acquitted. Ninety-eight were found guilty of manslaughter and thirty-eight were found guilty of murder. No information was available on the remaining ones.[8]

"One of Us Will Be Six Feet Deep"

It was about 8:00 P.M. when a neighbor called 911. Patrol cars rushed to the quiet neighborhood in Queens, New York, where they found the young woman kneeling on the sidewalk over her husband's body, crying hysterically. "It was a mistake!" she blurted out when the police arrived. Her two-year-old daughter was in the house when the killing happened. The child remained inside with a police officer while the family was contacted, and Mrs. Colon was taken to the police precinct. Once there, she confessed to stabbing her husband and signed a written statement. The assistant district attorney arrived a few hours later to videotape her confession.

It was never a question of whether Mrs. Colon was factually guilty of the crime. All the evidence pointed to her, and, of course, she had confessed, verbally, in writing, and on tape. Her attorney hired me to assess her for Battered Woman Syndrome (BWS) and an extreme emotional disturbance defense. I was to judge whether her stories were consistent and whether she fit the profile of a domestic abuse victim.

In New York State, if a defendant is found to have acted under extreme emotional disturbance, the offense is lessened from murder to manslaughter. BWS testimony can pave the way for an extreme emotional disturbance defense. The defense is most likely to succeed in cases where the defendant tried to escape or got an order of protection.

*   *   *

Mrs. Colon's attorney mailed me a package of materials to review in preparation for my first meeting with the defendant. There were hundreds of pages of hospital records, police records, and crime scene photos to review, in addition to the videotaped statement.

I decided to watch the video before tackling the pile of records. I pushed the tape into the VCR and she appeared on the screen, hunched over in her chair and running her hands through her long black hair. She was a small, childlike woman with dark circles of exhaustion under her eyes. Her eyes were also swollen from crying. Eventually she was able to stop crying long enough to describe what had happened.

There was no evidence that she was confused or unable to understand what was going on. She did not appear to be hearing voices and did not make any peculiar comments. She seemed distraught and remorseful, looking the prosecutor in the eye in a bid for his sympathy.

This was the story she told:

"I was cooking dinner that night. When I looked out the window I saw him get into his car with a strange woman in the passenger seat; I was convinced that she was his lover. I ran out of the apartment to confront him and forgot that I still had the cooking knife in my hand. I was nervous, scared, not really angry. I was feeling disrespected, cheap. When I saw the van, I saw this girl sitting here. He was half in and half out of the van with the door wide open. He was trying to tell me the girl was just a friend. I was asking him 'What's going on? Who is she?' The next thing I know he had a look on his face, that look he gets right before he hits me. And then he got up on the knife. He tried to get up on me. He tried to take the knife. When he grabbed my hand with the knife—he stepped into the knife. When he fell to the ground I saw the blood. Then I called the police."

I watched the tape a few times without seeing any signs of disturbed thinking or delusions. I moved on to the psychiatric records, which provided a detailed overview of Mrs. Colon's history. Unlike the majority of defendants I have interviewed, she had a childhood unmarked by any great tragedy. There were no records of foster care placements, investigations by the Bureau of Child Welfare, no special education placement, and no previous arrests.

Mrs. Colon was born in Mexico and immigrated to New York City at an early age. She and her brother and sister were raised by their single mother. By all reports it was a typical working class home. Mrs. Colon's mother worked two jobs and the children did well in school. The defendant graduated high school and worked for several years before marrying and becoming pregnant. Up until that time, she had no history of psychiatric treatment or counseling.

A few weeks after the birth of her daughter, however, she attempted suicide by overdosing on pills. Her husband found her and rushed her to a nearby hospital, where she had her stomach pumped. She was admitted to the psychiatric ward and diagnosed with adjustment disorder. Adjustment disorder is a relatively mild mental condition characterized by an excessive emotional reaction to an identifiable stressor—in this case, the birth of her new child.

Mrs. Colon was discharged within a few days with a prescription for Ativan, an antianxiety medication, and instructions to attend outpatient counseling. When I read through the psychiatric records, I was surprised by the quick discharge and questioned the diagnosis she was given by hospital staff.

Within a few weeks of her release, Mrs. Colon's condition worsened. She began acting strangely, talking to herself and staying up all night. Her husband and mother became concerned not only for her own safety, but also for the safety of her baby. They brought her back to the hospital, where she admitted to the staff that "strange things" had begun to occur after she was discharged. Initially she only heard whispers, but then she started to hear voices telling her to destroy her husband's property and to hurt herself.

The staff now recognized that this was *not* an adjustment disorder. The psychiatrist concluded that she was psychotic and diagnosed her with postpartum depression with psychotic features. Many women become severely depressed after childbirth, but very few hear voices or become delusional. Mrs. Colon had developed an extreme, psychotic form of the illness.

She was treated with antipsychotic and antidepressant medications and released after two weeks with instructions to continue in outpatient treatment. Since there were no records of any outpatient treatment, I concluded that she had not followed her doctor's advice.

This second hospitalization was her last; I had reached the end of the psychiatric records. Next I picked up the police records. I was looking for evidence of domestic abuse, but was surprised to see that the first police report had been filed by the defendant's husband. Six months after the birth of their daughter, he called to request an order of protection, explaining that he had separated from his wife and was being harassed by daily phone calls. They must have reconciled after that, because the second police report was dated a few years later. This time, Mr. Colon claimed that his wife had destroyed his property after an argument.

It seemed that the problems in their relationship were escalating. The third police report was filed only a few weeks later, but this time by Mrs. Colon who called to report an incident of assault. She claimed her husband had hit her during an argument. She was given an order of protection and her husband spent the night in jail.

Mr. and Mrs. Colon never separated, rendering the order of protection useless. A few years passed without any calls to the police. The next police documents in the pile were the records of her arrest for murder. I packed everything back in the box and began composing a long list of questions to ask her.

* * *

The interview took place a few days later in the counsel area of the Supreme Court building. Whoever designed these interview rooms certainly did not have privacy as a primary concern. The four rooms were no more than cubicles divided by thin walls that came up only three quarters of the way to the ceiling. There was so much noise in the room that it was difficult to conduct interviews. I almost had to shout to be heard, and because of this, people in the other cubicles could easily hear my conversations. The corrections officer sat right outside the door, further eliminating any illusion of privacy. I often complained about those interview rooms, yet they gave me the reassuring impression that help would be close at hand if a mentally ill defendant suddenly attacked me.

When she entered the interview room Mrs. Colon looked like a completely different woman. She was much prettier than she had appeared on the video. She explained that she had been placed on a mental observation unit at Riker's Island jail and had started taking antipsychotic medications again. Within a few days, the tormenting hallucinations had ceased and she was able to sleep.

I reviewed her history, questioning her carefully about her upbringing and relationships with her mother and siblings. Mrs. Colon described a conflicted relationship with her family, whom she rarely saw, though she did stay in touch with infrequent phone calls.

"Tell me about your relationship with your husband," I said.

She smiled as she recalled, "At the beginning it was great. He was real nice, real charming. My family loved him; he gave me anything I asked for."

She told me that her husband became possessive. "He'd sit there and listen to me on the phone," she said. "Sometimes he'd be on the other extension and I wouldn't even know."

"How were things after the baby was born?" I asked in a general way.

"I never returned to work after she was born," she replied.

"How did you spend your time?"

"My life was caring for my husband and child."

"What happened a few years ago," I asked, "after you had your husband arrested?"

"We were still living together," she said. "Because he was the one taking care of me. We ignored the order of protection and he came home the next day."

Her next remark perfectly reflected her total emotional and financial dependency upon her husband. She looked in my eyes, as if searching for my approval and said, "Everything I know is him."

Those five simple words spoke more to me about the life of a battered woman than all the extensive research I had done.

I switched topic and asked about her mental illness. Her story was consistent with her psychiatric records: she had been admitted twice to the psychiatric hospital after the birth of her child. What she said next, however, came as a surprise to me. After her baby was born, she said, she began hearing voices telling her to kill herself.

After the second hospitalization, her depression gradually lifted and for the next two years she lived a withdrawn but stable life. She ignored the doctors' advice to seek counseling. She rarely saw her family and spent most of her time home alone with her baby daughter. She continued to take the medication prescribed by her general practitioner but stopped approximately six months before she killed her husband.

"Why did you stop?" I asked.

"I didn't think I needed it anymore," she replied. "Then the voices came back. They said I was worthless and my husband had another woman."

"Is it possible your mind was playing tricks on you?" I said gently. "Maybe your husband wasn't unfaithful."

"No!" she said. "I know the difference between real voices and hallucinations."

"Did you tell anyone?" I asked.

"No. I knew they'd send me back to the hospital."

Then, she told me about puzzling and disturbing phone calls she received during this time. The caller never spoke to her, but the muffled sounds in the background were distinct enough that she could recognize her husband's voice talking to an unidentified woman. It seemed to Mrs. Colon that this "other woman" was taunting her with evidence of an affair. Listening to her outraged tone, I could not decide whether the phone calls were real or auditory hallucinations.

Mrs. Colon's voice rang with anger and betrayal when she talked about her husband's alleged infidelity. She reluctantly admitted that she had no objective proof of her husband's affairs. She frequently searched through his pockets and possessions but found nothing out of the ordinary.

She volunteered that her husband had been staying out late at night during the months leading up to her crime and that she had been feeling especially lonely and stressed while caring for their child without any help. Although she was certain that her husband had been cheating on her, I could never tell whether her belief about her husband's infidelity was delusional or not.

When I asked her about the abuse, her voice changed immediately. "He would hit me," she said in a hushed voice. "He gave me bruises. He'd apologize after he hit me and say things like, 'You drive me crazy because I love you too much.'"

She recalled how humiliated she felt by the bruises on her body. "I think the neighbors knew about it. I was embarrassed. I'd open my door before going out to see if anyone was there. If I did go out, I'd keep my head down."

She shamefully hung her head while admitting the beatings she had suffered by her husband. I wondered: was she really humiliated by the abuse or was she just a great actress? This was a question I kept in mind as I continued asking about her repeated claims of abuse.

"Can you tell me about the worst episode of abuse," I said.

"He was choking me and pulling my hair," she replied. "I tried to call the police but he pulled the phone jacks out of the walls. He hit me with a steel pipe and broke my arm."

The assault finally ended when their daughter came out of her bedroom, awakened by the screams in the living room. Mr. Colon backed off and the defendant was able to find her cell phone and call her sister, who quickly came over to take her to the hospital.

"Did you ever think he might kill you?" I asked.

She paused and said, "He kept that pipe in the bedroom. Right next to the bed. He used to tell me, 'One of us will be six feet deep, the other in prison.' He'd stare me straight in the eye and say, 'You know which one will be dead.'"

"How did you feel?" I asked.

"One minute we're talking, the next minute he'd be punching me. When I talked to him I was always scared."

I became aware of my growing feelings of sympathy as I listened to Mrs. Colon's stories of abuse and infidelity. But I reminded myself that I needed corroboration. She could be lying. I spent the next few minutes asking for her family's names and telephone numbers. We had been talking for hours and I was tired. Asking these questions helped diffuse the intense emotion in the room. It made it easier, at least for me, to say good-bye and watch the corrections officer handcuff Mrs. Colon and lead her back to the holding cell.

Over the next few days I reached out to those who knew the defendant best. I traveled to her family's home to interview her mother and sister. They brought me into the living room and offered me a cup of coffee. While waiting for them to join me I glanced around and saw a picture of the defendant and her husband at their wedding. They looked like a typical happy couple. I also saw many pictures of their daughter. Mrs. Colon's mother had temporary custody of the girl.

They told me that the defendant had confided in them about her

abusive relationship, though she never turned to them for help es-
caping her marriage. Both of them confirmed Mrs. Colon's story.
Her mother even told me that she had taken pictures of her daughter's bruises; unfortunately, she had lost them.

Mrs. Colon's sister supported her story about her fractured arm.
When taken to the hospital, however, Mrs. Colon told the medical
staff that her arm was injured during a mugging. This could indicate that she was lying about her husband's abuse, but I knew that
battered women often make up stories about their injuries to protect their abusers.

"Why didn't she just leave?" I asked her sister. She shrugged and
said, "My sister had no place to go. I guess she thought she had to
take it. He used to throw it in her face. He'd be like, 'Nobody's doing
anything for you; you have to do what I say.' "

The next day I called the prosecutor to ask for permission to interview the victim's mother about her son's relationship with the defendant. I wanted to hear about Mr. and Mrs. Colon's relationship from
someone not biased in favor of her. A few days later the prosecutor
called to tell me that Mr. Colon's mother refused to talk with me. I
was disappointed, but not surprised.

The second interview with Mrs. Colon took place the next week. I
asked her additional questions about the physical abuse and her psychiatric illness. Then I started to administer the psychological tests.
I find psychological testing is essential in confirming a diagnosis, as
well as ruling out exaggeration or outright faking. I administered
the Millon Clinical Multiaxial Inventory II[9] and a questionnaire to
measure post traumatic stress disorder symptoms.

The results of these tests confirmed my clinical impressions that
Mrs. Colon had a severe psychiatric disorder. I diagnosed her with
major depressive disorder with psychotic features and post-traumatic stress disorder. I believed Mrs. Colon's story. It seemed clear

that she had been severely physically and emotionally abused by her husband and that the pattern of abuse and mental illness had made her pathologically dependent on, and terrified of, her husband. She fit the classic picture of BWS.

I had reached my conclusions about her psychiatric illness and personality style. Now I needed to focus the interview on the most important forensic question—what was her mental state at the time she stabbed her husband? I needed to understand her behavior in light of her psychiatric illness and the circumstances of that night.

"How were things in the days before your husband died?" I said carefully. I figured if I avoided saying, "when you killed him," she would be less defensive and more revealing.

"I got more depressed and felt hopeless," she said. "I couldn't even get out of bed. I stopped cooking and cleaning."

"How was your appetite?"

"I didn't want to eat. I lost about ten pounds."

"And your sleeping?"

"I'd pace around all night. And when I finally fell asleep, I'd keep waking up."

"Were you having any other problems?" I asked, in a purposefully open-ended manner. I didn't want to suggest any symptoms or ask leading questions.

"The voices came back," she admitted, staring down at the table between us. "They were saying that I was worthless and my husband had another woman. They said to be careful of him. That he's going to hurt you."

Mrs. Colon had stopped her psychiatric medication six months before she killed her husband. I was sure she was depressed and psychotic on the night she stabbed her husband. But understanding her mental state was not enough to answer the pressing legal question. Was she also confronted with an acute trauma that overwhelmed her to the point where she acted in a state of extreme emotional disturbance? Did she kill him out of fear, rage, or a combination of both?

"Were you hearing voices that night?" I asked.

"I heard them all the time."

"What did they say?"

"I'm nobody, I'm nothing. The same things my husband used to say to me."

Mrs. Colon told me that she remembered she was in the kitchen when her husband rang the bell. She went outside to confront him but did not remember leaving with a knife. When she left the house she saw him sitting in his car with a woman she did not recognize. They began to argue.

"What happened next?" I asked.

"He told me the girl was a friend," she said. "I was asking him what's going on and who is she. The next thing I know he had that look on his face, I thought he'd hit me."

"How were you feeling?"

"I felt mad. And nervous. Scared. I felt disrespected. Cheap."

Mrs. Colon went on to tell me how her husband tried to grab the knife and they struggled. She remembered that her hand was in the air with the knife but could not explain how he was stabbed. At first, she did not even know he was injured. It was not until she saw the blood that she realized he had been hurt. She took his cell phone, called 911, and waited with him for the police to arrive.

The decisive legal question was what went through Mrs. Colon's mind during the moments before she stabbed him. I believed that she was experiencing flashbacks, a typical symptom of post-traumatic stress disorder and BWS. Her violent behavior did not result from any one factor. Instead, her attack stemmed from a psychiatric "perfect storm." Many years of mental illness and emotional and physical abuse left her vulnerable. When she stopped her psychiatric medications, she was tormented by hallucinations and delusions, which further weakened her already fragile psyche.

On the night of the murder, seeing an unknown woman in her husband's car, she broke. The threat of abandonment and betrayal was the final straw. I did not believe that she planned to kill her husband in any premeditated or calculated way. Instead, her violent behavior was influenced by intense emotions and provoked by an extreme stress. I concluded that Mrs. Colon was depressed and psychotic at the moment she stabbed her husband. She was acting under extreme emotional distress.

I prepared and submitted my report. I expected her case to go to trial, since she had no documented evidence of physical abuse and she never tried to escape. She did not even want her husband to leave her. Her severe mental illness was not in question, but the prosecutor could easily make a case that she acted out of jealousy, not extreme emotional disturbance. Without any corroborating evidence, I was not optimistic about her chances and doubted whether a jury would believe her. I started to prepare my testimony. The surprise resolution of the case occurred on the eve of trial.

Mrs. Colon's husband's parents wanted custody of their grandchild. An arrangement was offered. If the defendant agreed to sign over custody of her daughter to the paternal grandparents, the prosecutor would offer a plea of manslaughter in the first degree. Mrs. Colon quickly agreed, since manslaughter was the best she could hope for, even if she won an extreme emotional disturbance defense at trial.

Mrs. Colon was sentenced to ten years in prison.

"Everyday I Was Ready to Die"

Mrs. Chen was eight months pregnant when she cut both her wrists. Immediately afterwards, she called 911. Police and EMS were dispatched to her house where they found a gruesome scene. Mrs. Chen lay on the floor in a pool of her own blood, barely alive. Her husband's body lay on the bed in blood-soaked pajamas. He was stabbed twice and his head beaten in with a hammer.

Mrs. Chen had never been in any trouble before. She had recently emigrated from China and was completing a master's degree in business at a university in New York City. She had been married for a little over a year. Her defense attorney had retained an expert who concluded that Mrs. Chen was a battered wife who had acted under extreme emotional disturbance. I was hired by the assistant district attorney to give a second opinion.

I took the subway to Queens to pick up the records at the prosecutor's office. He wanted to meet with me before I interviewed the defendant. I had never worked with him before on a case and was surprised when he candidly began talking about the weaknesses of his case.

"She was eight months pregnant when she killed her husband," he said. "And after that, she cut her wrists. She almost died before the ambulance arrived." He told me that the EMS workers rushed her to the hospital just in time to perform an emergency cesarean and save the baby.

The prosecutor flipped through the crime scene pictures. The photos were brutal. Everything was red: blood seemed to have seeped into every corner of the room. I took a deep breath and looked at each one carefully, refusing to give into the temptation to rush through them. In my decades-long career, these crime scene photos were some of the most disturbing ones I had ever seen.

Especially jarring was a picture of the corner of the bedroom where the defendant had been found. It was evident by the carpet on the floor that she had almost bled to death. The pictures of the victim lying dead on the bed in his pajamas were equally horrific.

Before I could say a word, the prosecutor said, "I know, it certainly does seem like she was emotionally disturbed." And, he explained, there was more. When detectives searched through the files on the defendant's computer, they retrieved hundreds of demeaning and threatening e-mails from her husband.

"There is no objective proof he abused her," the assistant district attorney finished weakly, almost defensively.

"Show me the e-mails," I said.

The messages were vicious. None of them referred to any physical abuse, but most were filled with hateful attacks on his wife's appearance, intelligence, and abilities. He repeatedly called her worthless. His cruelty came through loud and clear. I sat there in the prosecutor's office, reading page after page of e-mails, and suddenly felt nothing but sympathy for the defendant, even though I had not even met her yet.

A few days later, Mrs. Chen walked slowly into the interview room of the District Attorney's office. She was 26 years old and about 5-feet 8-inches tall, with black hair and high cheekbones. Her eyes were already red from crying.

Extremely polite and demure, she spoke softly and in heavily-accented English. She was fluent, but paused often to search for the right word. I was grateful to be interviewing her in the private, quiet District Attorney's office as opposed to the crowded, noisy cubicles in the counsel area of the Supreme Court building. Even so, I had to strain to hear her.

Mrs. Chen confided in me in such a trusting manner that I felt uncomfortable. Concerned that she might not really understand the American adversarial court system, I repeatedly explained that her comments were not confidential and that I was hired by the assistant district attorney, whose job it was to prosecute her. She clearly knew I was not her ally or protector, yet she never assumed the defensive posture I am accustomed to seeing in defendants when I am hired by the prosecutor.

Mrs. Chen described what seemed an almost idyllic early childhood. She was the only child of professional parents who doted on her. Yet she grew to be a shy, inhibited teenager who had difficulty making new friends.

She recalled suffering panic attacks and periods of depression during adolescence. She considered suicide during periods of high stress, as when facing final exams or receiving anything less than an "A" grade. Whether as a result of the overly competitive academic environment at school or her eager-to-please personality, she became emotionally overwrought when she fell short of perfection. Her parents recognized that she was emotionally troubled but never sought treatment, perhaps because they viewed mental illness as shameful.

Mrs. Chen sat motionless and stared at the wall behind me as she calmly narrated the events of recent years. Upon entering college in China, she had struggled to find her social niche. She felt especially excluded as the other young women began dating. I asked her why the college social scene was so difficult for her and she explained that she was unattractive and never dated. "No one wanted me," she said, drying her eyes with the back of her hand. She was "undesirable" as a wife because she was tall and big-boned. I looked on skeptically as she explained her physical imperfections.

"Look," she said and pointed to her feet, "size nine." I tried not to look too obviously at my own equally large feet and concentrated on understanding her point of view. Listening to her and seeing the expression on her face no one could doubt her sincerity. I thought she was a very pretty woman but she saw herself as unattractive and unlovable.

Mrs. Chen told me that she moved to the United States to attend graduate school. Within a year she met the man who would become her husband. He was from a working-class family and had not graduated from college, but she convinced herself that she was lucky to have him. Initially, he was extremely attentive. He bought her flowers and called frequently.

"What was he like?" I asked.

"He was a gentleman," she said. "Very leading, he leads the decisions. He's in control of the situation."

"How did you feel about that?" I asked.

"I liked that. My father's like that."

The tears began in earnest as she next described her decision to accept his proposal. Though painfully aware she did not love him, she believed he was her only chance to marry and have a family. She felt she had no choice; only through marriage could she please and honor her parents and be respected in her community.

She was blinded to the red flags that would have been obvious to a more confident, independent woman. Her husband-to-be's excessive attentiveness was a clear warning sign of his possessiveness and controlling personality.

Mrs. Chen never consulted her parents about this important decision. She accepted his proposal. If her parents realized there were problems in their daughter's relationship, they did not have time to tell her. They only met their future son-in-law a few days before the wedding.

After a short honeymoon, Mr. Chen returned to work in a middle management position and she began graduate school. She did not tell her parents that her husband hit her, and they apparently never suspected anything was wrong.

"Why didn't you tell them?" I asked.

"They wouldn't have let me get married," she said. I must have looked unconvinced, because she went on: "Nobody saw me as attractive; I always get dumped after the first blind date. I never had a boyfriend. He's the first one who asked me and I'm almost 25 years old. I thought he'd change."

She held her hands out as if appealing for my sympathy. "It wasn't so bad at first," she said.

Before the wedding her husband had hit her only a few times. Each time he apologized and begged forgiveness afterward. She convinced herself that he would change after the wedding.

I knew what she would tell me next, even before she spoke. After they were married, the abuse became more frequent. The insults and threats now came on a daily basis. If she did not return home immediately after class, he would beat her. If she did not immediately return his calls or e-mails, he would beat her.

When he was laid off from his job, he blamed her. He frequently accused her of ruining his life and, eventually, she came to believe him. "I was cursed by God," she told me. "Because he married me, everything was not working out." He threatened to kill her if she told her family or friends about the abuse.

I continued asking questions about the most embarrassing events in Mrs. Chen's life. She told me that her entire life changed after she married. She was never extroverted, but she did have a small, close-knit group of Chinese girlfriends. After the wedding, however, her network of friends fell apart.

Her husband insisted that she come directly home after school each day. To avoid confrontation, she followed his commands and kept to herself. She withdrew from her friends and became isolated, leaving the apartment only to attend classes and returning home quickly to avoid a nightly beating. The pattern became more entrenched. She kept following his commands to keep the abuse a secret, but the longer she stayed silent, the longer it was allowed to continue.

"Did you tell any of your friends about the abuse?"

"I wouldn't tell my friends," she said. "That's like spitting on my own face. In front of my best friends, I wanted to look great. No one likes a depressed friend."

"Why didn't you just divorce him?" I asked.

"Divorce is a shameful thing in my community. On my mother's and father's side of the family, we only know two people who divorced. For men to get a divorce is not such a big deal, but for a woman to get a divorce it is shameful. My aunt, she is beautiful, rich, but got divorced twice. Now, nobody wants to talk to her. She's like an outcast."

"What's more," she said, "the Bible forbids divorce." I was tempted to confront her interpretation of religious doctrine, but stopped myself. What really mattered was *her* interpretation of the Bible.

"What about your religion forbids divorce?" I asked.

"That's my family background," she explained. "In my religion, divorce is not an option. God says 'I hate divorce.'"

She told me that she approached her pastor for help, but she must have downplayed the problems in her marriage and avoided all mention of the physical abuse because her pastor's advice was "to pray a lot."

Mrs. Chen told me that she hid the bruises and tried to convince herself that her husband would stop hitting her after she became pregnant. On the contrary, he became even more physically and emotionally abusive. He continued to beat her, even as she pleaded with him not to cause a miscarriage.

I recognized that Mrs. Chen's experience was hardly unique. Unfortunately, it is not unusual for abusive men to increase the frequency and severity of abuse when their partners become pregnant. They frequently resent the woman's attention toward the unborn child and are unable to accept the changing dynamic of their relationship. Already prone to jealousy, their possessiveness only increases during the pregnancy. Their resentment of the unborn child manifests itself through abuse of the mother.

"How did your husband react to your pregnancy?" I asked.

"He said I had to abort the baby if it was a girl," she replied. "He insisted that I have an abortion if the sonogram showed I was carrying a female baby."

"What did you do?"

"I postponed the sonogram three times because I was so afraid of the results. But he made me go. I was so relieved when the results showed the baby was a boy."

"Did that change things?"

She paused a long moment. "I thought, now that he knows he will have a son, he will stop hitting me."

*   *   *

Of course, the abuse did not stop. Mrs. Chen's husband threatened to kill her and the baby if she allowed her parents to visit after the birth. Alone in New York City, unaware of or unable to utilize the resources available to her, she made no effort to escape as the delivery date rapidly approached.

The stress of the pregnancy and the physical and emotional abuse took its toll. Before, she had been a relatively contented and successful young woman, but now she was barely passing her courses. She dreaded the birth of her first child. She was anxious, depressed, unable to sleep, and suicidal.

"Why didn't you call your parents?" I asked.

"I was so ashamed," she replied, staring down at the floor and sobbing softly.

"How were you feeling in the days before . . . ?" I let my words trail off.

"Every day I was ready to die," she replied in a deadened tone.

I needed to focus the interview on the most salient issue—what motivated her to kill her husband and attempt suicide on that particular night. I asked, and she told me the same story she had told everyone: the police at the hospital, her attorney, and the defense psychologist.

That night her husband was working on assembling the crib and left a hammer on top of the dresser in the baby's bedroom. He insisted they have sex, and, when she resisted, hit her a few times in the face. To force her compliance, he threatened her with a knife, which he then left on the nightstand by the bed. She gave in, afraid the beating would only get worse.

Afterward, while he slept, she was plagued with catastrophic thoughts: What will happen when the baby comes? What will he do to my parents? What will he do to me? During the next few hours she was overwrought and unable to sleep. She paced the apartment from room to room. She told me that she did not remember everything that happened after that.

"Tell me what you do remember," I prompted.

"I was feeling like a zombie, everything became like a dream. I just wanted to die. He was lying down. The lights were off. I went to the other room, saw the hammer, I'm thinking, why is the hammer still in the room? We already fixed the crib. I just picked it up. I took the hammer, went into the room and hit him over the head. Then I saw the knife he had left on the nightstand. I stabbed him twice."

Through the tears, Mrs. Chen recounted how her husband barely fought back. The first blow must have incapacitated him. She told me that she was not sure how much time elapsed between the moment she stabbed him and when she turned the knife on herself.

"What happened after you stabbed him?"

"I think I remember cutting myself, but I can't remember when," she replied. "I wanted all of us to die. It would be more peaceful to be dead."

Mrs. Chen was convinced that she and her baby should die together. She cut both wrists, sat down, and waited to die. Then, for reasons she could not explain, she called 911. The EMS workers were easily able to get into her bedroom since there was no knob on the door. Her husband had removed it one night after she locked him out of their bedroom.

Mrs. Chen's story was similar to those I have heard so often with women who kill their husbands or boyfriends. I might have doubted her if there was no corroboration of her story. When I reread the pile of e-mails her husband sent to her, I was convinced that she was being truthful. His written words told it all.

Many of Mr. Chen's e-mails were threatening and he frequently made reference to the Bible, including text with the words "revenge" and "avenger" in bold faced type. He referred to her as his "worst enemy" and "the greatest curse" in his life. Often, in what seemed to me a bizarre twist of logic, he wrote comments indicating that he actually viewed himself as a good husband. In one e-mail he reminded her that she was lucky to have him.

I believed Mrs. Chen's story. Her story and the e-mails were powerful evidence of physical and emotional abuse. I concluded that she fit the pattern of BWS. Her already weakened mental state was complicated by the hormonal changes of pregnancy.

But very few victims of BWS ever kill their abusers. What had led her to this desperate act? I believed that she could not face the birth of her son. Death for all three was her only solution. I agreed with the defense psychiatrist that Mrs. Chen had acted under extreme emotional disturbance. I called the assistant district attorney to report my conclusions.

"Once the jurors hear those e-mails," I warned him, "they'll hate the victim and conclude he got what he deserved."

"I can't say I'm surprised," he admitted.

We both agreed that this was indeed a case in which a jury would feel sympathy for the defendant.

Mrs. Chen's case never went to trial. Instead, the assistant district attorney offered one of the best pleas I had ever heard of. His proposal: if she agreed to leave the country with her infant son and never return, he would allow her to plead to manslaughter and he would recommend probation and no prison time. Not surprisingly, Mrs. Chen agreed and this is exactly what happened. She left the country a few weeks later.

I have often wondered about her and her son. I hope that she was able to build a happier life for herself and her son back home in China. When I think about the night she killed her husband, I remembered a comment made by one of my favorite mentors, Dr. Richard Weidenbacher. After we interviewed a woman charged with killing her abusive boyfriend, he looked at me with his characteristic mischievous grin and said, "Some men almost ask to be killed."

Chapter 6

THE MAN WHO KNEW
TOO LITTLE

The 911 call came through late in the afternoon. When the police arrived at the small two-family house, an older woman opened the door, her hair undone and her clothes wrinkled and slept in. She told the officers that her grown son had stumbled downstairs carrying his one-year-old daughter, mumbling incoherently, "Something's wrong, Ma." The police entered the downstairs living room, where they found the dazed looking man slumped in a chair. The officers went upstairs to the bedroom, where his wife lay dead on the floor next to their unmade bed. She had been stabbed over twenty times and there was blood splattered on the floor all around her. Since there was no sign of forced entry, the killer's identity was never in doubt. It should have been an open-and-shut case.

"Mr. Abrams insists he doesn't remember anything about the murder," his attorney told me over the phone. "Could you take a look at him and tell me if he's for real?"

"Of course, I'll see him," I said eagerly. I could not pass up the opportunity to evaluate a defendant claiming amnesia.

It is very unusual for a defendant to be genuinely unable to recall committing a violent crime. Many defendants insist, "I can't remember," but most are lying. Genuine amnesia usually occurs only in the event of a severe head injury, brain damage, alcohol intoxication, or sedative drug use. A different type of amnesia is linked to emotional trauma. An individual can become psychologically unable to remember an overwhelmingly traumatic event. According to Freudian theory, individuals use repression as a defense mechanism against post-traumatic stress. This kind of amnesia usually lasts for a few hours or days; the memories are typically recovered, although certain aspects or details may be lacking.

The next day I took the subway to Manhattan to meet with the attorney at his office downtown. I had never worked with him before, but knew him by reputation as a well-respected lawyer with over thirty years of legal experience. I arrived at his office suite and he came out to the waiting area to greet me. Dressed in a tailored suit, with longish white hair, he looked every bit the part of the successful trial attorney. I presumed the defendant's parents had tapped into their savings to pay for their son's defense.

"The police immediately knew there was something wrong with him," he said. "They took him to the hospital to get him checked out. As soon as the family hired me, I asked for a competency evaluation."

"What was the result?" I asked.

"The court-appointed doctors diagnosed my client with depression and concluded he wasn't competent. He was sent to a forensic psychiatric hospital, where he's been held for the past year."

The attorney filled me in on the details of the murder. Mr. Abrams claimed to be unable to remember much about that evening but recalled that he was pacing and unable to sleep. He woke his wife and she gave him a pill. He did not know what kind.

Mr. Abrams' next clear memory was "coming to" in the psychiatric hospital. Not only did he have no recollection of killing his wife, but he did not remember being arrested or questioned at the precinct. He thought someone else must have killed her.

"What do you make of his story?" I asked.

"There is no evidence of an intruder," the attorney shrugged. "The only possible defense is insanity or extreme emotional disturbance."

He handed me an impressively heavy box of psychiatric records, along with police and autopsy reports and crime scene photos. The sheer quantity of psychiatric records convinced me that Mr. Abrams had a long history of severe psychiatric illness. The box contained the records of the two psychiatric hospitalizations prior to his arrest in addition to all the evaluations that took place afterwards.

As I read through the older psychiatric records, I realized that Mr. Abrams' mental illness surfaced during major life upheavals. He could not cope with the normal stress of change. His first depressive episode occurred at age eighteen when he graduated from high school, the second episode, a few years later, when he separated from his first wife. His third and last episode began about six months after the birth of his daughter by his second wife. His depression worsened over a period of months, but he delayed starting treatment until a month before he killed his wife.

I scheduled my first appointment with Mr. Abrams who had returned from the forensic hospital a few weeks earlier. The hospital psychiatrists had diagnosed him with major depressive disorder with psychotic features, and concluded he was finally competent to stand trial.

I arrived at the Supreme Court building at 11:00 in the morning and headed toward the corrections department holding area. Once I passed through security I found an empty interview room, took a seat, and waited. When Mr. Abrams walked in I was taken aback by his dramatically altered appearance. In his mug shot police photo, he looked like an old man, unshaven and haggard, with a dazed expression. Today, he was clean cut, well groomed, and alert. He appeared almost jaunty as he reached out to give me an enthusiastic handshake. Even in his baggy orange jumpsuit, his athletic build was evident. Why the jail-issued jumpsuit? Most jail detainees are permitted to wear their own clothes; he must have been on special suicide watch.

My first, mostly positive, impression changed dramatically when he started to speak. Throughout the first interview session, he complained loudly about his treatment by corrections staff and bemoaned his fate. I could now understand why so many staff had written critically of him. In their notes they often described him as manipulative and immature.

"Tell me about your first psychiatric admission," I said.

"I got depressed right after high school. It was awful, and the antidepressants didn't help. It got so bad that the doctor admitted me to a psychiatric hospital for ECT treatment." He paused dramatically. "ECT was the only thing that worked."

Electroconvulsive therapy (ECT), also known as "shock therapy," is an effective treatment for severe depression and is often recommended for those who do not respond to, or are unable to tolerate the side effects of, antidepressant medications. The patient, while under anesthesia, is given an electrical pulse applied to the scalp to generate a seizure.

Many people are biased against ECT. When first introduced, patients were inadequately anesthetized and many were injured with broken bones and teeth. An anti-ECT bias was reinforced by the treatment's negative portrayal in media. For example, ECT was given as a punishment to the main character, Randall McMurphy, in the movie *One Flew Over the Cukoo's Nest* based on the novel by Ken Kesey.[1] The graphic images of McMurphy, played by Jack Nicholson, undergoing the treatment were certainly horrifying.

I certainly understand why many depressed patients will not

consider ECT. Despite its negative portrayal in the media, ECT is viewed by most in the medical community as a safe and effective treatment for depression. The patient is under anesthesia and experiences no pain. As with most treatments, there are side effects. Some patients complain of headaches, nausea, and brief mental confusion. Some complain of lingering memory problems. None, however, experience the global amnesia claimed by Mr. Abrams.

The defendant told me that his first course of ECT was miraculous. His depression lifted and he was quickly discharged home from the hospital. His mental illness did not recur for many years. He married and he and his wife lived in the upstairs apartment of his parents' house.

Mr. Abrams became depressed when his marriage fell apart. His response to treatment was the same this second time around; his depression resolved itself only after a course of ECT. He returned to work and continued to live upstairs from his parents. His life returned to normal.

Mr. Abrams talked proudly about his work ethic and steady employment at the hospital. He completed a master's degree in social work and worked on a psychiatric unit. I already knew much about his history, but his obvious delight in his accomplishments surprised me. He was acting as though I was interviewing him for a job, I realized.

Mr. Abrams' years of employment on the psychiatric unit was an intriguing part of his legal case. With years of direct contact with the mentally ill, he knew what depressive and psychotic symptoms looked like, and was certainly capable of faking mental illness.

Mr. Abrams told me that years passed uneventfully after his second depressive episode. He met and married the woman who became the mother of his child. The trouble began when he was forty years old, a few months after the birth of their daughter.

"Tell me what your life was like after the baby was born," I prompted.

"Everything changed," he said with a sigh. "My wife quit her job and we couldn't pay our bills. I transferred to the night shift."

"Why?"

"To earn extra money. The hospital paid a differential for working the graveyard shift. But even with the extra money, the bills kept coming. I couldn't keep up. My wife kept spending on the baby."

"Do you think working nights was a good idea?" I asked.

"My family told me I shouldn't work nights," he acknowledged. "But I had no choice. We were broke."

The change in his sleep-wake cycle undoubtedly contributed to his depression.[2] But I had to give him credit; he continued working, even as he sank into his third major depression. He started taking antidepressants, and still showed up on the job. Finally, a week before he killed his wife, he agreed to go on medical leave.

"I felt exhausted working the night shift. I couldn't sleep during the day," he said. "And my wife, she wasn't paying much attention to me. All her attention went to the baby. There was nothing for me. It was like the baby took my place."

As he grumbled about his deceased wife's behavior, I fought the increasingly strong urge to say to him, "What about *her* needs?"

I wondered whether his self-absorption was a symptom of his emerging depression or a sign of something more troubling. Perhaps it was merely a sign of his immaturity and dependency, qualities I had detected earlier when he talked about living at home with his parents. His jealousy of the new baby was not, after all, an uncommon reaction. Many new fathers feel left out and neglected when their wives become pregnant or give birth. Many couples separate or divorce around these times. Some men do more than leave.

The case of Laci Peterson came to mind. Laci was seven-and-a-half months pregnant when she disappeared in 2002. When her body and the body of her unborn baby Conner washed ashore, suspicion fell on her husband Scott. The case gathered enormous press attention and the public was transfixed by the events of the investigation, arrest, and trial. Although the defense raised the idea that Laci was killed in a satanic ritual, most people did not buy it. Instead, it was commonly believed that it was Scott's dread of becoming a father that motivated him to kill. The exposure of his extramarital affairs at trial also did not help his case. Although the evidence was mostly circumstantial, he was convicted of first-degree murder of his wife and second-degree murder of his son. Currently, he waits on death row at San Quentin prison.

Laci's disturbingly radiant pregnancy picture lingered in my mind, but I did not find her case had much in common with Mr. Abrams'. I believed him when he told me how much he treasured his daughter and loved being a father. Did his feelings of jealousy and insecurity overpower his love for his family?

"What happened the night your wife died?" I asked.

"When I got out of the shower I started having palpitations. I think I was suffering from extreme anxiety," he recalled. "I told my wife I couldn't breathe. She said she'd call the doctor in the morning. She gave me a pill. I told her I loved her and said good night."

"What type of pill was it?"

"I don't know. My wife always gave me my medicine." He explained that his wife was in charge of his medication regimen because he was too distracted and forgetful to take responsibility for it.

"What time did you take this pill?"

"One-thirty in the morning," he said. "The next thing I remember, I woke up in a wheelchair. I didn't know where I was. I asked the doctor why I was handcuffed."

I shot him a skeptical look, and he repeated emphatically that this was all he could remember. Did Mr. Abrams really suffer from amnesia or was he faking? He hadn't suffered any type of head injury and was not drinking alcohol or using sedative drugs at the time of his alleged amnestic episode.

I looked at his face carefully, and surprisingly, I found him believable. All the forensic evidence pointed to the irrefutable fact that he and he alone had killed his wife, but Mr. Abrams was unable to accept it—it was too overwhelming for him. He began telling me an elaborate story, seemingly for his own benefit, about how a killer could have broken into his apartment, killed his wife, and escaped without leaving a trace. It reminded me of the plot of a *Mission Impossible* movie.

I began to ask him questions about the weeks before his wife was killed. He told me that he was falling apart and he felt helpless.

"Did you have any unusual thoughts," I asked.

"I was thinking that people could read my mind," he admitted in a faint voice, as if he had travelled back in time.

"Who could read your mind?"

"My wife, my ex-wife. I was thinking that my ex-wife wanted to break up my marriage. I believed she had control over me and that I was possessed."

I noticed his momentary slip—wife and ex-wife—but decided to let that go.

"Tell me more about your ex-wife," I prompted, eager to follow the thread of his paranoid ideas.

"She thought she was telepathic and could talk to the dead. I know now that, in reality, my ex-wife couldn't read my mind."

"She thought she could talk to the dead?" I asked.

"She was into black magic and voodoo. When she abandoned me, she left all her books on Santeria in the garage."

I knew that Santeria is a religion based on the fusion of Catholic beliefs and the religious tradition of West Africa. It is a folk religion with many negative associations, chiefly related to magical practices and animal sacrifice. The magical practices are thought to bring good luck to friends of the worshiper and harm to his or her enemies.

"Why didn't you throw out these books?" I asked.

He explained that these books did not trouble him at the time of the divorce. The books sat boxed up in the garage, all but forgotten. Only years later, in the months before he killed his second wife, did his thoughts return to these books. He became preoccupied with the power he believed these books possessed.

This was as good a time as any to end the first session. We had been talking for about two-and-a-half hours. Before I left, I asked him to sign a form granting me permission to discuss his case with the psychiatrist who had been treating him before he killed his wife.

A few days later, I called the psychiatrist who treated Mr. Abrams for a month prior to his arrest. I explained who I was and why I was calling, but before I could even ask my first question, he interrupted me. "I never saw any symptoms of psychosis or threat of violence."

"Uh, I'm not—"

"There was no reason to believe he was dangerous to himself or his wife," he continued in a breathless voice. "He wasn't in need of hospitalization on an emergency basis."

I heard the tone of urgency in his voice and wondered if he was trying to convince me or himself. It was a psychiatrist's worst nightmare to find out that one of his patients had killed someone. I considered the difficult position he was in, and felt sorry for him.

I faxed the defendant's signed Release of Information Form and the psychiatrist quickly faxed back his case notes. I examined the pages, looking for unusual alterations in penmanship, abrupt changes in spacing or line quality. Handwriting analysis is certainly not my field of expertise, but I could see no evidence that the psychiatrist had changed anything in his notes.

The only problem was, I could not read them. The psychiatrist had a typical doctor's penmanship, and I could not make sense of many of the words. I called him back to ask a few questions.

The psychiatrist told me that he treated the defendant up until the day he was arrested. During the first visit, he prescribed a standard dose of Paxil for depression and Ativan for anxiety. A week later, during the second session, he wrote that his patient was somewhat better. He raised the Paxil dosage and added Ambien, a common sleep medication. The next week, he noted that his patient was less depressed and less anxious, yet added a low dose of Seroquel, most likely as a sedative. Seroquel is effective in treating psychotic symptoms, but a low dose is typically prescribed for agitation.

The next session was scheduled for five days later. The psychiatrist noted that his patient was crying and depressed. He increased the dosages of Seroquel and Paxil. During the next session, a few days later, he noted that his patient was anxious and crying. He recommended ECT and referred Mr. Abrams to another psychiatrist who could perform the treatments on an outpatient basis.

One of the psychiatrist's entries grabbed my attention. He recommended psychiatric hospitalization and noted that he had contacted the facility, but Mrs. Abrams adamantly opposed this option.

The fateful decision was made. Mr. Abrams received ECT treatment as an outpatient a few days after the last session with his psychiatrist. Four days later he killed his wife.

Since the defendant was not able to or would not tell me what had happened that night, I needed to talk with the people who knew him best. I met with his family and found that his sister's memories were the most distinct. She told me that her brother's mental state was deteriorating for months before his arrest.

"What did you observe?" I asked.

"He switched his work schedule. I saw him struggling. He was getting quite irritable, not sleeping."

"What else did you notice?"

"His look was different," she said. "He had a faraway look. I'd be talking and he wouldn't know what I was talking about."

"What about after he started treatment? Did anything change?"

"No, he wasn't getting better," she recalled. "He said to me, 'I feel like I'm in a tailspin.'"

"Anything unusual?" I asked, careful not to put words into her mouth.

"My brother felt that people were talking about him all the time, even the people at work. And he talked about his ex-wife a lot."

"What about his ex-wife?"

"He asked me the strangest question," she said. "He asked me whether I was afraid of his ex-wife. Then he went off rambling about her voodoo books. He told me he was afraid of those books."

"What happened to those books?" I asked.

"He wanted me to search the garage for the Santeria books," she recalled. "He asked me to burn the books. But I didn't."

"Did he describe anything else that seemed strange?" I asked.

"He told me that his ex-wife came to him, even when he was awake. I think he was hearing voices."

"What gave you that impression?"

"He said to me that his ex-wife was angry and told him not to get rid of those books."

"What was he like when he said this?"

"He was all sweaty and clammy," she recalled. "He was afraid. He asked me to go upstairs with him when he took a shower."

"What did he say, exactly?"

"He said, 'I'll leave the bathroom door open so I'll know you're there.'"

Mr. Abrams' sister told me that she tried to get her brother admitted to the hospital. Her voice took on a pleading tone; she seemed afraid that I would accuse her of not doing enough to prevent this tragedy.

"What was your brother like in the days after he had the ECT treatment?" I asked.

"I took him for the ECT treatment. He had some trouble with his memory afterwards. He went out with the car to visit our aunt.

She called to tell me that he was there, but when he left, he couldn't remember where he parked the car."

"Did you notice anything else?"

"He was pacing all that night, he couldn't sleep. The day before . . ."

"What?" I encouraged, after a long minute had passed.

"The day before, he told me, 'I'm so sick. Do you think the second treatment will help me?' He cried and cried. That's the last time I saw him . . . before . . ."

Again, she let the word hang, too choked up to finish her sentence.

"Did you see him after he was arrested?" I jumped in to rescue her.

"When I got home I saw him, sitting in the chair, not moving. He didn't answer me. He was just staring. I don't think he blinked his eyes. His eyes were very glassy. It didn't look like him at all. When the police took him out of the house, he looked catatonic, frozen."

She took a long, shaky breath before continuing, "I guess my sister-in-law didn't appreciate how sick my brother was."

Mr. Abrams' parents told me a similar story. They said their son was losing weight and crying constantly in the weeks before his arrest. The father, who was the last one to see the defendant, described their brief exchange: "It was the night he killed his wife. When he parked and came into the house, he told me, 'Dad, my head feels like it's going to explode.'"

"Did you notice anything else?" I asked. I felt terrible when I saw the tortured look that crossed his face.

"My son was an excellent driver," he said. "But that night, the car was parked with one wheel on the curb."

I met with Mr. Abrams five more times. I administered a full battery of psychological tests, the results of which indicated, unsurprisingly, that he had severe dependency needs and struggled with strong feelings of inadequacy.

His case continued to puzzle me. Of course, I considered the possibility that he was lying about his amnesia, but in my gut (not scientific to be sure), I believed him. It was not only intuition. Mr. Abrams just did not fit the classic picture of a malingerer.[3] He did not exaggerate or make up symptoms and he never claimed to be suicidal. Well aware of what real psychotic symptoms look like, he did not try to fake psychosis. He described vague paranoid ideas, but only when I asked; he never volunteered. He also never mentioned that he heard voices until I confronted him with his sister's story.

I started to write his report, but could not make up my mind about his psychiatric diagnosis. I knew he was severely depressed when he killed his wife, but I was not sure if he also fulfilled the diagnostic criteria for a psychotic disorder. I looked back at the records from the hospital where he was admitted after his arrest. Upon admission, he was diagnosed with depression. The court-appointed competency doctors also diagnosed him with severe depression. Yet, the psychiatrist who discharged him diagnosed him with adjustment disorder.

Adjustment disorder is a mild diagnosis. Most perfectly healthy people who are going through a rough patch in life could be diagnosed with adjustment disorder, and none of them should be in a mental hospital. I did not expect to see this diagnosis given to a man charged with the murder of his wife.

The psychiatrist who discharged Mr. Abrams was a good friend of mine. He was a seasoned forensic specialist with over twenty years' experience treating mentally ill defendants. We had worked together back when I was a staff member at that hospital ward. Reading through his notes, I was sure that he neither liked Mr. Abrams nor believed his story about amnesia.

Mr. Abrams was transferred to a long-term forensic hospital after he was found not competent to stand trial. He was diagnosed there with major depressive disorder, recurrent, severe, with psychotic features. A list of the symptoms observed upon his admission included depression and a paranoid delusion that people were talking about him. His depression did not lift for many months and he was treated with several medications. He was prescribed Klonopin for anxiety, Paxil and Effexor for depression, and Zyprexa, a major tranquilizer and antipsychotic.

Putting all the pieces of this puzzle together, I diagnosed Mr. Abrams with major depressive disorder with psychotic features. I concluded that he was insane and not criminally responsible for killing his wife, though I could find no rational explanation for his apparently motiveless crime. My report summarized my opinion in this way:

> Unfortunately, he is unable to recall his exact thoughts and feelings at the time of the offense. His statements to family indicate that he was very depressed, frightened and psychotic. He was experiencing paranoid delusions, specifically that he was being talked about and threatened by others. He described hearing his ex-wife's voice. He was feeling very frightened and agitated.
>
> In his agitated and psychotic state he was unable to adequately judge reality. In my opinion, Mr. Abrams' psychotic symptoms caused him to lack substantial capacity to know or appreciate the nature and consequences of his conduct or that such conduct was wrong.

The months passed and the case stalled. Mr. Abrams became depressed again. His attorney requested a second competency exam and the court-appointed doctors concluded that he was, again, not competent to stand trial. The presiding judge concurred and Mr. Abrams returned to the forensic hospital for treatment.

Almost a year after I completed my evaluation, Mr. Abrams recovered to the degree that he was found competent. Then, the assistant district attorney hired a psychiatrist to interview Mr. Abrams. Not surprisingly, the psychiatrist did not agree with my conclusions. He diagnosed Mr. Abrams with major depressive disorder, but did not believe that his mental illness precluded his ability to appreciate the wrongfulness of his actions. In his opinion, Mr. Abrams had not been experiencing psychotic symptoms. He concluded that Mr. Abrams was responsible for killing his wife and that he killed her because of "acute stresses" and his underlying personality features.

He wrote that Mr. Abrams' mother-in-law, brother-in-law, and work supervisor had described the defendant as self-centered, easily angered, argumentative, and verbally abusive. Mr. Abrams' work supervisor told the psychiatrist that she had seen Mr. Abrams only three days before he killed his wife and saw no signs of psychosis.

As I read through his report, I searched for mention of what I considered "the elephant in the room." What did the prosecution's psychiatrist make of the defendant's inability to recall stabbing his wife?

The psychiatrist wrote that Mr. Abrams' amnesia was "selective" and not a "genuine loss of memory." It was a cautiously worded sentence, but it meant that he did not believe the defendant.

But—I still did.

"Can you hire a psychiatrist?" I asked the defense attorney. "I think we need a medical opinion about this amnesia."

"Sure," he said. "Who do you recommend?"

"Lawrence Siegel is excellent," I said. "He and I have worked together on a number of cases. He's diligent and never misses a detail."

Dr. Siegel agreed to see the defendant. Over the next year, however, Mr. Abrams' mental state fluctuated, and he was readmitted several times to the forensic hospital. Dr. Siegel did not have an opportunity to meet with him for two more years—three-and-a-half years after I had evaluated him.

A few months after Dr. Siegel's first interview, the defense attorney called to tell me about a surprise discovery. The prosecution had "found" a tape of Mr. Abrams' statement, filmed at the police precinct right after he was taken into custody. The attorney had no explanation as to why the tape was turned over four years after his client's arrest. Was it lost or somehow purposefully misplaced? Of course, we were all suspicious.

The attorney had only one copy of the tape, so Dr. Siegel and I scheduled a time to meet at his office. Eager to see this mysterious tape, I hopped on the subway early. Dr. Siegel was already there, but the attorney was late. We, of course, began talking about the case.

"Do you think Mr. Abrams was psychotic when he killed his wife?" I asked.

"Well, I can't be sure. But did you see the hospital records from last year?" Dr. Siegel asked.

"No, I never saw those notes."

"You didn't? Cheryl, they're very important! Out of the blue, Mr. Abrams became psychotic. He was delusional and told hospital staff that his parents were murdered and that fluid had been taken out of his brain.

"The staff realized Mr. Abrams was hearing voices," Dr. Siegel continued, searching for the notes in his briefcase. "No one knows why, but his psychosis remitted after three days."

Dr. Siegel pulled out the file and handed it to me. I quickly rifled through the papers to find the highlighted portions. It was exciting, and, frankly, a bit of a relief, to read about the defendant's odd three-day psychotic break. Prior to this event, Mr. Abrams' sister was the only one to witness his paranoid delusions and hallucinations. Now, I had more corroboration. His psychotic state had been observed by many clinicians on the psychiatric ward. No one there suspected that he was malingering. It confirmed my opinion that he was mentally fragile and psychotic when he killed his wife.

Both Dr. Siegel and I had years of forensic experience and had interviewed dozens of men who had killed their wives. We agreed that Mr. Abrams' lethal attack on his wife was totally out of character.

"He had no rational motive for this crime," Dr. Siegel said.

"It's true. The crime doesn't fit his personality or history."

"People who are violent tend to have a prior history of violence," Dr. Siegel added. "Mr. Abrams has no documented history of violence. And most violence is committed by young men. At the time he killed his wife he was almost forty-five years old. But I just can't be certain he was psychotic when he did it," Dr. Siegel continued. "Because he tells me he can't remember."

Dr. Siegel, like me, was convinced that Mr. Abrams' amnesia was genuine. We spent a good deal of time discussing what could have caused his memory loss. Was it psychological or was there some medical explanation?

"I've recently seen reports about Ambien and sleep disturbances," he said.

"I've seen them too," I replied. "There were reports of people eating, cooking, and driving while asleep. When they woke up the next morning, they had no recollection of their behaviors."

"Did you read the news reports about Representative Patrick Kennedy?" he added. "Kennedy claimed that his use of Ambien caused him to be unable to remember crashing his car."

"Mr. Abrams was taking Ambien," I said, "Do you think—?"

"Well, it certainly is possible," he said cautiously. "But I haven't read any studies linking Ambien use to violence."

At that moment, the defense attorney arrived and ushered us into his office. Watching Mr. Abrams' image transported us back in time. I momentarily forgot about the Ambien as we started watching Mr. Abrams' confession, recorded over four years earlier. The video revealed a completely different side of the man I had met and interviewed.

Mr. Abrams was disheveled, unshaven, and appeared to be in a stupor. Staring blankly ahead with dead eyes, he barely responded to the assistant district attorney's questions. "I need help. I need help," he mumbled as the tape abruptly cut out.

Dr. Siegel and I had no doubt that the assistant district attorney had ended the interrogation as soon as he realized that Mr. Abrams' zombie-like expression could not help him at trial. Perhaps that is also why the tape went "missing."

Dr. Siegel completed his evaluation and diagnosed Mr. Abrams with major depressive disorder with psychotic features. His report concluded:

> While I cannot make a firm statement based upon firsthand information that Mr. Abrams lacked substantial capacity to know or appreciate the nature and consequence of his conduct or that his conduct was wrong, it is my professional opinion with a reasonable degree of psychiatric certainty that the balance of probabilities point in that direction.

A few weeks after Dr. Siegel submitted his report, the defense attorney called to tell me that the prosecution had made an offer of twenty years for manslaughter. He advised his client to take it, but Mr. Abrams insisted on going to trial with an insanity defense.

Dr. Siegel called a few months before the trial was scheduled to begin. His enthusiasm was contagious. He told me he had been searching for reports on Ambien and had unearthed journal articles that totally altered his thinking about the case.

Dr. Siegel e-mailed me these articles. One of them described twenty-one cases of psychotic symptoms associated with Ambien use. Some patients reported visual hallucinations.[4] Another article described two patients who experienced auditory and visual hallucinations as well as delusions after taking Ambien. Neither patient had any history of psychosis.[5]

Dr. Siegel also forwarded me a recent letter addressed to healthcare professionals on the subject of Ambien. "Visual and auditory hallucinations have been reported as well as behavioral changes such as bizarre behavior, agitation, and depersonalization," the letter warned. "Patients usually do not remember these events."[6]

Reading through these articles was literally an "aha" moment for

me. It was exciting to find an explanation for Mr. Abrams' uncharacteristic violence and amnesia. He had told me that his wife had
given him a pill when he was unable to fall asleep the night of the
murder. The pill—very likely Ambien—and his mental illness were
a lethal combination.

Finally, Mr. Abrams' case came to trial. I arrived at the courthouse
at 9:30 A.M. and sat on the bench outside the courtroom. I waved
to Dr. Siegel who came in moments after I did. The court officers
unlocked an empty conference room, and we went inside to wait for
our turn to testify, taking turns going downstairs to get refills from
the coffee truck. We tried to guess who would be called first to the
stand.

"Look what I put together," Dr. Siegel said, taking out a large
binder and dropping it on the table. AMBIEN RESEARCH read the label on the side. He wore a satisfied smile on his face and was clearly
itching to explain his research about Ambien and psychosis to the
jury. I imagined him up on the stand with the large binder in front
of him, the label clearly visible. It would make a powerful impression on the jury.

As it turned out, I was called to testify first. I glanced at the jury
as I walked down the center aisle toward the witness box. There appeared to be a mix of ages, genders, and backgrounds. I felt fairly
comfortable, in part because I was familiar with the room and the
judge. I had testified in that courtroom many times and recognized
a number of faces in the gallery rows. Since psychiatric cases rarely
go to trial, many attorneys and clinicians were there to watch.

After a brief good morning from the judge, I remained standing
with my right hand raised as I was sworn in. Then I took my seat
and waited for the defense attorney's questions.

The defense attorney posed the first round of questions, called
the direct examination. He took me through my qualifications
and then asked me to describe my evaluation and conclusions. I

had prepared a timeline highlighting the crucial weeks and days before Mr. Abrams killed his wife. The new courtroom was equipped with all the latest technology, and my timeline was displayed on an overhead projector for everyone to see.

During the direct examination I testified about my diagnosis of the defendant and gave my opinion that he was not legally responsible when he killed his wife. The direct examination lasted only an hour. Then the court broke for lunch.

After lunch, I returned to the stand. The assistant district attorney stood up and addressed me. "Good afternoon," he said pleasantly. Just a few minutes into his cross-examination I could see where he was going with his questions.

"Doctor, on your direct [testimony] you used a term that has been used to describe the defendant, histrionic. Correct?"

"Yes."

"That was a word that was used to describe the defendant in a series of medical records that you have read over the past years. Correct?"

"Yes."

"What does that word mean?"

"Well, it's expressing emotion, being very dramatic, needing a lot of attention, being very needy, clinging. It's what they call personality or character traits."

"It can mean overly dramatic in behavior and speech?"

"Yes."

"For effect, correct?"

"In that he needs a lot of attention, yes."

"He wants the effect to be that people believe that he is sick?"

"I would view it that he is very needy and wants a lot of attention."

"Okay. But in the dictionary, they describe it as a person acting for an effect and being insincere and [displaying] an exaggerated expression of emotion. Would you agree with that?"

"Yes."

"And it's a deliberate effect by someone, it's on purpose?"

"Well . . . I am not sure how much control he has over it or how much is on purpose. But he is a very, very needy guy, and at times he becomes quite emotional in a 'can somebody listen to me and take care of me' way."

"Right, but that's also a description used by doctors in this case over a period of time, by several different doctors, correct?"

"Yes."

"But they also made several descriptions of him . . . and here are those words: 'he was demanding, intrusive, hostile, needy, aggressive, manipulative, selective and evasive about information, [preoccupied] with perception, and *consistently, but not credibly, stating he had no recollection.*' [italics added] Those are what was written in the [hospital] record within days of him arriving there, correct?"

"Yes."[7]

The ADA was asking leading questions, giving me very little chance to elaborate on my answers. It was clear that he was trying to convince the jury that Mr. Abrams was neither seriously mentally ill nor even likeable.

Later, the assistant district attorney began asking questions about Mr. Abrams' memory loss and his use of Ambien. Once again, his questions required little more than a "yes" or "no" from me.

"So, one of the things that the defendant spoke about was his lack of memory about what happened that night [to] Mrs. Abrams or into the day Mrs. Abrams was killed, right?"

"Yes."

"He's told you he has no memory, right?"

"He's told everyone that," I replied.

"Right, everyone. But aside from those moments when he doesn't remember the actual stabbing, he does remember certain things?"

"It's not moments. It looks like he has lost memories for hours."

"Well, he remembers in talking to you [that] he gave you a full history, correct?"

"Yes."

"He gave doctors a full history, the doctors he's been to, of the depression he had, that he worked for [the hospital]. These are people he is talking to just a day or so after [Mrs. Abrams] was killed, right?"

"Yes."

"So he can provide that history to them?"

"Right, but that's what the [researchers] describe [about] Ambien. You lose memories for hours around the time after you have taken the Ambien, but there is no memory problems before you take the Ambien or the next day. It doesn't cause long-standing problems learning and remembering. It's just [for] that period of time when the medication is in you."

"But you don't have any indication that Ambien was in him at that time other than a prescription that he was given?"

"He told me that his wife gave him another medication."

"You don't know what that is though, right?"

"I'm not sure, that's correct."

"But, Doctor, you talk about Ambien, Ambien, Ambien, you don't even know if he took it that night, do you?"

"Well, not 100 percent, but if someone wasn't sleeping and the prescription was for Ambien, a sleep medication, I don't think it's a stretch that that's what his wife would give him."[8]

I was aware that my answer was not what the prosecutor wanted to hear, but he did not seem rattled. He maintained a professional and respectful attitude throughout.

"Doctor, is it also possible that he has just decided not to remember? Isn't it possible?"

"Well, anything is possible."

"Thank you."[9]

With that, I was dismissed. It was after three o'clock and I expected the court would adjourn until tomorrow for Dr. Siegel's testimony. To my surprise, he called me later that evening.

"They called me to the stand at three-thirty," he said. "I couldn't believe it. I finished my testimony in about an hour."

"Direct and cross-examination?" I asked.

"Yes," he said. "I expected to testify for hours. The prosecutor didn't ask much, which was no surprise. But even the defense attorney didn't have many questions. I didn't have the chance to tell the jury about all of the research on Ambien."

I went back to court the next day to testify for a different case. Dr. Alan Perry, an old colleague of mine, stopped me outside the elevator.

"Have you heard?" he asked. "The jury already reached a verdict. They found him guilty."

"Oh," I said, deflated. It was not a complete shock. Most insanity defenses are unsuccessful, and I had prepared myself for this outcome. What was startling, however, was to learn that the jury had only deliberated for two hours. I realized that Dr. Siegel's and my testimony must have not been very convincing.

Dr. Perry noticed the expression on my face and rushed to reassure me.

"It wasn't you," he said. "The defendant was talking to his attorney during a lot of the testimony. When he did that during the coroner's testimony, it looked really bad, like he didn't care about his wife's death."

"But did you think he was mentally ill?" I asked.

"I don't know. The guy seemed too well composed, too smug and complacent. I didn't 'smell' mental illness."

Later that day I met Mr. Peck, the mental health expert of the Brooklyn Legal Aid Society who had also been in the courtroom during the trial.

"What did you think about Mr. Abrams?" I asked.

"He just didn't look upset enough," he said. "Not even when the pictures of his wife's body were shown."

* * *

In my experience, no matter how convincing the psychiatric testimony, jurors are always swayed by their personal feelings toward the defendant. They had watched Mr. Abrams for days during the trial. His coldness and composure made a powerful impression. The testimony about his "manipulative" and "histrionic" personality must have also been persuasive. In a case like this one, jurors will acquit the defendant only if they feel sympathy for him. The judge seemed similarly unsympathetic; he sentenced Mr. Abrams to twenty-five years to life.

This case continued to trouble me. Apparently, the jury did not see him as psychotic or believe his amnesia was genuine. I had expected that his severe mental illness and the research on Ambien would be compelling testimony in his defense. I could even imagine how the headlines would read if he had been acquitted: AMBIEN ON TRIAL! Instead, it was Mr. Abrams' character that was on trial, and that, in the end, convicted him.

PART 2

*Evaluations of Competency to Stand Trial
and Waive Miranda Rights*

D oes the defendant understand the charges against him? Does he understand the roles of court personnel and courtroom procedures? Can he assist his attorney in the preparation of his defense? The next part of *The Measure of Madness* addresses these fundamental psycho-legal questions.

The competency to stand trial evaluation assesses whether a defendant has "sufficient present ability to consult with his lawyer with a reasonable degree of rational understanding and whether he has a rational as well as factual understanding of the proceedings against him."[1] It is the most common type of forensic evaluation.

The fairness of our adversarial system of justice depends on a defendant's right to meaningfully participate in criminal proceedings. When a defendant is found incompetent, all legal proceedings stop. He can not resolve the case through trial or plea. His fate is determined by the severity of the legal charges. If he is charged with a misdemeanor, the criminal charges are dropped and he is admitted to a state psychiatric hospital. An incompetent defendant charged with a felony, on the other hand, is sent to a secure forensic hospital. He is treated and returned to court to face his charges after he is considered improved and competent to stand trial.

The defendants described in this section of the book were evaluated by two or more forensic psychologists or psychiatrists. Mr. Arkin's case was so complex that five psychologists and one psychiatrist testified at his competency hearing. He was charged with the killing of a young woman and claimed he was falsely arrested because the police wanted to deprive him of a substantial inheritance. Mr. Lawrence was also delusional but his conspiracy involved a plot to destroy the world. Mr. Cowen, on the other hand, seemed rational, but the more we talked, the more psychotic he began to appear.

The final case in this part concerns a defendant's competency to waive his Miranda rights and give a confession. The Miranda rights are familiar to most people from countless police dramas on television. The Miranda rights require that an individual in custody "must be warned prior to any questioning that he has the right to remain silent, that anything he says can be used against him in a court of law, that he has the right to the presence of an attorney, and that if he cannot afford an attorney one will be appointed for him prior to questioning if he so desires."[2]

The Supreme Court's ruling in the precedent setting case of Ernesto Miranda identifies procedural safeguards known as Miranda warnings. If the prosecutor is unable to show that the warnings were given and the defendant waived his Miranda rights, "no evidence obtained as a result of the interrogation can be used against him . . . [the suspect must] knowingly and intelligently waive these rights and agree to answer questions or make a statement."[3]

Guilt or innocence? So much rides on the confession. Jurors are powerfully swayed by a defendant's statement; they typically believe it to be genuine. The layperson is convinced that no one would confess to a crime he or she did not commit. Research has proven, however, that this bit of common sense is flawed. Confessions given by a mentally ill or mentally retarded suspect are of special concern. That is why this type of psychological forensic assessment is so important.

I have found that the videotaped statement is the single most important piece of evidence showing the defendant's state of mind at the time of the offense. The video is typically filmed within a few hours of the defendant being taken into custody and I may not be called into the case for months after the arrest. Defendants can change dramatically during those months, for the better or the worse. Many defendants who were psychotic when they committed their crimes, for example, start on antipsychotic medication after their arrests. By the time I interview them, they are much improved. Typically, they are no longer obviously psychotic. Therefore, the video statement taken at the time of the arrest is the best snapshot of the defendant as he or she was on the day of the crime.

Mr. Almeda, a chronic schizophrenic, waived his Miranda rights and confessed to setting hundreds of fires. His attorney hired me to answer three issues: Did Mr. Almeda possess enough knowledge, information or intelligence to understand his rights at the time he was making his statement? Was his waiver of rights the product of a rational reasoning process? Was his waiver voluntary?

Over the past twenty-five years I have interviewed thousands of defendants to assess competency issues. I chose the following four cases because each illustrates, in a different way, how challenging competency evaluations can be. While many defendants are clearly either competent or incompetent, these four defendants were perplexing. All were psychotic, but clearly understood how the court system worked and none wanted to be sent to psychiatric hospitals.

Chapter 7

THE BRAIN CHIP

The victim was not hurt much, only a few scratches. When the police arrived, Mr. Cowen admitted that he had chased his girlfriend and pushed her to the ground. He was charged with assault in the third degree, a misdemeanor, and released without bail. His case should have been resolved quickly. He could have pled guilty and received probation. With so little at stake, why did his attorney ask for a competency to stand trial evaluation?

Dr. Weidenbacher and I read through the criminal complaint form before the defendant arrived. My colleague was a 68-year-old psychiatrist with over thirty years of forensic experience. He had served as a "father" for most of us working with him. He never married and seemed to live for the job. He was usually the first one to arrive at work every day, greeting each of us with a cheery "Good morning!"

Dr. Weidenbacher was an eccentric man. His now white hair was usually uncombed. His suit was technically appropriate for court, but on closer scrutiny the shirt cuffs and collars were often frayed. I was not surprised to learn that he bought his clothes at a thrift store. While he did not care much about his appearance, he cared very much about the job.

I called Mr. Cowen's attorney before the defendant arrived. He explained that the case involved a "simple" domestic dispute.

"What do you know about him?" I asked.

"He has no history of psychiatric treatment and he has a job. But there is something strange about him. I'm not sure whether he's competent."

Mr. Cowen, a 39-year-old white man, had no criminal record and his attorney expected that he would be offered a plea of probation. Most defendants in his situation accept probation in order to get released from jail quickly and avoid the risk of going to trial.

"This should be a short interview," I said to Dr. Weidenbacher.

"Yes," he agreed, "This is a good way to start the day. The defendant's only charged with a misdemeanor."

Mr. Cowen was on time for his appointment. I was immediately struck with how vigorous he appeared—muscular with a ruddy complexion and cheerful expression. I could easily imagine him at the beach were it not for the sterile court building office in which the interview took place.

Mr. Cowen's brightly colored T-shirt of tropical birds was distinctly upbeat—casual, yet clearly attention had been paid. He reached out to shake my hand in a confident, assertive manner. Not surprisingly, he had one of those "good handshakes" I like, with a warm, strong grip.

The interview was going along effortlessly. Mr. Cowen was cooperative and seemed practical. "I know I shouldn't have pushed her. I'll take the plea offer of probation and time served," he volunteered.

I was almost ready to conclude Mr. Cowen was competent. So far, so good, I thought, my mind already drifting onto cases scheduled for later in the day.

"Have you discussed the case with your attorney?" Dr. Weiden-bacher asked.

"I can't talk with him," he replied matter-of-factly. "They're listening."

There was a long pause before I could form a question.

"They?"

"No conversation is confidential because of the 'implanted chips,'" he replied.

Struggling to maintain a calm and unemotional tone, I asked "What chips?"

Out it all came, a slew of bizarre comments about electronic chips implanted in his brain. He was eager to tell us his story which began when he was incarcerated a few years earlier on a different charge. While in prison he was having bouts of stomach pain and had undergone a routine gastrointestinal endoscopy. This is a medical procedure where a tube is inserted through the mouth and down the throat to examine the tissue. He was convinced that during this minor procedure the surgeon implanted "mind and auditory control devices."

Mr. Cowen rambled on and on, endlessly detailing other "scientific" research that proved that the implanted devices in his body were real. He described brain electrode experiments conducted by the U.S. military and the CIA. The more he told me about this research, the more apparent it became that his delusions had begun many years earlier.

Pulling papers out of his backpack, Mr. Cowen showed us a community newspaper article about how the government had experimented with him by implanting "paramagnetic" computer chips in his body. He had underlined journal articles about animal research on brain stimulation and emotion. He had also extensively researched the science behind brain implants and, as frequently observed in paranoid patients, real scientific research had been misinterpreted to support his delusions. His psychosis fueled his "homework" and he was able to bolster his beliefs by finding grains of truth in the medical literature and then liberally peppering them throughout the pseudo-scientific documents.

As is the case with many psychiatric patients I have interviewed, Mr. Cowen's psychotic delusions were influenced by popular culture. I listened to his story and was immediately impressed with the resemblance between his story and one of my favorite movies, *The Manchurian Candidate*. I was not surprised when he pulled some papers out of his bag and showed me his own writings which included comments about this movie and Denzel Washington's performance as a man with an implanted electronic chip.[1] In between his entries, he included the comment, "Welcome to *The Matrix*," referring to another recent futuristic movie about mind control.[2]

Mr. Cowen decided to have an MRI because, in his words, "I felt something inside me. I was hearing voices, like a white noise, like the hissing of a transmitter. The voices were trying to disturb my life and make me dysfunctional. They were using auto-suggestions to create anxiety and monitor my activities."

The expression on his face mirrored his outraged feelings as he insisted that an MRI scan had "found" the implanted devices. I knew Mr. Cowen was paranoid, but I did not understand why he thought the government chose him for this experiment. I am always fascinated to discover why a person believes he or she was chosen by a conspiracy. When defendants describe paranoid delusions, their enemies are threatening them for a reason.

"Why were you the target?" I asked, without betraying my doubt of the premise of his bizarre story.

"I deduced that I'm a good subject. I'm intelligent. I think they're interested in my memory."

"How do they monitor you?"

"Audiosemetrics basically. I have several chips, electronic chips in my head. I hear them."

I was momentarily distracted by that term and wondered

whether audiosemetrics was a real word. Psychotic people often use made-up words. In psychiatry, these words are called neologisms.

"What do they say?" Dr. Weidenbacher asked.

"They use basic words," Mr. Cowen explained. "This disrupts my activities and makes me think they're going to harm my family. They say my children are plotting against me."

Listening, I became truly alarmed. Mentally ill patients with paranoid delusions can become violent. Although I was not asked to determine whether Mr. Cowen could be violent, I felt concern for his children. I also thought about the doctor he blamed for implanting the devices.

The 1976 Supreme Court decision in Tarasoff v. Regents of the University of California, is frequently known as the psychotherapists' "duty to protect" or "duty to warn" standard.[3] Ms. Tarasoff was murdered by graduate student Prosenjit Poddar who had told his psychologist, Dr. Lawrence Moore of the Berkeley University Health Service, about his plans to kill her during a therapy session on August 18, 1969. Dr. Moore conferred with the assistant director of the clinic and then contacted the university police. Unfortunately, campus police spoke only briefly with Mr. Poddar and did not take him to a hospital for a psychiatric evaluation. Mr. Poddar killed Ms. Tarasoff on October 27, 1969.

Ms. Tarasoff's parents sued Dr. Moore, the other clinicians involved in Mr. Poddar's treatment, the University of California and the university police. The California Supreme Court ruled twice on this case. In 1974 the court ruled that the doctors treating Mr. Poddar had a "duty to warn" Ms. Tarasoff. In a later 1976 decision, the court revised this ruling to a "duty to protect." A duty to protect includes warning or taking other alternative steps to protect the identified victim.

I was not Mr. Cowen's treating clinician. But with the duty to protect in mind, I needed to carefully explore his risk of dangerousness.

I looked at him and asked, "Have you done anything about those electronic chips?"

"Yes, indeed," he said without hesitation. "I've tried a few things already. I filed a lawsuit in Eastern District Federal Court, charging the U.S. government with invasion of privacy and conspiracy to commit murder."

"Anything else?" I asked, hoping his answer did not include anything about buying a gun.

"I contacted a few surgeons to have the devices surgically removed," he replied.

A frustrated expression crossed his face as he confided that no doctor had agreed to operate on him. My anxiety rose as I thought— what would he do when he was unable to find a surgeon to remove the devices? My concerns were confirmed when he blurted out what I most feared. He had considered confronting the doctor who had performed the endoscopy.

Mr. Cowen did not say he planned to hurt that surgeon, but he did admit that the implants were "pressing" him into violent action. He recounted how voices were "trying to tell me to do things. Like I'll have blanket protection to do something that would be against the law." Dr. Weidenbacher and I questioned him about this comment, but he reassured us that he would resist any voice that told him to hurt people.

But could he resist? Listening to him ramble anxiously, another implanted chip case came to mind—Ralph Tortorici.[4] Tortorici was born with a congenital deformity of his urethra. This is the tube connected to the bladder for passing urine. He had three operations but the condition was not cured. During adolescence he became convinced that the government had implanted microchips in his penis during these surgeries. He complained that he heard voices commanding him to sexually molest young girls and he believed that these voices were transmitted from these microchips. He was hospitalized numerous times and diagnosed with paranoid schizo-phrenia.

Even with this history Tortorici was permitted to purchase a semiautomatic rifle. On the morning of December 14, 1994, dressed in military fatigues, with a hunting knife and eighty rounds of am-munition, he entered a university lecture hall of the State University of New York at Albany and kept thirty-five students hostage. His stated goal was to meet with the president and governor. The two-hour siege was ended when several students overpowered him. One student was shot and Tortorici was charged with attempted murder, kidnapping, assault, reckless endangerment and criminal possession of a firearm.

Tortorici pled not guilty by reason of insanity. At his trial a num-ber of psychiatrists testified that he was insane. The prosecution could not find a single expert willing to testify that Tortorici had *not* been insane at the time of the offense.

The jury deliberated for only one hour and convicted him of all charges. The judge sentenced him to the maximum term, twenty to forty-seven years. Although everyone involved in the case agreed that Tortorici was schizophrenic, he was not kept in a psychiatric hospital. Mr. Tortorici committed suicide by hanging himself with a bed sheet.[5]

Dr. Weidenbacher interrupted my thoughts about Tortorici and steered the interview back to the issue of competency. "Do you know what you're charged with?" he asked.

Mr. Cowen nodded and said: "I told my girlfriend to leave, she was yelling at me and on the way out she picked up a rock and threw it through the window. I chased after her. She ran across the street and I tried to grab her. I guess I pushed her. She ran into some car and fell down."

Mr. Cowen had an excellent understanding of his case. He de-scribed the events in detail—an important criterion for competency to stand trial. He maintained that he had never slapped his girl-friend, but acknowledged that he should not have chased her and that she may have been hurt when she fell.

"Do the voices discuss your legal case?" I asked.

"The people who are transmitting in my ear through the micro-chip implants influence my decisions," he said. Then, all of a sudden, he broke eye contact and looked off to the side. He appeared to be hallucinating.

"You seem distracted," I pointed out, bringing him back to *our* conversation.

"The implanted microchip voices are discussing my case," he ad-mitted.

"What did they say?"

"The voices were just laughing and carrying on," he blandly re-plied.

We continued to discuss these voices as if hallucinations were an ordinary experience. He told us that the implantation of devices was part of a larger conspiracy. He believed it was possible that his ex-girlfriend was somehow connected with the conspiracy against him and that she was pressing charges against him in order to derail any future lawsuit against the surgeon. He also thought that his at-torney "could be involved in the conspiracy." Clearly, his delusions about the "implants" contaminated his ability to view his legal case in a rational manner.

I questioned him again about whether he would agree to discuss his case with his attorney. He patiently explained that he could *never* discuss his legal case with his attorney, since "others" were listening. Although he wanted to accept a plea, he would not discuss it with his lawyer because he had, in his words, "no hope for privacy."

As we continued to question him, I carefully watched for signs that he might involve us in his paranoid system. I scanned his face for expressions of anxiety or fear, but found quite the op-posite. He looked me straight in the eye and smiled in a winning way. Most paranoid defendants I have interviewed were wary and defensive. He surprised me again when he laughed and admitted that his beliefs certainly sounded crazy. I found it remarkable that Mr. Cowen, while clearly delusional, on some level was able to see himself objectively.

Mr. Cowen did not fit the stereotype of a mentally ill man. He was not disheveled or incoherent. He did not behave bizarrely. He was enjoyable to talk with and had a good sense of humor. If I did not know about his delusions, he would have seemed perfectly normal. He was unique because he was clearly psychotic but appeared rational on the surface. Once he started talking, however, even those with no clinical experience would recognize he was ill.

Dr. Weidenbacher and I asked a few more questions and ended the interview on a polite note. Everyone shook hands and wished each other a nice day. Mr. Cowen did not ask about our conclusion, and we did not offer it.

Dr. Weidenbacher and I then launched into an animated discussion about Mr. Cowen's diagnosis. His delusions and hallucinations pointed toward a diagnosis of schizophrenia. Schizophrenia is a mental illness affecting approximately one percent of the population; the onset of the disease is usually between late adolescence and the mid-thirties. Schizophrenics often experience delusions and hallucinations. Delusions are false ideas such as the belief that one is being followed or has a special mission in life. Hallucinations are false sensations such as voices. Patients experience severe problems in their everyday functioning, in their relationships, at work, and at school. Many are unable to work for sustained periods; most never marry.[6]

Mr. Cowen did not seem to fit the criteria for schizophrenia. He had a steady work history and close family and romantic relationships. He was never treated by a psychiatrist. Dr. Weidenbacher and I discussed whether Mr. Cowen had a delusional disorder.

Delusional disorders are quite rare, accounting for only 1 to 2 percent of admissions to psychiatric hospitals. An essential criterion of a delusional disorder is the presence of "non-bizarre" delusions without impaired social functioning or disorganized speech or behavior. Non-bizarre delusions are not "clearly implausible" and typically involve delusions of being poisoned, followed, infected by a virus, etc.[7]

Was Mr. Cowen's delusion about the implanted computer chips a non-bizarre delusion? We considered the role of culture, and specifically the influence of the movies. Was it possible that some of these ideas had filtered down and were accepted as a possibility by many individuals? It occurred to me that many normal people were convinced that they had been abducted by aliens.

Mr. Cowen did not fit either diagnosis perfectly, but Dr. Weidenbacher and I decided to diagnose him with a delusional disorder. Dr. Weidenbacher, in his characteristic 'I can remember every case I ever heard of' style, then told me about a little known, yet similarly bizarre Brooklyn case from many years earlier. As he filled in the story with details, I, as usual, was impressed with his uncanny ability to recall minutiae.

This defendant was convinced that a device had been implanted in his eye during routine cornea surgery. He disguised himself as a Hassidic Jew in order to get past the security guards at the hospital where his surgeon worked. He then confronted and shot the doctor, who luckily survived. After he was arrested, he told the examining psychiatrists that he believed the doctor was an Israeli Mossad agent who stole eyes of non-Jewish people to send to Israel for experimentation. I was surprised to learn that his insanity defense was unsuccessful; he was convicted and remains in prison today.

"Do you think we have to warn anyone about Mr. Cowen?" I asked Dr. Weidenbacher.

"I don't think so," he replied. "He isn't saying that he is planning to do anything to the surgeon. But, I'm certainly going to include a comment about Mr. Cowen's potential for taking revenge in my report."

We agreed that it was impossible for Mr. Cowen to assist in his defense. He could not even confer with his attorney because of his delusion that his attorney might be involved in the conspiracy. Even though his desire to accept a plea was certainly a practical and legally sound one, we concluded that he was not competent to stand trial.

I knew Mr. Cowen needed treatment, but I still felt ambivalent about recommending psychiatric hospitalization. I often feel conflicted when I advocate involuntary treatment for defendants like Mr. Cowen, individuals dead set against admission. I knew he would not want to go to the hospital—he was convinced that the "implant" was real and that he had no mental illness. But I could not think of any alternative for him. He would never voluntarily seek outpatient treatment and, without treatment, I was convinced he could be dangerous.

A judge reviewed our reports and ruled that Mr. Cowen was not competent. Since Mr. Cowen was charged with a misdemeanor, his criminal charges were dropped and he was admitted to a state psychiatric hospital.

To this day, I wonder if my concern that Mr. Cowen might attack his surgeon had an effect on my finding him not competent. I remember escorting him out of the clinic after the interview was over. I wished him a good day but never told him that I believed he needed hospitalization. I generally tell defendants what I will be recommending to the court. Sometimes, I even try to sell them on the idea and explain all the benefits of treatment to them.

Not so for Mr. Cowen. I never told him directly what I thought or what my conclusions were. Was it because I hated the idea of him being locked up against his will? Or was it because we were meeting in an outpatient setting, with no corrections officer to rush in if he got violent? I knew that Mr. Cowen's attorney would tell him about my conclusions—later. Still, I felt a bit like I was passing the buck.

I have often wondered how Mr. Cowen has fared since. Delusional disorders are difficult if not impossible to treat effectively. I later discovered that he was committed to a psychiatric hospital but I never heard whether he was released. For many months I found myself looking for his name as I read through the metro section of the local newspapers. I was relieved that I never found his name mentioned.

Chapter 8

THE GOOD SAMARITAN

A young father was beaten by a stranger outside a coffee shop where he and his son had just finished breakfast. As he was taken away by ambulance, the officers at the scene spoke to the irate man identified by the crowd. Mr. Lawrence pointed to the ambulance's brake lights and insisted that the person who should be arrested shouldn't be him. It should be the man on the way to the hospital. "I was upset for the little boy because he was sexually violated," Mr. Lawrence explained. "My initial reaction was to protect the boy. I wasn't trying to be aggressive." The officers arrested Mr. Lawrence and took him to the precinct.

Mr. Lawrence was charged with assault in the second degree. He told his attorney that he only "grabbed" the complainant. According to police records, however, the victim's rib was broken and his lung punctured. The attorney asked the judge to order a competency to stand trial examination after she heard her client's strange story.

I picked up the judge's order when I arrived at the Supreme Court building in the morning. Glancing at the thin file, I expected it would be a relatively simple interview. Mr. Lawrence's attorney arrived a few minutes later, and we discussed the case while walking to the pens, the area where the defendants are housed.

I sat down on a metal chair in the small interview room. I read through the paperwork and barely noticed the dirty cinderblock walls. I looked up from the papers as the corrections officer brought in the defendant.

Mr. Lawrence was a slim, handsome 32-year-old, African American man. He looked out of place in his button-down business shirt and khaki pants. My first thought was that he looked more like a successful attorney than a defendant. He did not seem shy or uncomfortable. He looked me straight in the eye, and after the corrections officer unlocked and removed the handcuffs, reached out to shake my hand.

It was easy to get Mr. Lawrence talking about his past. He matter-of-factly described a fairly ordinary childhood; his parents were loving and he did well in school. He never married and worked in a variety of blue collar factory jobs. In a slow, southern-accented voice, he explained how he had left his family in Georgia and moved to New York City to look for his "pot of gold."

I was lulled by his likeability and understood why the staff at Riker's Island had housed him in general population instead of a mental observation unit. He seemed entirely rational—that is, until I asked about his move to New York City.

"I came here because of a family issue; I'm a trust fund beneficiary. I was trying to unseal court documents to show my inheritance."

That comment got my attention. Nothing he said was obviously alarming, but I felt uneasy. I was no expert in trusts and estates but his story seemed odd nonetheless. His manner of speech changed dramatically as he described his lost inheritance. Whereas before he spoke in a slow, almost-relaxed manner, he now grew quite animated.

"Tell me about your lost inheritance," I said.

"I'm involved in a situation and I don't know how to tackle it," Mr. Lawrence said, leaning forward. His voice became more urgent. "There is a gag order imposed on me. They're against me and they're trying to steal my inheritance."

By this point, I knew he was psychotic. The mood in the once comfortable room changed and my questions became more direct.

"Who is against you?"

"They're organized crime and they're worth twenty billion dollars. They have enough power and money to manipulate the others."

"Who is against you?" I repeated.

"The party I'm fighting against is trying to destroy the world," he said. "They've accepted the devil."

"Have you heard voices when no one was there?" I asked.

"Of course I don't hear voices!" His eyes opened wide and he appeared startled and insulted. He quickly added, "I'm not crazy."

Mr. Lawrence was clearly delusional and paranoid. Now I needed to find out whether he was competent to stand trial. The law states that a defendant is competent if he has "sufficient present ability to consult with his lawyer with a reasonable degree of rational understanding."[1]

What would be reasonable or rational in this odd case? I wondered.

"Tell me what happened," I said.

"I was eating in a coffee shop when I noticed this young man sitting in the next booth," Mr. Lawrence said. He paused, and then continued, "He had a little boy, and he was fondling him."

"What happened next?"

"When the two left the restaurant, I followed them out. I confronted the man and tried to hold him for the police. The man struggled and tried to run."

"Did you punch him?"

"No, somehow he fell to the ground."

He insisted that he had only grabbed the complainant and denied causing him any serious injuries. I knew Mr. Lawrence's story was not factually true, but I did not know whether he was lying or just was unable to remember what had happened. Many defendants minimize the severity of their violent behavior. Psychotic defendants, on the other hand, often misperceive or misinterpret events. Some are confused; others are paranoid and weave their perceptions of the events into a preexistent delusional world.

"Does this incident relate somehow to what you told me earlier about the conspiracy?" I asked.

"Absolutely," he replied, nodding his head. "This guy went and grabbed his penis with the boy's hand. He did that a second time. This refers back to what I said about all pedophiles keeping this gag order. They're all trying to keep me from getting my money."

He insisted that "the devil" must be involved and that there was more at stake here than only his freedom—his inheritance and the world's existence hung in the balance. I listened carefully but could not understand how the victim's behavior connected to Mr. Lawrence's delusions about stolen money, organized crime, and the devil.

His thinking was not bizarre throughout the interview. He talked intelligibly about his childhood and family. He was able to recite the exact legal name of the charges against him. He could even describe the physical layout of the diner in a coherent way. Yet when he began talking about the victim, he became overly excited, and his thinking went off on tangents like a pinball after it has left the chute. His comments veered off to ping from one delusion to the next.

I was confused and asked him to repeat the sequence of events one more time. In his retelling, he puffed up, seeming proud of his behavior. He claimed to have acted in a "proper and brave manner."

"I know it's against the law," he reluctantly agreed when he saw my doubtful expression. "But I've been wronged. It wasn't my fault; it was the pedophile's fault—he should be the one on trial here."

Mr. Lawrence insisted that he wanted a trial to prove his innocence and accuse the victim of sexually assaulting the boy. His attorney and I pointed out that his actions could land him in prison, but the advice never seemed to truly register. His smile, however, slowly faded and he appeared deflated.

The defense attorney then read the long list of people that could be called to the stand to testify in court—the coffee shop eyewitnesses, the police officer first at the scene, and the complainant himself. She then showed him the victim's medical records to prove that he was badly hurt.

Mr. Lawrence argued with his attorney, but could not rationally explain how both the coffee shop eyewitnesses and the first officer on the scene could all be so wrong while he was so right. He insisted a jury would find him innocent at trial.

I felt frustrated and asked a bit provocatively, "Okay, and how would you prove you're innocent?"

"Maybe there are other witnesses. Maybe with that, we could indict that man," he replied.

I knew that in order to get out of jail, Mr. Lawrence needed to forget about arresting the victim. He did not grasp the risks of going to trial, that he could be convicted and sentenced to prison. The defense attorney brought up another issue. In order to be found not guilty, his client would have to testify. Defendants are never *required* to take the witness stand, since the burden of proving guilt rests on the prosecution. In this case, however, the attorney argued that Mr. Lawrence would need to explain his behavior.

I imagined the defendant on the witness stand and was convinced that no judge or jury would believe his story. Chances were they would do just the opposite. Seeing him "live and in person," they might be as concerned about him getting free as I was and decide to convict him.

Catching the lawyer's eye, I could see that she did not think her client's chances of winning at trial were good either. She tried a different tack and started with good news. Since Mr. Lawrence had no criminal record, the assistant district attorney was willing to offer him a very generous plea—probation with mandatory mental health treatment.

She explained that his case could be transferred to Mental Health Court—this new and innovative program was part of a specialized court designed to help mentally ill defendants. Psychiatric treatment was offered as an alternative to incarceration. He would not have to go to jail if he successfully completed a one-to-two year outpatient program. His conviction would also be changed from a felony to a misdemeanor.

The defense attorney was selling the mental health court program to her client like a matchmaker trying to set him up on a blind date. I was not surprised to see that Mr. Lawrence did not share her enthusiasm. His face was now sullen and he mumbled, "I'm not crazy."

Mr. Lawrence clung to the belief that he was mentally stable. The label of "mental patient" obviously stung to the point of clouding his better judgment. Again, he insisted he was wrongly accused and was not going to consider the plea bargain. His mind was made up and he was eager to go to trial. He believed it was his only chance to prove his innocence, accuse the pedophile, and obtain his inheritance.

The interview was over. I told Mr. Lawrence, as gently as possible, that I thought he was emotionally disturbed and needed the treatment program. I explained that another doctor would be interviewing him soon and stood up to leave. He politely thanked me for my time and shook my hand good-bye. The corrections officer came to put on handcuffs and lead Mr. Lawrence away. The scene was surreal. He acted as if he had just finished a job interview.

I diagnosed Mr. Lawrence with delusional disorder and concluded that he was not competent to stand trial. He fit the criteria for delusional disorder spelled out in the psychiatric "Bible," *The Diagnostic and Statistical Manual-IV*.[2] A patient with a delusional disorder can appear normal since he does not have any of the classic symptoms of schizophrenia such as hallucinations or disorganized speech.

Mr. Lawrence fit this picture. His hygiene was good and he

dressed appropriately. He was able to function in society and hold down jobs. He did not hear voices or see things. The jail staff had not noticed any of his delusions or referred him for a psychiatric evaluation.

I submitted my report. A second doctor, a psychiatrist, interviewed the defendant a few days later. I was surprised when I found out that he came to the opposite conclusion. He agreed that the defendant was psychotic and delusional, but believed Mr. Lawrence could work with his attorney.

The psychiatrist was an old friend of mine. When he told me his conclusion I was tempted to say, "How could you possibly think that?" But I reminded myself that forensic experts often come to different conclusions. The third doctor, a psychologist, agreed with my friend. He, too, found the defendant delusional but competent.

A few weeks later the assistant district attorney called me to discuss my testimony. He said he was new at his job and had never done a competency hearing before. He also told me that Mr. Lawrence had requested a new lawyer. An older attorney, with years of trial experience, had been assigned.

I entered the crowded courtroom a few days later for the competency hearing. I glanced around and looked for friendly faces. The other doctors were already there. Smiling their welcome of professional camaraderie, they moved over to make a space for me between them in the second row. We joked with each other, even though we were about to testify about our opposite opinions. I noticed several attorneys I had worked with before and wondered if they would stay to watch us testify.

I looked over at the defense attorney and felt a jolt of nerves. He was close to 60 years old, gray-haired but slim, with an athletic build. He had a reputation as a tough litigator. I knew he would not be easy on me. His client did not want to be found incompetent, and he had to fight for his client.

The case was called. The defendant was brought into the courtroom and his handcuffs removed. I was called to the witness stand. As I walked between the prosecution and defense tables, I quickly looked over toward the defendant. Dressed in a suit, Mr. Lawrence seemed even more like a successful attorney than before. He appeared like a second seating defense counsel, not a defendant.

Of course, I suspected that the defendant was still delusional. He had not been prescribed any psychiatric medications in jail. Delusional disorders do not resolve quickly, even when a patient takes antipsychotic medication.

Yet Mr. Lawrence appeared mentally balanced sitting at the defense table. He was neatly dressed, well-groomed, alert, and attentive. I wondered how his appearance would affect the outcome of the hearing. If he did not testify, he would look—at least on the surface—as sane as the rest of us.

I was called to the witness stand. The atmosphere in the crowded courtroom was simultaneously intimate and intimidating, but my nerves were somewhat calmed when I looked upward at the bench. I had testified in front of this judge many times and knew what to expect. I stood in front of the witness chair and waited to be sworn in by the senior court clerk.

I was a bit surprised to find my heart beating fast. After years of testifying in court, I knew this sometimes happened during the first few minutes. Luckily, those minutes are spent swearing in— "Do you solemnly swear or affirm the testimony you are about to give this court is the truth, the whole truth and nothing but the truth?" recited the clerk. "I do," I replied, and sat down.

The judge smiled down at me. "Good morning, doctor, how are you today?" he said jovially. I was relieved to be in front of a judge I knew would keep the hearing professional and polite.

I looked over at the defendant. He sat perfectly still. Glaring at me from behind the defense table, his look of hatred was unmistakable. I knew he had seen my report. He had read my conclusion and my recommendation—psychiatric hospitalization.

The assistant district attorney stood up and began what is termed the direct examination. Many attorneys schedule a mock run-through with me to practice the questions they will ask me during the direct examination. However, I had not practiced with this prosecutor. He was carrying a legal pad with a long list of pre-planned questions. I guessed that he had done some research or had some coaching.

I knew what was coming. He posed typical competency questions. How had I conducted the evaluation? What diagnosis did I give? Why had I concluded the defendant was incompetent? As I answered these routine questions, I relaxed. My heart rate returned to normal.

One brief period of excitement occurred when I glanced down at my notes. The defense attorney jumped up and interrupted the prosecutor: "Judge, I object to the witness reading from her notes. She should answer from her recollection."

I refused to let this rattle me. The defense attorney was using a common strategy to throw me off. Newly licensed psychologists often make mistakes when they fall into the trap of relying on their memory. I knew better, and waited. The judge ruled that I could look at my notes if I needed them to "refresh" my memory. Taking my cue, I said, "I would like to use my notes to refresh my memory." This allowed me to read the defendant's actual words to bolster my point. I made sure to mention one especially bizarre comment he made during the interview: "The devil will be in court."

Then it was time for the cross-examination by the defense attorney. My anxiety rose as he stood to approach me. His face was set and determined with a bulldog expression. I did not know exactly what he would ask, but I knew the tone of his questions would be adversarial. He would definitely focus on Mr. Lawrence's strengths and probably try to discredit me so that my comments would carry less weight with the judge. He might even try to find mistakes in how I had conducted the interview, or imply that I was biased or inexperienced.

"Did the defendant know his charges? Yes or no?" he asked.

"Yes."

"Did the defendant understand the roles of court personnel? Yes or no?"

"Yes."

"Did the defendant understand his defense options? Yes or no?"

"Yes."

He was using a typical legal strategy. He asked questions in a "yes" or "no" format to prevent me from explaining what I thought. We both knew that the defendant understood the facts of the case, but defense counsel was not letting me explain that, in my opinion, it was his client's *interpretation* of the facts that was the problem.

"Doctor, would you change your mind about the defendant's competency if you knew he was working with his attorney? Yes or no?"

While this sounds like an innocent, factual question, I knew better; it was another trap. It was a question I could not, or should not, answer with "yes." My thinking about Mr. Lawrence's ability to work with his attorney was complicated. I knew I had to be careful to keep my answer brief, but I did not want to answer with a "yes" or "no."

A long moment passed while I considered how to answer. I wanted to say, "I might change my opinion and conclude the defendant is competent if I knew he was working with his attorney with a rational, non-delusional understanding of the case." Or I might answer, "If the defendant remains insistent upon taking the stand and testifying about the worldwide conspiracy of pedophiles, then, no, I wouldn't change my mind."

Gamely, I tried to explain my thinking, but defense counsel interrupted. "Will you answer the question I asked? Yes or no?"

I was feeling irritated even though I was aware that he was just putting on an act for the judge. I knew he was trying to fluster me so I kept my voice calm. "It isn't a question that I can answer with a 'yes' or 'no.'"

He shook his head in exasperation and sarcastically asked, "Can you answer *anything*, doctor?"

I was angry now because I realized he was trying to cast me as a "clueless academic." I refused to rise to the bait and waited silently.

The judge jumped in. "May I rephrase?" he said in a conciliatory manner. Without waiting for the defense to respond, the judge continued, "Doctor, if you believed that the defendant was no longer delusional and was able to work with his attorney, would your opinion change?"

Now that was a question I could answer. "Yes," I said.

This essentially ended my testimony, and I was dismissed. I was not permitted to remain to watch my colleagues on the stand. The defense attorney had requested that none of the doctors stay in the courtroom while the others were testifying.

Later that day, I bumped into one of the other doctors in the courthouse and asked about the judge's ruling. He seemed surprised that I had any doubts as to the results of the hearing. "Of course the judge ruled that the defendant was competent," he said. "It was two to one." It is true that in a split (two doctors versus one), the judge generally rules with the majority. But it is not always a sure thing. The ultimate decision of competency rests with the judge. He must not have been convinced by my testimony.

Now that the hearing was over, I felt comfortable discussing the evaluation with my friend. He agreed that Mr. Lawrence was mentally ill and his judgment was poor. "But he deserves his day in court," the doctor said.

"But what about his delusional obsession with the victim?" I asked, "Wouldn't that distort his thinking about the case?"

"Plenty of defendants make bad decisions and ignore their lawyers' advice," he remarked. "Besides, the defense attorney certainly indicated at the hearing that he believed he could work with his client."

"But what if the defendant is convicted and sentenced to prison?" I persisted.

He shrugged. "The competency issue could always be revisited. As the case progresses, if defense counsel has qualms and believes his client is irrational, he could request a second evaluation."

He flashed a sudden smile at me. "Besides," he said, "maybe Mr. Lawrence just has problems with women."

I let that comment go. I knew he was just teasing me.

I left the courthouse that day in a philosophical mood, hoping that Mr. Lawrence would agree to enter into treatment through the mental health court rather than take the case to trial. I recalled some of his last words to me—"The devil would be there during the trial."

Weeks later, I learned what had happened to Mr. Lawrence. Originally he was charged with a felony—assault in the second degree. After the competency hearing, the assistant district attorney offered a plea of assault in the third degree which is a misdemeanor. The prosecutor also offered a conditional discharge, which meant that Mr. Lawrence would be released from jail.

I did not understand why the assistant district attorney offered Mr. Lawrence such a good deal since the victim had been badly injured. Did the victim agree with the offer? It occurred to me that the victim probably was not eager for a trial. Most people do not relish the idea of being publicly accused of pedophilia.

I never found out why Mr. Lawrence changed his mind about going to trial. His attorney probably advised him to take the deal. I did not believe that his psychosis was resolved, but for some reason Mr. Lawrence had the good sense to take his lawyer's advice.

Almost two years later I found a note left on my desk. "There is news about Mr. Lawrence. Call me." It was signed by his first attorney. I reached her on her cell phone and she told me the news.

"I ran into the attorney who replaced me—the one who represented Mr. Lawrence at the competency hearing," she said. "He told

me that a year after the case was over, his client committed suicide."

"How?"

"He bought a gun, put it in his mouth, and pulled the trigger."

I was shocked. I had imagined many scenarios for Mr. Lawrence's future, but not this. It was so sad that this young man, tormented by delusions, did not get the help he so desperately needed. I knew he belonged in a psychiatric hospital. I was tempted to call my friends, the two doctors who testified that Mr. Lawrence was competent, but decided against it. I did not want them to feel it was their fault. No one could have predicted that he would kill himself.

Chapter 9

A DESCENDANT
OF BRITISH ROYALTY

The next door neighbors heard sounds of a violent struggle and called 911. Two police officers were on patrol nearby, arrived quickly, and saw a man rushing away from the apartment building. Inside, they found a middle-aged tenant strangled to death in her living room. There were no signs of forced entry, but an end table was knocked over and a lamp broken. The police were able to raise fingerprints from the door knob. Through records, the police identified the defendant. They quickly found and arrested him.

The defense attorney probably realized that his client, Mr. Arkin, was mentally ill when he confided to him that he was the direct descendant of English kings and was "born of natural selection." Mr. Arkin also claimed that his arrest was part of a plot to steal his inheritance. In light of these declarations, defense counsel requested that his client be evaluated for competency to stand trial.

Mr. Arkin was evaluated by two court-appointed doctors who both agreed that he was competent. The defense attorney reviewed their reports but still had doubts. That was why he called me.

"Doctor," he said, "my client is charged with murder and tells me he is a descendant of kings. He says he is of royal blood. Can you evaluate him for an insanity defense?"

"Royal blood," I repeated, pulling out a pad of paper to take notes. "That's a new one. How can I resist? Of course, I'll see him. But are you sure he's competent to stand trial?"

"No, I'm not. But the court-appointed doctors concluded he was competent, so I need to work on a psychiatric defense."

The attorney sent me Mr. Arkin's psychiatric records and the competency reports. A few days later, I began to review these records.

I am never happier than when I make myself cozy on a couch with a box, or two or three, of old psychiatric records. Reading the charts, page by page, I imagine myself sitting in on hospital staff meetings, privy to their discussions. Reading detailed descriptions of a patient's behavior, I feel like I am there watching him in the day hall. Hospital staff observe patients twenty-four hours a day for months on end. Their notes often contain valuable clues about whether a defendant is lying, truly psychotic, or a combination of the two.

As I scrolled through page after page of notes, I found no indication that Mr. Arkin was malingering (faking mental illness). One staff member quoted Mr. Arkin as saying that he had a rare blood type which indicated that he was born of "natural selection." Luckily, the staff member asked him to explain the comment. Mr. Arkin said it meant he was better equipped to deal with the world; it would be easier for him to find a mate and to defend himself in his environment.

The records showed that Mr. Arkin's early childhood was unremarkable. He was frequently truant in high school, however, and dropped out at age seventeen. There was never a question of a learning disability or low I.Q., and he successfully completed his GED (Graduate Equivalency Diploma).

Mr. Arkin joined the Navy at age seventeen, completed his

A DESCENDANT OF BRITISH ROYALTY   153

service four years later, and was honorably discharged. After he left the service his life began to unravel. He enrolled in college, but dropped out after his freshman year. During the next few years, he started a series of jobs but never held one for long. He came to rely on his mother's financial support.

I read Mr. Arkin's earliest records, wondering when his delusions emerged. It seemed that the seeds of the delusions were sown while he served in the military and he noticed in his medical records that his blood type, Type B+, was labeled "Special." Somehow, he became convinced that he was unique and born of "natural selection."

Mr. Arkin took his first trip to Europe in search of evidence of his lineage when he was 22 years old. The trip was a failure and he descended into a deep depression. The next year he attempted suicide. There followed a series of psychiatric hospitalizations.

The majority of mentally ill people never become violent, but Mr. Arkin did have a prior criminal record. At age 24, he struck his sleeping father four times in the head with a hammer. He was arrested for assault in the second-degree and criminal possession of a weapon.

I thought Mr. Arkin was very lucky to be charged only with assault and not attempted murder, considering the viciousness of the attack. This arrest was the first sign that he could act violently on his delusions. He was found not competent to stand trial and transferred to a forensic psychiatric hospital. Those records were the most revealing of all.

The psychiatrists diagnosed Mr. Arkin with paranoid schizophrenia and treated him with antipsychotic medications. He improved and returned to court a few months later, at which time he was declared competent to stand trial and accepted a plea of three years.

After completing his sentence, Mr. Arkin returned to live with his mother—his father had passed away while he was in prison. He was now 27 years old. He did not attend outpatient treatment or take any psychiatric medications.

Mr. Arkin was arrested for sexual assault a year later. He followed a woman walking up the subway stairs and grabbed her buttocks. Two bystanders attempted to help, and during the struggle, he sprayed one of them with mace.

This was certainly an odd crime. Although it was a relatively minor offense, there were many similarities between this second arrest and the murder case I was working on. First was the choice of target: both victims were women he had never met before. Second, both appeared to be crimes of opportunity, without much planning or any attempt to conceal his identity.

Why did he need these weapons? Who was he afraid of? Unfortunately, I could not answer these questions since, at the time, his attorney had not requested a competency exam. Since no psychological examinations had been conducted, all I could glean from the criminal records was that Mr. Arkin had accepted a plea of one to three years. After serving a three-year sentence, he again returned home to live with his mother.

Mr. Arkin was now 31 years old, unemployed, and not under any psychiatric care. I read through interviews with his mother where she described how her son would seclude himself in his room and mostly come out for meals. He was so distrustful, she said, that he would not allow anyone into his room. She also mentioned that he occasionally had outbursts of rage and trashed the apartment.

Over the next seven years, Mr. Arkin's erratic and violent behavior took its toll on his mother so much that she insisted he move out. I could just imagine how painful it must have been for her. Since he had no place to go or any money to live on, he slept in shelters and wandered the streets. He was arrested for the murder a few days later.

I had spent hours reading through the box of materials. After I turned the last page, I put the box aside and scheduled my first appointment.

I arrived at court in the middle afternoon and went to the holding cells to see Mr. Arkin. As he entered the interview room, my first impression of him was "harmless." He was a small-built, white, 38-year-old man. I seated him at the table across from me in the cubicle, in a room that barely fit a tiny table and the two chairs. The walls did not reach the ceiling so the corrections officer on duty outside could listen in if he wanted to.

This lack of privacy did not deter Mr. Arkin. He talked so fast it was difficult to transcribe his words. He spoke in a style referred to in psychiatry as pressured speech.

"Tell me about your royal heritage," I said.

"There were people following me," he told me. "I was being directed, being told who I was and what to do."

His story came out in a rushed monologue, and once he got going it became increasingly difficult for me to interrupt. As he talked, he squirmed in his seat and appeared anxious, full of excess energy, and almost unable to contain the jumbled thoughts that threatened to spill out. He was manic.

I was quite taken aback when, within the few minutes of talking to him, I realized that he was psychotic and paranoid. I knew that the court-appointed doctors concluded that he was competent to stand trial. They did not mention any paranoid delusions in their reports. I was perplexed. I knew the excellent reputation of both doctors and wondered how both could have missed such prominent delusions.

Comparing their reports with the defendant sitting across from me, I thought I understood what had occurred. The court-appointed doctors did not have access to Mr. Arkin's psychiatric records. They never realized he was psychotic since they did not ask him about his grandiose and paranoid delusions. Mr. Arkin, like many other paranoid schizophrenics, had "faked good." Faking good is a clinical expression describing the behavior of a mentally ill person who purposefully hides or minimizes the severity of his or her psychological problems.

When I interviewed him, however, Mr. Arkin seemed eager to tell me that officers of the court, including his own defense attorney and the prosecutor, were conspiring against him to prevent him from claiming his millions in inheritance. It was like the proverbial opening of Pandora's Box. Once Mr. Arkin's core delusional beliefs were uncovered, he was excited to fill me in on all the details. With an animated gleam in his eyes, he recounted all his "evidence" that proved he had royal blood and an unclaimed inheritance. He was determined to convince me that he was the descendant of British kings.

Mr. Arkin pushed some crumpled papers across the table. "Read these," he insisted. I paged through the copies of many letters he had written to various political figures. The letters were a laundry list of delusions, detailing his "special blood type," his royal lineage, his European real estate holdings, and his unclaimed inheritance.

I searched Mr. Arkin's papers for any indication that he was exaggerating or malingering. All his writings went on and on in a similar incoherent style and the more I read, the more convinced I became that no person could just make this stuff up.

"Do you ever hear voices when no one is in the room?" I asked.

"Yes," he nodded. "I could be in the living room and they would know where I was at. They knew what part of the apartment I was in. I don't know who they were."

"What would the voices say?"

"I would hear them talking. Sometimes they would lie and say I'm gay," he replied.

"How do you explain these voices?" I asked.

"I'm still trying to figure out how that apartment got bugged. Did they rig it up? If they have that kind of power, who knows what these people are capable of."

I tried to direct the conversation back to the question at hand—was Mr. Arkin insane when he killed the woman? Yet a nagging thought kept intruding. Was he competent to stand trial as the court-appointed doctors had concluded, or were his delusions so pervasive as to make him incapable of helping in his defense?

In rare cases, delusional defendants can be competent. I had once evaluated a 70-year-old woman who was convinced that she was pregnant. She was charged with a misdemeanor, entering the subway without paying. Her delusion of pregnancy was totally un-related with her legal charge and did not interfere with her ability to work with her attorney and quickly resolve her case. I found her competent.

I needed to determine how Mr. Arkin's psychosis affected his thinking about defense strategy. He clearly knew the charges against him and the roles of court personnel. He also understood the na-ture and seriousness of the charges. "If I'm found guilty, I could get twenty-five to life," he told me.

"Do you know the evidence against you?" I asked.

"They say they found my fingerprints."

"Is there other evidence against you?"

"Well," he hesitated, "two police officers say they saw me coming out of this woman's building."

"How do you plan to deal with the prosecution's case?" I asked.

"I don't have an alibi and my lawyer is saying I should do an in-sanity defense. But I don't want to."

"Why not?"

"Because I'm not sick."

"Wrong!" I wanted to say, but restrained myself. It never works to confront a delusion head on. I believed that he understood, factually, what his lawyer said. He knew there was overwhelming evidence against him. He knew he had no alibi. But, did he appreciate the risk of refusing the insanity defense?

Defendants refuse to consider an insanity defense for a variety of reasons. Some understand they are mentally ill, but do not want to be admitted to a psychiatric hospital for an indeterminate period of time. Defendants found not guilty by reason of insanity are admitted to a secure forensic psychiatric hospital until deemed not a danger to themselves or others. Many mentally ill defendants have good reasons to fear that they may never be released, and therefore decide to risk going to trial. Others prefer to accept a guilty plea, especially if the assistant district attorney offers an attractive plea to a reduced charge.

Mr. Arkin's mental illness was more than obvious to me, but he seemed to have no inkling that he was delusional. In a matter-of-fact manner, he categorically denied having any psychiatric illness and told me and his attorney that he would "not even consider an insanity defense."

His reasoning troubled me. An insanity defense, he said, would thwart his efforts to obtain his inheritance. His logic was twisted. I felt like confronting him with, "Don't you know you'll never get any inheritance, whether you are or are not found insane?" Instead, for the moment, I pretended to accept his story.

"How will a psychiatric defense interfere with your inheritance?" I asked.

"If I do an insanity defense, it will go in the records," he said in a machine-gun delivery. "Then I won't be able to inherit this wealth. I might as well commit suicide."

I concluded that Mr. Arkin was not competent. I believed he was unable to realistically appreciate the advantages and disadvantages of a psychiatric defense. I informed the defense counsel of my opinion and wrote a report.

Defense counsel submitted my report to court and forwarded a copy to the two psychologists who conducted the court ordered competency exams. They were probably pretty surprised to read my report, since apparently they were totally unaware of the defendant's extensive psychiatric history and delusional beliefs.

A few weeks later I learned that these doctors decided to re-examine the defendant. They reversed their opinions and wrote second reports concluding that the defendant was, in fact, not competent to stand trial. After their reports were submitted to court, the case became even more complex.

Defense attorneys and prosecutors are legally permitted to hire private experts to examine defendants and testify during competency hearings. The assistant district attorney in Mr. Arkin's case did that. He was apparently displeased with the new findings of the court-appointed doctors and hired an independent psychologist.

Approximately one month later I received the prosecution-retained psychologist's report. He was aware that the defendant was deluded and wrote about Mr. Arkin's belief that he was a descendant of British royalty. He understood Mr. Arkin's reason for refusing a psychiatric defense—that it would make him ineligible to collect his inheritance.

Although the prosecution-retained psychologist agreed that the defendant was a paranoid schizophrenic, he concluded that Mr. Arkin's mental illness was in partial remission. Mr. Arkin told the psychologist that there was only a fifty percent chance that he was related to royalty. He also said he would consider taking a plea, although he preferred going to trial.

I also learned from the prosecution-retained psychologist's report that Mr. Arkin did not mention his concern that his attorney and the government were working in collusion to convict him of a crime he did not commit. Instead, he couched his dissatisfaction with his attorney in a seemingly rational way, stating that he did not agree with his attorney's advice to use an insanity defense. He wanted an attorney who was eager to prove that he did not commit the murder at a trial.

As I reached the end of the prosecution-retained expert's report, I was not surprised to read his final conclusion that Mr. Arkin was competent to stand trial. He even wrote that, despite Mr. Arkin's insufficient insight into his mental illness, his judgment pertaining to his legal situation was "excellent."

Excellent? I figuratively fell off my seat when I read that. I could not imagine what this psychologist could have meant by calling Mr. Arkin's judgment "excellent." I was convinced that going to trial was a losing battle. I believed Mr. Arkin's only viable defense was a psychiatric one.

I considered the possibility that Mr. Arkin's mental state may have improved in the five months since I interviewed him. I learned that, during that time, he had been admitted to a forensic psychiatric hospital. He refused to accept antipsychotic medications when he was hospitalized but his treating doctor applied for a medication override. They went to court to request legal permission to force him to take medication. The judge agreed that Mr. Arkin was dangerous and granted this override. Mr. Arkin was given medications against his own will during the course of his hospitalization.

Weeks passed and a date was set for the competency hearing. The case had become a battle of the experts. The defense called four psychologists to the stand to testify that the defendant was not competent. The prosecution called one psychologist and one psychiatrist to testify otherwise. The psychiatrist who testified for the prosecution had not evaluated the defendant for competency. She was the defendant's treating doctor from his most recent psychiatric hospitalization.

It is unusual to call a treating psychiatrist to the stand to offer an opinion on competency, but legally it can be done. Many people believe that the roles of treating clinician and forensic evaluator must be kept separate and distinct, since the psychotherapy relationship encourages a patient to divulge details of the crime. Perhaps I was being overly judgmental, but I wondered if the psychiatrist felt any conflict of interest.

The morning of the hearing I walked toward the courthouse and wondered how the judge would rule. Four experts would testify that

Mr. Arkin was incompetent and two that he was competent. The judge could decide either way.

A forensic expert always needs to be aware of the risk of losing perspective during a hearing and becoming wedded to his or her opinion. While being grilled on the witness stand, it is crucial to remember the most important aspect of one's role as a forensic examiner—to remain neutral and to keep in mind the reality that your opinion is just an opinion. The ultimate ruling on competency rests with the presiding judge.

While mentally rehearsing my upcoming testimony, I thought about the tragic and complex case of Colin Ferguson. He was charged with shooting and killing six people and injuring nineteen others on the Long Island Railroad in Garden City, New York, in 1993. Two psychologists testified he was competent to stand trial and one psychiatrist testified he was not. The judge ruled he was competent. Legally, this meant he was also competent to serve as his own attorney (go *pro se*). Mr. Ferguson went to trial and represented himself. He was convicted and sentenced to 315 years and 8 months. Many observers believed he was psychotic, not competent to stand trial, and the trial a travesty.[1]

My testimony during Mr. Arkin's competency hearing was relatively short. I stated my opinion—that he was not competent. I was not permitted to remain in the courtroom to hear the other doctors testify.

The defense attorney called me a few days later to tell me that the judge had ruled that his client was competent to stand trial. We discussed Mr. Arkin's adamant refusal to consider a psychiatric defense and his determination to protect his inheritance. Every defendant who is competent has the right to a trial, even if his chances of winning are slim. Since Mr. Arkin had been found competent, he was able to refuse an insanity defense.

My role in his case was over.

Even so, I could not help but consider whether Mr. Arkin could have successfully used a psychiatric defense. Was his mental illness in any way related to the crime? I recalled puzzling comments in reports from a competency evaluation that had been conducted after he assaulted his father. The doctors had documented Mr. Arkin's claims that he was being threatened by a group of homosexuals.

Could Mr. Arkin have sexual delusions? Could that explain why he murdered the victim? With this question in mind I re-read his psychiatric records and found other references to sexual delusions. He frequently told clinicians he was afraid of being raped by homosexuals. One clinician noted Mr. Arkin's complaints that people were putting saltpeter in his food to cause impotency. I wondered if he delusionally concluded his impotence was caused not by his own anxiety, but instead, by the malicious intentions of others? Maybe he had repressed homosexual urges.

I considered a possible scenario for the murder: Mr. Arkin followed the victim to her apartment, broke in, and attempted to rape her. He was unable to get sexually aroused because he was not truly attracted to women. He never planned to kill her. Instead, he was overwhelmed with self-hatred when he could not perform sexually and he took out his rage on the victim.

This was just a hypothetical scenario. Yet this case had several loose ends that simply refused to tie together. Despite my extensive work on the case, I was unable to resolve the question of how Mr. Arkin's sexual delusions might have played into the murder.

As the date for Mr. Arkin's trial approached, I continued to have nagging doubts. Was he really competent to stand trial? Did his delusions cause him to kill, or was it merely a botched rape or robbery?

Mr. Arkin stood trial still insisting that he was factually not guilty. I did not envy his attorney, who tried to dispute all the physical evidence and the eyewitness testimony.

Not surprisingly, he was convicted.

*   *   *

I saw Mr. Arkin in the holding cells a few weeks later and asked the corrections officer to bring him out of his cell to talk with me. His trial was over, but I wanted to speak with him one last time before he was sentenced and sent to prison. I knew this might be my only chance to resolve some of my lingering doubts.

The sterile, tidy conference room seemed unusually small as we sat across from each other at a table. We quickly dispensed with the niceties. I sensed eagerness in Mr. Arkin's hushed tones as he inched closer to me with every question and answer. It was almost as if he needed the closure of our final good-bye as much as I did.

Mr. Arkin glanced around the room to see if anyone was listening. In a hushed voice, he told me that, while he was still convinced he was a descendant of royalty, he had, in fact, killed the woman. He said he added the lies about the conspiracy in a purposeful and calculated strategy to avoid being tried and convicted.

Immediately, I realized I had been tricked. Then he told me the "real" story about why he killed:

"I had taken enough of static from these people. I didn't know who they were, but I felt they had been trying to turn me into a homosexual for some time. I decided that if I sacrificed someone, it would prove that their mind games didn't control me. Then they would back off and leave me alone.

"So, that's what I did. I followed her to her apartment and broke in. The next thing I knew I was strangling her. I didn't want to kill her. I was just thinking about getting these people off my back. If I didn't take the action I would end up being the corpse."

I was stunned and had nothing to say in response. The corrections officer called out his name to get on the bus back to the Riker's Island jail. Mumbling a polite good-bye, I ended what turned out to be our last meeting.

Mr. Arkin still seemed delusional, yet I certainly realized the distinct possibility that he was still conning me. I was not going to be so easy to dupe a second time. Was he insane at the time that he killed the woman, or had he committed a robbery that got out of control? I've never been able to answer this questions. But the complexity of this case taught me an important lesson. A delusional person isn't "crazy" all the time and can be quite skilled at fooling the experts.

Chapter 10

THE ARSONIST

For almost eighty years, very little changed in this quiet, family-friendly neighborhood in Queens, New York. Children grew up, families moved out, and new families moved into the two-story wooden frame houses. The peace remained largely undisturbed until one night when one of the homes was set ablaze. Thankfully, no one died, but one elderly woman fell and suffered minor injuries as she tried to escape. She was lucky to get out alive. The residents of the neighborhood were shaken, and the police were baffled. Over the next three years, the arsonist set fire to ten more houses, and still the police had no leads.

Mr. Almeda's defense attorney called me late one afternoon.

"My client confessed to the fire marshals that he set all those fires," he said.

"How did the police find him?" I asked. I got up and closed my door so I could hear better.

"They didn't. He called the fire marshals himself," the attorney replied.

"Why did he call?"

"He was desperate to get out of the hospital, but the doctors wouldn't discharge him. He'd been locked up at the state psychiatric

165

hospital for over six months. He asked to see his social worker. Then he asked his social worker to call the fire marshals. Can you believe the social worker actually called them!" the attorney exclaimed in a tone of indignation. "When the marshals arrived, my client gave a full confession. I need you to interview him to find out whether he was competent to waive his Miranda rights when he confessed."

It was one of the first times I had been asked to assess a defendant's competency to waive Miranda rights. I knew it was a very different type of exam from the competency to stand trial evaluations I had been doing for years. Competency to stand trial assessments require that I focus on the defendant's mental state at the time of the interview. In order to assess whether Mr. Almeda was competent to waive his Miranda rights, I needed to travel back in time. I had to understand his state of mind when he gave his statement, months before I was assigned to the case.

I pulled out a pad of paper to take notes as the attorney briefly explained the events leading up to his client's arrest and indictment for arson and attempted murder. Mr. Almeda was admitted involuntarily to a psychiatric hospital months before he confessed to the arsons. The hospital staff concluded he was psychotic and denied his repeated requests for discharge.

Mr. Almeda's behavior was unpredictable. He was so dangerous that he was on a one-to-one level of observation. In hospital jargon, this meant a staff person was assigned to be physically near him at all times to prevent suicide attempts.

Mr. Almeda refused to take the prescribed medication and his doctor went to court for what is termed a medication override. Psychiatric patients are granted many rights, but under certain conditions they can be legally medicated against their wishes. The judge granted a medication override based on the doctor's testimony that Mr. Almeda's psychosis was unlikely to resolve without medication. He was forced to take intramuscular shots of antipsychotic medications.

As I listened to the attorney's description of Mr. Almeda's situation, I was reminded of the classic Greek myth. Two sea monsters named Scylla and Charybdis lived on opposite sides of a narrow channel. Men sailing through the channel confronted an unsolvable dilemma. The strait was so narrow that by avoiding one monster, they put themselves in dangerous proximity to the other. This myth is thought to be the basis of the saying "caught between a rock and a hard place."

Mr. Almeda was caught between the proverbial rock and a hard place. If he confessed, he would be sent to prison. If he stayed silent, he would be trapped in a psychiatric hospital. But did he set those fires? Or did he confess to those crimes because he was desperate to get released from the hospital? Could an acutely ill, hospitalized man truly understand the risks of such a confession?

"Can you send me all his records?" I asked the attorney. "I want to read them before I meet your client."

I had no idea what I was getting myself into when I asked for *all* the records. When the box arrived in the mail, I realized that this case would require me to do more than just interview the defendant and review a few files. Mr. Almeda had over fifteen years of psychiatric hospitalizations.

I was pleased to find out that his confession had been taped. I grabbed the tape cassette from the box and sat down on my couch to watch it. The tape brought Mr. Almeda to life in a way that the reams of reports could not. It was immediately obvious to me that he was a very sick man. I watched the tape over and over and saw things I had never seen before or since.

Every videotaped statement I had ever seen had been filmed inside an interview room of a police station. Mr. Almeda's confession, however, took place in a large, sterile conference room of the psychiatric hospital. Even more remarkable were the people present in the room. The camera panned across the room to show the fire marshal and the patient—and the patient's psychiatrist.

I leaned in closely just to be certain. What was Mr. Almeda's psychiatrist doing there? In all my years of forensic work, I had never seen anything like that. Doctors are notoriously court-phobic, yet this doctor was placing himself right in the middle of things.

This tape was unique. The first person to be questioned was not the defendant—it was the psychiatrist! The doctor was sworn in, then stated his opinion—that his patient had the mental capacity to give informed consent to participate in the interview and make a video-taped statement.

What was he thinking? I wondered. He was not a forensic specialist and was not trained in assessing competency to waive Miranda rights. What was his role in the interrogation? He appeared to be functioning as an agent of the state, not as a protector of his patient. Did the fire marshal or hospital administrators coax him into making this statement, or did he volunteer to do so? All I knew was, I was glad I was not the one making such a pronouncement, especially not on videotape.

Finally, the camera zoomed in to focus on Mr. Almeda. He was an emaciated, small-boned Hispanic man with long, disheveled corkscrew curls. He looked exhausted, and his eyes darted here and there around the room. His face was deeply lined and he seemed much older than his 34 years. I also noticed many superficial scars on his forearms. He had been cutting himself, another sign that he was mentally unstable.

Throughout the interview, Mr. Almeda was shaking visibly and had a continuous tremor of his head and limbs, a severe Parkinsonian tremor. It was evident that he suffered a common and very disagreeable side effect of antipsychotic medications. Now I better understood why he had fought against receiving medications.

The fire marshal read the Miranda rights aloud on the tape, but Mr. Almeda did not even seem to be listening. Mr. Almeda answered in a monotone: "Yes—Yes—Yes," in response to each warning. It was as if talking was a burden and he wanted the interview to be over with as quickly as possible. It was not the tone of a man looking to unburden his soul with a revealing confession.

Mr. Almeda robotically waived his Miranda rights. Then something unexpected occurred. "Do you wish to talk with us now?" the fire marshal asked.

"Not really," he answered.

The marshal looked a bit stumped. "You don't want to?"

"Yes. I don't know," Mr. Almeda said slowly. "I'm tired of speaking."

Perhaps the marshal should have ended the interview then. Instead, he leaned over in a friendly, supportive way and said, "Only a few questions." He quickly moved on without waiting for Mr. Almeda's assent. Then Mr. Almeda grudgingly started to answer his questions.

He proceeded to confess to setting numerous houses and cars on fire. With crumpled papers he showed how he had placed newspapers underneath the wooden porches, lit the paper with a match, then withdrew to watch the occupants flee as the fire trucks arrived. He described the fires in detail, sounding almost proud of his work.

I watched his face for signs of embarrassment and guilt, but saw only exhaustion and resignation. He did not seem psychotic during the interview. He had no trouble understanding the questions, and his answers were coherent. He did not appear to be hearing voices, and he did not utter any delusional statements.

Midway through the questioning Mr. Almeda's voice took on an anxious tenor. "Are you going to arrest me?" he asked.

"I'm not out here to arrest you," the fire marshal replied. "I don't arrest people."

I could not help smiling at that. His answer was technically correct, but completely misleading. No, the marshal would not be the one physically arresting the patient, but certainly he would be intimately involved in the decision to have Mr. Almeda arrested.

The marshal's attitude and demeanor gave away no clues as to his thoughts or feelings. I wondered what was going through his mind at this moment. Did he think Mr. Almeda really appreciated the seriousness of confessing? Did he feel a twinge of guilt that he might be taking advantage of a mentally ill man?

It seemed that Mr. Almeda still did not understand or appreciate the implications of his confession, because a few minutes later, he repeated the question: "Are you going to arrest me?"

"We're just out here to talk to you," the marshal said without pause. "An arrest may happen, it may not happen. We just want to talk to you about the fires."

The marshal's second response was consistent with his first. It was evasive and misleading, if not downright deceptive.

After watching the videotaped confession a few times, I turned to the box of psychiatric records.

Mr. Almeda's psychiatric history was almost as long as his criminal history. At age seventeen he was admitted for the first of many psychiatric hospitalizations. At first he was diagnosed with major depression, but in the past twelve years he had always been diagnosed with schizophrenia.

Schizophrenia is a devastating disorder which affects approximately one percent of the population. Schizophrenics suffer from a variety of psychotic symptoms such as delusions, hallucinations, disorganized or catatonic behavior, and disorganized speech. They often experience a flattening of emotions and difficulty making and carrying out plans.[1]

When he was younger, Mr. Almeda experienced what in psychiatry is termed the positive symptoms of schizophrenia—auditory hallucinations and disorganized thinking. In the few years before his arrest for arson, however, he exhibited the primarily negative symptoms, including withdrawal, isolation, and flattened emotions. Many schizophrenics have long periods of remission and are able to live in the community. Others, like Mr. Almeda, are not so lucky and need long periods of hospitalization. Psychiatric staff described him as a man without the normal range of emotions, a man who took no pleasure in life.

I knew that Mr. Almeda's schizophrenic illness did not in and of itself make him incompetent to waive his Miranda rights. Mental illness creates unique weaknesses in each defendant. I analyzed his psychiatric records to determine whether his schizophrenia demonstrably impaired his ability to resist pressure or made him abnormally vulnerable or suggestible.

I skimmed through thousands of pages of hospital records, slowing down to read the last weeks of notes more carefully. Missing one crucial sentence could lead me astray. I needed to piece together the chain of events that led to his interrogation. I knew that Mr. Almeda had not been a suspect until he called the fire marshals. His attorney told me that the police had had no clue that his client was the arsonist until he made that fateful phone call. With that I mind, I searched the hospital notes for mention of the call.

I examined the most recent pages of Mr. Almeda's hospital records, trying to determine who had called whom. When was the call made and what was actually said? I found a very short note written by his social worker buried in the documents. It was only a few lines long and merely reported that Mr. Almeda had requested help making a call to the fire marshal. I read the lines a few times, wondering what the social worker was thinking when he documented this extraordinary request. He must have wondered why his patient wanted to call the fire department.

I was working on a psychiatric ward at Kings County Hospital when I was hired on this case. Patients often approached me with specific requests. Each morning I would turn my key to open the heavy metal door of the unit. Patients flocked to me as soon as

I walked onto the day hall. Most were anxious for their freedom, home, or drugs. Many simply asked me for food or cigarettes; others just wanted to talk. Inevitably, most appealed to me to discharge them, some less politely than others. I was frequently asked to make phone calls for them. Thankfully, no patient ever asked me to make a call like the one Mr. Almeda asked of his social worker.

From what I could deduce, the social worker did, in fact, "help" Mr. Almeda place that call. Before the marshals arrived, it appeared that plenty of staff knew what was going to happen—their patient was going to confess to a crime.

The most puzzling aspect of this case was the role played by the Mental Hygiene Legal Services (MHLS) attorney. New York State law requires MHLS provide hospitalized psychiatric patients with advice and representation relating to their hospitalization. There was a note in Mr. Almeda's hospital records indicating that his MHLS attorney had visited him a few hours before he made his confession. I had no idea what she said to him, but I hoped she at least recommended that he call the criminal division of the Legal Aid Society.

I could not understand why his MHLS attorney did not contact the Legal Aid Society herself. Since her client was declared dangerously mentally ill, he was, by law, not competent to make many of his own medical decisions or leave the hospital. Legally, the psychiatric staff served as surrogate, making medical decisions for him. But who was really looking out for Mr. Almeda? Who had his best interests at heart?

Years later, I mentioned this case to Bob Peck, an attorney in the criminal division of the Brooklyn Legal Aid Society. He told me that if Mr. Almeda's MHLS attorney had contacted him, he would have advised her to tell her client not to make a statement. "If he talks to the police, he should say: 'I want an attorney present!'" Bob said emphatically.

*   *   *

I noticed some very peculiar hospital notes written on the day of Mr. Almeda's confession. He refused to take his antipsychotic medication on the morning before he met with the fire marshals, but I did not see any note to indicate that he had been forced to take it.

Mr. Almeda had been on a one-to-one level of observation for many months. On this particular day, however, he was removed from this level at 12:30 P.M. This was only two hours before he confessed to the fire marshals.

Later that evening he was placed back on one-to-one observation. This seemed much too coincidental to me. After weeks of one-to-one observation, did Mr. Almeda really suddenly and dramatically improve, confess, and deteriorate, all in one day? It appeared that members of the psychiatric staff were collaborating with the police. And, if the doctors were not protecting their patient, who was?

The hospital records convinced me that Mr. Almeda was severely mentally ill when he confessed, but they did not answer the legal question. When assessing competency to waive Miranda rights, I always examine the interrogation itself to understand what happened before and during the questioning.

It was crucial to determine whether the fire marshals took advantage of Mr. Almeda's mental illness. Direct coercion and physical abuse are not permissible. They cannot physically threaten or make concrete promises of leniency. Indirect coercion, however, is a more nuanced strategy. It is permissible for the interrogators to assume a non-adversarial style or use persuasion. They can employ different forms of trickery to coax or intimidate suspects into confessing. Some minimize the seriousness of the charges or the import of waiving the Miranda warnings.[2]

Which approach did the fire marshals use with Mr. Almeda? I looked forward to asking him this question during our interviews. I was scheduled to meet with him the next day. He had already been incarcerated for a few months and had stopped taking all psychiatric medications.

I watched Mr. Almeda carefully as he walked into the small interview room and took a seat across from me. Physically, he appeared better than he had on the videotaped confession. He walked quickly, was less tremulous, and had gained some weight. He did not seem to be hearing voices but he certainly was not *fine*. His clothing was torn and dirty and he looked disheveled. The negative symptoms of schizophrenia, the sense of emptiness and the detachment from other people and his own emotions, were still apparent. I recalled a hospital note from his voluminous case file that captured his demeanor perfectly. A nurse wrote that Mr. Almeda had a sort of vacant and hollow quality about him.

I noticed faint, random cuts on his forearm. Farther up he had carved a homemade tattoo—his own name—more deeply into his arm. Curious, I asked him to roll up his sleeves. He obliged, revealing the professional tattoos of various rock bands on his upper arms. I had no idea what to make of them.

I began the interview with questions about his childhood. His parents were not perfect, but they were not abusive. He was the second of four children and the self-described black sheep of the family. His parents divorced after years of arguments and rancor when he was in high school. Mr. Almeda blamed their marital problems on his father's alcoholism. His mother died ten years earlier, and he did not even know whether his father was alive or dead. His siblings were also out of the picture.

"I think they moved," he said.

"Why didn't you stay in contact with them?" I asked.

"They were reading my mail," he said blandly.

A long moment passed while I considered this. There it was—the paranoia I had read about in the hospital records.

Mr. Almeda talked about his childhood in a flat tone, until I asked him about his mother. "She was the man of the house; my

father was a coward, a scapegoat, a jackass!" he blurted out an-
grily. I was beginning to suspect that his arsons were the result of
unacknowledged, perhaps unconscious, displaced rage against his
family. It could hardly be a coincidence that the houses he burned
were all in the neighborhood in which he was raised.

Mr. Almeda told me that he attended general education classes
and was never held back. He started smoking marijuana and cutting class in high school. He left school after the tenth grade. His
life went downhill after that. He never completed his GED or held
a steady job. He barely eked out an existence from family hand-
outs and petty theft. Prior to his most recent hospitalization, he was
homeless, living in shelters and in abandoned buildings. His long
list of arrests dated back to his eighteenth birthday and included
misdemeanor offenses such as entering the subway without paying
as well as trespass, petty larceny, and possession of stolen property.

Mr. Almeda's life was completely empty. He had no friends or
contact with family. He had never had a girlfriend, had never been
intimate with a woman, and had never had sexual intercourse.
When I asked him what he thought about his psychiatric problems,
he insisted, "I'm perfectly normal." His comment demonstrated a
classic symptom of schizophrenia—impaired self-reflection.

I was not able to establish a rapport with him. The whole time
we talked, he was irritable and hostile, as if I was annoying him.
There was no way to gain his confidence. He repeatedly asked me,
"You're not against me, are you?" Throughout the interview he
interrupted the conversation with suspicious questions. "You're
talking everything negative. You should talk positive. Why? Are you
getting paid?"

He obviously did not think very highly of me or my questions. I
wondered if he felt the same about his attorney.

"What do you think of your lawyer?" I asked.

"People don't want to help me." He glared at me. "My attorney,
he's probably having a couple of beers right now."

"And what of the judge?"

"I never saw the judge before in my life," he said. "What did I do to him? Who is he to judge me? Does that make sense?"

I was stumped, not quite sure how to respond to this nonsensical rant. I ended the interview at that point. I was exhausted and out of ideas on how to get him to open up.

When he walked into the tiny counsel room for the second interview, he carried a packet of papers with him. I felt a small glimmer of hope. I knew from experience that a careful reading of a defendant's private papers could uncover hidden aspects of his personality.

I asked to see his papers after a particularly tense point in the interview. It seemed time for a break, and I thought I would change tack for a little while. He tossed the papers onto the table as if it didn't matter to him whether I read them or not.

He had filled page after page with chaotic scribbling, disorganized rants, and bizarre pronouncements. His sentences were disjointed and written at random, but all expressed a common theme: his hatred for humanity. Sometimes he became startlingly intuitive, as when he quoted a Dean Koontz poem. "At the point where hope and reason part, lies the spot where madness gets a start."[3]

His writings confirmed for me that he was psychotic. But it was not enough that I simply diagnose him with schizophrenia, since each schizophrenic has a distinctive pattern of symptoms and beliefs. I administered a battery of psychological tests to get a picture of who Mr. Almeda was and what he thought and felt about himself and others. I gave him an intelligence test and several projective tests which would tap into his unconscious or unacknowledged feelings. Psychologists use these projective tests to examine personality characteristics and emotional functioning and to detect any confused or bizarre thinking.

The Rorschach or "inkblot test" is frequently used in forensic settings.[4] The test consists of a set of ten cards, five dotted with black ink, two with red and black ink, and three with multicolored ink.

The psychologist takes into account several parts of the test-taker's responses, including location, form quality, and content. Location corresponds to the parts of the blot to which the test-taker responds. The term "form quality" refers to the degree to which the test-taker's responses conform to the actual appearance of the inkblots. The content is what the person sees on the Rorschach cards.

Emotionally healthy individuals perceive a variety of living and inanimate objects and integrate colors into their responses. For example, the test-taker might report seeing a yellow flower or strawberry ice cream. Good Rorschach responses describe images in motion; the best answers mention humans doing something positive together, like dancing or cooking. A person who only sees animals in the blots and never describes a human image is most likely immature or regressed.

Mr. Almeda's responses to the Rorschach test were pathological in the extreme. The images he described were powerful evidence of his psychotic thinking and emotional turmoil. I showed him a particularly colorful card and he said, "This looks like the inside of somebody's body. It's dissected. The stomach, chest and inside of his stomach." On other blots he saw a skull, two people without legs, a demon, and the bones of a rib cage. His bleak responses turned my stomach.

Then I asked Mr. Almeda to complete another widely used projective personality test, the House-Tree-Person Test.[5] The test-taker draws a picture of a house, a tree, a man and a woman. These drawings are actually representations of himself and his world view. The walls of the house and the trunk of the tree represent the test-taker's ego strength. The roof of the house represents his fantasy life. The ground underneath the house and tree, his sense of emotional stability. The doors and windows of the house, the branches of the tree, and the arms of the person all reflect the test-taker's relationship to the outside world. A tree without branches, for example, indicates barren and desolate feelings. A house drawn without a door indicates that the person is unwilling or unable to relate to others.

A healthy individual typically draws a house with details that reflect a warm, satisfying family and home life. Mr. Almeda's house was just a box. With no line indicating a ground or foundation, the house seemed to float in space, reflecting an overall sense of instability. Inside the box were two squares cut with a cross for panes and a simple door. There were no curtains, plants or shrubs, no path leading to the house to welcome guests. The house seemed cold and foreboding, with no significant details of family life. It was the type of house drawn by what we in the field call a "burnt-out schizophrenic." Mr. Almeda had little emotional warmth or connections with other people.

Mr. Almeda's man and woman looked like gingerbread figures. They were childlike, lacking in sexual details and clothing. Neither figure had a neck; the lines for the heads continued directly to the shoulders. The neck represents a healthy separation of the head, which represents thought and cognition, from the body, which represents drives and needs. Mr. Almeda drew himself without a neck; he would have difficulty using his intelligence to control or modulate his feelings.

The results of the psychological tests fit with Mr. Almeda's history and the data I had gathered during our interviews. I was certain that he had been severely mentally ill at the time of his confession.

Now I needed to explore what specifically occurred during the questioning.

"Why did you confess?" I asked.

"I had to get out of the hospital. They were juicing me up on medication."

We continued discussing what led to his decision to call the fire marshal. He then glared at me suspiciously and again exclaimed, "You're not against me, are you?"

Without waiting for an answer, he immediately continued, "I just wanted to get out of the hospital. I didn't care what they charged me with. I wasn't worried about what would happen next."

And with that comment, it seemed time to end. The second interview was over and I went home to weigh all the information I had. It was time to reach a conclusion. Was Mr. Almeda competent to waive his Miranda rights when he confessed?

His vulnerabilities and weaknesses were almost too many to count. He was hospitalized against his will, suicidal, and acutely psychotic. The interrogation certainly took place in an unusual setting. And what about his psychiatrist's contribution to the entire peculiar setting? Was he there to encourage or condone his patient's confession? He certainly was not there to help his patient.

I believed that Mr. Almeda's psychosis, particularly his disordered thinking, interfered with his understanding of the interrogation and his decision to contact the fire marshals and ultimately make a confession. I concluded that he did not voluntarily waive his Miranda rights.

I am usually sympathetic toward a defendant who was coerced into confessing, but I had not felt much compassion for Mr. Almeda. Even so, I had been curious to know what he felt about going to trial, and had told him so, glancing up from my notes to see his reaction.

"I don't care if they throw the book at me," he had said. "But I wish I'd never confessed."

"Would you rather have stayed in the hospital?" I then asked.

"No," he said. "I'd rather be in prison than in a hospital, juiced up with drugs."

"What are your thoughts about prison?" I asked.

"What's the difference if I get a long sentence?" he had said in a flat voice. "I'm not going to get paroled. They'll talk to the parole board. They'll never let me out."

Mr. Almeda never appeared very upset by the prospect of incarceration and was realistically pessimistic about his chances of being paroled. He actually seemed almost at peace with the idea. Perhaps he was tired of surviving on the streets and welcomed the relative security of prison, where he would have a bed and receive three meals a day. I briefly considered the possibility that he felt guilty and needed to do penance. I seriously doubted it.

When I called his defense attorney and told him my opinion, he asked me to write a report for court. He told me he would request a pre-trial hearing to determine whether his client's confession was admissible at trial. In New York State, such a hearing is called a Huntley hearing.[6]

During our phone call Mr. Almeda's attorney raised an entirely different legal question: his client's mental state at the time of the offense.

"Do you think there is any psychiatric defense for the arsons?" his attorney asked.

"It is well known that arson is frequently a 'psychological' crime," I began.

"Even if Mr. Almeda wasn't 'crazy' enough for an insanity defense," he interjected, "perhaps his mental illness could be enough of a mitigating factor to use in negotiations with the prosecution."

I was not surprised by the attorney's questions. All along I had wondered whether Mr. Almeda's attorney would recommend an insanity defense. Defense counsel confided to me early on that his client certainly appeared guilty of the crimes. I realized that, although defense counsel was fighting to have the confession thrown out, at the same time he was also maneuvering for the best plea offer possible.

I considered what I knew about arson. Research has determined that the typical arsonist is a young man from a broken home with a prior criminal record and impaired social relationships. Arsonists are frequently mentally ill and most often diagnosed with schizo-

phrenia, substance abuse, mood disorders, personality disorders, or
mental retardation. Many arsonists are motivated by revenge, thrill-
seeking, profit, or pyromania.[7]

People tend to use the word "pyromaniac" to describe anyone
who sets fires, but true pyromania is rare. Individuals diagnosed
with pyromania experience irresistible impulses to light fires and
derive pleasure or sexual satisfaction from watching the fire burn.
Was Mr. Almeda a pyromaniac?

I needed to delve into his state of mind when he set those fires, so
I scheduled a third session to evaluate Mr. Almeda for the insanity
defense. A defendant is found to be insane or not responsible for a
crime if, "at the time of such conduct, as a result of mental disease or
defect, he lacked substantial capacity to know or appreciate either:
(1) the nature and consequences of such conduct; or (2) that such
conduct was wrong."[8]

I told Mr. Almeda why I was seeing him for the third time. He
quickly confessed to me that he committed some of the house
arsons and set approximately 200 cars on fire. He giggled in a hu-
morless, chilling way when he talked about the fires. His blank face
lit up; his voice became animated and strangely gleeful.

"How did you feel setting the fire?" I asked.

"Fire is nice; I like to watch," he said. "When a person wakes up
and finds his car burned, I find it fun. Sometimes I go back the next
morning, for fun, not to hurt anybody."

It was evident to me that Mr. Almeda's motivation for setting
fires was psychological, not for profit or to hide another crime. His
background and his own words indicated that he fit the profile of a
revenge arsonist. For him, arson served as a displacement of intense
anger onto innocent victims. As I listened to him talk excitedly
about the arsons, I realized that he also fit the description of a pyromaniac. He set fires to gratify his sexual frustration and add some
excitement to his empty life.

I could not decide why he set fire to these particular houses. He shrugged when I asked him. "I just think because they were wooden, to tell the truth," he said.

Then he veered off into a peculiar digression about "people from deep space" who knew why he set fires. I began to consider the possibility that he was following commands from auditory hallucinations.

"People from deep space?" I asked.

"They know why I did it," he said. "The people that got powers. The people from deep space. We're just mortals. They know what I did. They respect me for it. If I didn't do it, they wouldn't respect me. They told me so; whispered it in my head. They enticed me. They were with me, laughing."

I wondered if he was making this stuff up. He had denied hearing voices during our first two sessions. The hospital records also showed that he had consistently denied experiencing hallucinations. And even if he was hearing voices, that did not necessarily mean he was insane at the time he set the fires.

I concluded that, since he chose homes within the neighborhood where he was raised, the link was symbolic. I believed he displaced his rage from his family onto the homes of strangers. I was convinced that his mental illness played a huge part in his fire setting. But, he certainly knew and appreciated what he was doing was wrong.

I decided that Mr. Almeda did not fulfill the legal criteria for the insanity defense. His whole defense now rested on the admissibility of his confession. Without it, the prosecution had no evidence, no case.

I told his attorney that I could not be of any help during the actual trial but would be able to testify at the Huntley hearing. If the judge concluded that Mr. Almeda was not competent to waive his Miranda rights, the videotaped confession would be excluded. This would make it much more difficult for the assistant district attorney to prove the defendant's guilt at trial, since there was no direct evidence linking him with the arsons. If the judge concluded that Mr. Almeda was competent to waive his Miranda rights, his confession could be shown at his trial.

Later that day, I sat down at my desk and began to look through my notes. It was time to write the report. I described the reasons I believed Mr. Almeda was unable to voluntarily waive his Miranda rights at the time of his confession. Even though the fire marshal did not directly coerce the confession, I was convinced that Mr. Almeda's severely impaired mental condition, in combination with the circumstances of his involuntary hospitalization, effectively deprived him of his will to resist.

For his part, the prosecutor had hired his own expert, a very experienced and well-respected psychiatrist. We knew each other well, having frequently worked together and on opposing sides. The psychiatrist prepared a ten-page report, which was short compared with other reports of his I had read. As always, it was well-written, detailed, and succinct. He also diagnosed Mr. Almeda with schizophrenia. With no wishy-washy "maybes" or "perhaps," he also gave Mr. Almeda the diagnosis of antisocial personality disorder and concluded that he made his statements knowingly, intelligently, and voluntarily.

The psychiatrist noted that Mr. Almeda never appeared to be hearing voices, and he never acted delusional or confused. He concluded that the defendant was not vulnerable to suggestion or coercion. In fact, he insisted that Mr. Almeda was "impervious" to these interrogation tactics.

What I found missing from the psychiatrist's report, however, was any consideration of the coercive quality of the hospital setting itself. The report made reference to Mr. Almeda's serious psychiatric illness, but it did not mention how his mental illness impacted his decision to call the fire marshals. It did not discuss his severe psychopathology in depth or acknowledge the psychotic symptoms revealed through the psychological tests I had given him.

As so often occurs in forensic examinations, two experts hired by the prosecution and defense had looked at the same evidence and come to radically different opinions. It is true that we did not interview the defendant together, so the information we gathered during the interviews was not identical. It is possible that Mr. Almeda had been more forthcoming to one of us or had evoked different emotional reactions in us. Perhaps he and the psychiatrist had been able to build that rapport which was so sorely lacking in our relationship, but I doubted it. Mr. Almeda was not an easy defendant to like.

After we submitted our reports, a hearing was scheduled. The prosecution-retained psychiatrist and I testified during the day-long hearing. My direct testimony and cross-examination went smoothly and relatively quickly. As I waited for news of the judge's ruling, something very unusual occurred. The defense attorney called me and told me that the judge was seriously considering excluding the videotape and had strongly "encouraged" the prosecutor to make a good plea offer. The assistant district attorney followed the judge's lead and made an offer that Mr. Almeda accepted. After that, the case was resolved quickly.

In the end, the judge never issued a ruling on the admissibility of the confession. The question of whether or not Mr. Almeda's confession was voluntarily given remained unanswered. It felt anticlimactic. I would never know if my testimony had convinced the judge to throw out the statement.

This turned out to be a unique case in many respects. In the first place, confessions are almost never excluded. Also, I am unaware of any other case involving a hospitalized psychiatric patient who was assessed for competency to waive Miranda rights. This case highlights some unanswered issues faced by psychiatric patients concerning both their rights as well as what legal protections they should be granted.

Mulling over these complex, unresolved questions, I recalled my last meeting with Mr. Almeda. He had showed no remorse and pro-claimed:

"I don't care if they convict me. I don't care as long as I got them back. I got back at the system. They made me hate everybody. Those wicked superiors. People that dress like you. The higher ups. I don't know what they're doing in their laboratories and what stuff they make in labs—chemicals, pills and liquids. They're Nazis. I had a lot of vengeance."

With these last hateful words we said our good-byes. It was the last time I spoke with him. He pled guilty and was sentenced to twenty years. It was sobering to realize that Mr. Almeda might never have been caught if he never made that fateful call.

In the end, like so many others, the case of "the serial arsonist" left me with as many questions as answers. The big question: would the judge have thrown out the confession if Mr. Almeda had not taken the plea?

PART 3

*Evaluations of Juveniles and Assessments
of Dangerousness and Malingering*

W ill a released offender commit another violent crime? Should juveniles be treated differently in the criminal justice system? Can a defendant fake mental illness? In many cases, the courts have turned to forensic experts to answer these controversial questions. This last part of *The Measure of Madness* includes a number of cases where I explore these very issues.

I know that many people falsely believe that a defendant found not guilty by reason of insanity is "getting away" with murder. Some believe that he or she is released after the verdict or is treated in a psychiatric hospital for only a brief period of time. Quite to the contrary, research has shown that defendants found not guilty by reason of insanity (insanity acquittees), are likely to serve longer periods of time in psychiatric hospitals than if they were convicted and sent to prison. Even those who are psychiatrically stable, without symptoms of psychotic illness, often remain in a secure forensic hospital for years.

New York State law places the legal burden on the prosecutor to prove, by a preponderance of the evidence (in other words, more than a 50 percent chance), that the insanity acquittee requires retention in a secure facility. Hospital administrators, doctors, prosecutors, and judges are leery about recommending their release or transfer to state hospitals. In these less secure settings the patient will be granted increasingly more freedom and privileges and eventually be released to the community. With this freedom comes the chance to commit new crimes.

For a man who had stabbed his own mother, Mr. Russo was the warmest and friendliest person I had ever evaluated. At the time of the offense, he heard a voice instructing him to "bleed" his mother to save her from eternal damnation. He obeyed this command. There was never a question whether he was psychotic; he was found not guilty by reason of insanity and admitted to a forensic hospital. Seven years later, I was asked to evaluate him to determine whether he was still dangerous or could be transferred to a state psychiatric hospital.

One chapter describes the cases of two adolescents charged with murder. Miguel was seventeen when he was arrested, and Anthony was only 15 years old when he killed his grandmother. It was painful for me to listen to their childish explanations for their behaviors. They were so young that I felt the tugs of motherly compassion during both evaluations. However, I had to objectively assess their psychological functioning, emotional maturity, and intellectual abilities. The legal question I addressed was whether their age affected their mental state at the time of the killings.

The last chapter details five suspected fakers. Mr. Allen claimed to suffer from multiple personality disorder. It is a controversial diagnosis that many experts consider to be very rare; some don't believe it exists at all. When he asserted that "Tom," another personality, had strangled his ex-girlfriend, his attorney called me to see him. Mr. D'Martino reported brain damage due to a stroke, and Mathew, a diabetic, insisted that the police refused lifesaving medical treatment to force him to confess. Mr. Gates spit at one attorney and threatened the second.

The eight cases I include in this last part raise different psycholegal issues. Two were some of the youngest defendants I'd ever seen and one was a senior citizen. Most had no history of psychiatric treatment yet raised psychological issues during their legal proceedings. What they all shared was that each was a challenging example of some of the more controversial and newly emerging areas in forensic psychology.

Chapter 11

THE DUTIFUL SON

The nursing home was understaffed, and no one thought to search Mr. Russo before he left for a home visit with his family. As a result, no one noticed the knife he had concealed in his clothing. Mr. Russo passed the first few hours of the visit quietly. Patient and calm, he waited for a chance to be alone with his mother. When the moment came, he stabbed her three times, methodically, until her cries alerted other family members. He later told his attorney that he had heard the voice of God commanding him to "bleed" his mother to save her from an eternity in hell.

The defendant never went to trial. The assistant district attorney offered an insanity plea, and without much fanfare or publicity, Mr. Russo was admitted to a forensic hospital. Seven years later, the psychiatrists at the hospital recommended that Mr. Russo be transferred to a state psychiatric hospital. The assistant district attorney had to make a decision, whether to allow the transfer or to get another opinion. That is when he called me.

A few days later a box of psychiatric and legal records arrived. I quickly realized that Mr. Russo was not a typical insanity acquittee. He wasn't schizophrenic or bipolar. Raised by both parents in what he described as a happy home, he never had any medical or psychiatric problems until he turned thirty-five. That year, he got caught in the crossfire of a barroom shoot-out. Mr. Russo was shot twice in the head, sustained extensive damage to his temporal and frontal lobes and was in a coma for ten days. After a year in rehabilitation, he was left with partial paralysis on one side of his body, a seizure disorder, and impaired vision, speech, and hearing.

Mr. Russo's brain damage caused drastic changes in his personality. As I read through the records, I thought of the famous case of Phineas Gage, who was working as a construction foreman when an accident occurred. A tamping iron was blown through his head and landed almost thirty yards away. Amazingly, he survived this devastating accident, but he suffered severe brain damage to his frontal lobes. His personality changed drastically and his friends commented he was "no longer Gage." A polite, hard working man before the injury, he was unable to return to work because he was unreliable, impatient, moody, and unsociable.[1]

Like Gage, Mr. Russo's personality changed for the worse. Previously restrained and polite, he was now impulsive. He drank too much and began smoking marijuana. During the next twenty years he tried to kill himself a few times and was admitted to psychiatric hospitals over twenty times. Considering the amount of brain damage he suffered, no one was surprised by Mr. Russo's personality change. It was shocking and totally unexpected, however, when he began to hear "the voice of God."

Most brain-damaged individuals, like Phineas Gage, never become violent. Perhaps that is why no one realized how dangerous Mr. Russo could be. Twenty years after he was shot, he unexpectedly attacked his mother with a knife. Luckily, her injuries were superficial. He was charged with a misdemeanor assault, found not competent to stand trial, and admitted to a forensic hospital.

I read the psychiatrist's report from that admission. Mr. Russo told his psychiatrist that he stabbed his mother because "she had not repented for her sins." According to Mr. Russo's interpretation of the Bible, his mother needed to "bleed" in order to be cleansed of her sins.

Mr. Russo was discharged from the forensic hospital after a few months. He was placed in a nursing home, and soon he seemed stable enough to begin making home visits. Years passed without incident so no one realized that he was still hearing voices. No one searched his room to discover the knife he hid there.

Mr. Russo was home on a visit when he heard the command to "bleed" his mother. Then, without any warning, he stabbed her. Fortunately, she again survived her son's unprovoked attack. His symptoms preceding the attack were identical the second time around. He explained to the police, his attorney, and the psychiatric experts that he never intended to kill his mother; he was only following God's instructions to "bleed" her in order to guarantee her place in heaven. He stabbed her not because he was paranoid or angry, but because he "loved her so much."

After Mr. Russo accepted the insanity plea, he returned to the same forensic hospital. He faithfully took his antipsychotic medications. However, his symptoms were not easy to treat, and he continued to hear voices on and off throughout the next few years.

By the time the assistant district attorney called me, Mr. Russo's psychiatrists believed that medication and psychotherapy had eliminated his symptoms. They concluded he was no longer dangerous and recommended his transfer to a less secure facility.

Sometimes, I think I am a bit compulsive when I read psychiatric records. I look at each note carefully to make sure I do not miss anything crucial. In light of the psychiatrists' recommendations, I was surprised to see that the hospital records were not uniformly positive. Buried deep in hundreds of pages of notes, I found mention of an alarming incident. A few months ago, Mr. Russo punched another patient, claiming that God had mandated the unprovoked attack. "God told me to bless him by hitting him," he said, his words reminiscent of those he had used to justify his stabbing his mother. I jotted down a note to remind myself to ask him about this incident and mentally reviewed the issues I needed to address in the interview. Was Mr. Russo compliant with treatment and psychiatric medications? Was the medication effective in eliminating the hallucinations? Was he in control of his behavior? Would he comply with psychiatric treatment after transfer? Did he know what to do if he heard voices again?

I finished reading through the records and packed for my trip upstate. The forensic hospital is located a few hours northwest of New York City, between quaint towns and outlet malls. New visitors might be charmed by the sight of wild deer grazing in the woods nearby and have the impression of the hospital as a pleasant retreat—a retirement community, perhaps—until they inevitably notice the barbed wire. I was not under any such illusions. The hospital is, in many ways, like a prison. The insanity acquittees are legally innocent, but they are not free.

According to New York Criminal Procedure Law, insanity acquittees must remain hospitalized until they are no longer dangerous. At that point, due process and the right to liberty require that patients be transferred to a non-secure state psychiatric facility, and ultimately get released. This process usually takes years.[2]

I parked my car and wandered around until I found the correct building. When I arrived, security staff reviewed my identification and paperwork and assigned me a locker for my pocketbook, phone, and pager. I was not permitted to bring anything into the facility other than papers and a few pens. I passed through the metal detector and then followed my escort through the winding hallways and outside into a courtyard. Walking along the cement path, I glanced over at a group of patients sitting at tables and milling around. What would I do if I recognized one of the men I had evaluated in the past? Wave? Seeing no familiar faces, I continued onward, through more hallways and a locked door into a private conference room. Mr. Russo's attorney was already there to observe the evaluation. We chatted while waiting for the patient to arrive.

Soon, there was the click of the door unlocking, and Mr. Russo walked unsteadily into the room. He leaned on his cane, and a therapy aide gripped his right elbow to protect him from falling. His left arm was curled from the paralysis. His aide settled him into a chair, and then went to sit in the corner opposite the attorney.

Mr. Russo was one of the most amiable and cheery individuals I had ever interviewed. His pink face split into a wide smile when he saw me; I felt like we were striking up a conversation on a park bench somewhere. I tried not to notice that he was drooling. He carefully dabbed at the corner of his mouth frequently during the interview.

Even after I explained that I was hired by the district attorney, someone most insanity acquittees are wary of, he seemed eager to chat. He was thoroughly entertaining throughout the interview. Like many other brain-damaged patients I have evaluated, he was silly and overly friendly. He started to sing a few times to show me what a strong, clear voice he had and I was tempted to join in. I appreciated why the staff liked him so much.

Mr. Russo seemed like he was trying to answer all my questions honestly, but many of his statements contradicted each other. "I haven't heard the voice in a year or two," he said at one point in the interview, and then, a short while later, he said that he spoke with God yesterday.

"Does this voice tell you to do things?" I asked.

"I have to listen to the voice of God. If I ignore his commands, I'm going to end up committing suicide."

"Do you hear any other voices?"

"Sometimes I hear the Devil's voice; I don't want to follow him. He tells me to commit suicide."

The Devil? I thought. I had not read anything about the Devil in his records.

"I saw the Devil a few months ago," Mr. Russo said.

"What did he say?" I asked.

"He was saying I should kill myself, I should hang myself."

Mr. Russo's smile slowly dissolved. He looked victimized and aggrieved, insisting to me, "I ain't hanging up for nobody."

The doctors believed that Mr. Russo had not heard voices in over a year. My heart sank. I liked Mr. Russo very much, but his mental stability was looking worse by the minute.

"Why did you hit another patient a few months ago?" I asked.

"That patient spit at me one time," he replied. "God doesn't forget; God wants his children to be victors, not victims."

I looked for any signs in his words or on his face indicating an awareness of how bizarre his experiences were. There were none. His saintly smile had returned. He wore the serene look of a man basking in God's love and approval.

"Are you thinking of hurting anyone now?" I asked.

Mr. Russo leaned over to shield his voice from the others in the room. "I want to kill somebody in the hospital but God tells me not to kill any therapy aides," he whispered.

His voice was actually audible to everyone in the room. His attorney sat up in her chair and interrupted excitedly: "He didn't say that!"

"Oh, yes he did!" called out the up-to-then silent therapy aide.

Mr. Russo did not seem to understand what had just happened, but he did have a sense that it could get him in trouble. He looked chagrined when I asked who he wanted to kill and he pouted like a child about to receive a scolding. "I don't want to say," he muttered.

I steered the interview back to what I believed was the crucial issue: why had he twice stabbed his mother? He patiently explained that he was acting on God's commands. "I stabbed my mother in the arm for religious reasons," he said. "God told me that my mother had sinned and would go to hell if she did not repent. I gave her time to repent and she didn't want to repent. God told me that if she bled, she would be saved. So I had to bleed her. I wanted her to go to heaven."

I then asked Mr. Russo whether he had discussed his unusual experiences with the treatment staff. Yes, he said, but the staff had told him repeatedly that these voices and visions were not real. Then he lowered his voice.

"I believe my doctor is making a mistake," he said anxiously, as if afraid of getting in trouble.

"What mistake?" I asked.

"I told him God told me to do it, to hit that patient, and my doctor said 'No, God didn't tell you.'"

"Did you believe your doctor?"

"No. So I just decided to stop telling him about the voices."

So much for the therapeutic relationship. But was Mr. Russo still dangerous?

"Would you follow God's commands if he told you to kill someone?" I asked.

"But God wouldn't say that," he patiently explained. "It's against one of the commandments."

"What would happen if you didn't follow God's commands?"

"I'd end up committing suicide, which I don't want to do. It's a dilemma."

I agreed. It certainly was. "Would you follow God's command to *bleed* someone again?"

"Yes, I think I would," he replied.

"Do you think you could hurt others if you were able to get a knife?" I asked him.

Mr. Russo gave it some thought. "It's better for me not to be around knives," he said in a matter-of-fact tone. "I could get a message from God to hurt someone. And I don't want to do that, not again."

He seemed to have no idea of the significance of what he had just said. He had actually just told me that he was dangerous and needed to be closely supervised. I patted him on the forearm and nodded in agreement, reassuring him that I also did not want him to hurt anyone. He seemed comforted by that.

Clearly, years of psychotherapy and psychiatric medications had not altered Mr. Russo's core delusion. He was still as psychotic as ever.

I contacted the assistant district attorney and described the interview. I told him I believed that Mr. Russo was still dangerous and needed to remain in the forensic hospital. A retention hearing was scheduled to decide whether or not Mr. Russo would be transferred to a state hospital.

I spent hours preparing my testimony. I made a list of questions the attorneys would likely ask me on the witness stand, and then practiced how I would answer each one. Every time one of my family passed by my office, I wondered what they thought of me talking to myself.

The courthouse was located in a small town south of the hospital. As usual, I left home early to allow myself plenty of time to get lost. When I arrived, I sat down on a hard wooden bench outside the courtroom, trying not to eavesdrop too obviously on the two men in suits sitting nearby. I realized fairly quickly that they were the hospital psychiatrists called to testify that Mr. Russo was no longer dangerous. "But the patient is much better!" one of them exclaimed. "He's not hearing voices to kill anyone!"

I squirmed a bit, wondering if it was appropriate to interrupt their conversation with a few pointed comments of my own. Should I tell them it was never about "killing" his mother, it was all about "bleeding" her to save her from eternity in hell? Or, should I just be collegial, walk over, and introduce myself? But before I could make a decision the court officer called us all into the courtroom.

The judge had some surprising news for us. He had already made a decision without even hearing our testimonies. Referencing my report, he expressed concern about Mr. Russo's recent attack on another patient. I wondered if the judge noticed that this assault took place *five* months after Mr. Russo's psychiatrists had written their reports and that they had not updated their reports after the assault took place.

The judge suggested canceling the hearing. He said he was in favor of ordering a six-month period of continued treatment in the forensic hospital. He said that he was willing to proceed with the hearing, but would, in that case, most likely order a year-long period of treatment. Both attorneys agreed to cancel the hearing and have Mr. Russo reassessed in the future.

It turned out to be one of those all too frequent, "All dressed up with no place to go" days. I packed up my notes and prepared for the long drive back home.

Almost a year passed before another box of records arrived at my doorstep. The psychiatrists were again recommending Mr. Russo's transfer to a state hospital and the assistant district attorney wanted me to interview him again. I reviewed the new psychiatric notes and was saddened to discover that Mr. Russo's mother had died and his medical condition had worsened in the past year.

Mr. Russo had been admitted twice to a medical hospital for pneumonia. He was physically weaker and unable to walk independently. On a positive note, his psychiatric medications had been changed and he was less religiously preoccupied. A year and a half had passed since his last unprovoked attack on a patient, and he denied hearing voices or seeing God or the Devil.

I drove back up to the hospital. The grounds were even prettier with the trees decked in brilliant fall colors. It was heartbreaking to see Mr. Russo being rolled in a wheelchair when I recalled how recently he had been able to walk on his own.

Mr. Russo was both gracious and welcoming; his smile was as

wide as ever and he seemed to remember me fondly. I guess he held no grudges, or did not realize that I was the one who had recommended continued treatment at the forensic hospital. Either way, we were like old friends reuniting, laughing and singing a few songs together. He said he was feeling "hunky-dory."

After a short while, I settled into interview mode. "Tell me about hearing voices," I said. I asked the question in several different ways, but his story was consistent. Since starting on new medications, he no longer heard voices. He told me that he would always continue to take his medicine because he no longer wanted to hear the voice of God or the Devil. He had even stopped watching evangelical shows on TV. "Too much religion isn't good for me," he said, and added that watching Jimmy Swaggart had prompted him to stab his mother.

Mr. Russo never quite acknowledged that he had a mental illness but he did admit to needing help. "I'm ready to go home," he said. His attorney explained that the most he could hope for was a transfer to the state hospital, and he readily agreed this was a good plan.

"Why do you want this transfer?" I asked.

"Because I want to smoke," he succinctly replied.

Mr. Russo's attorney seemed a bit put out. As she patiently explained to her client that he could not smoke in a state hospital, I wondered if she wished he had a higher motive for wanting the transfer. Perhaps I was trying to raise her spirits because I found myself listing all the benefits of a state hospital. "You can visit your family more often," I said. "And you can spend holidays with them."

I was feeling increasingly hopeful that Mr. Russo was no longer dangerous.

"What will you do if the voices return?" I asked.

"If the voice was telling me something I didn't like, I'd have to tell the staff," he said.

All his answers that day indicated that he was no longer dangerous—until my last few questions. Then it became clear that he still believed that his past hallucinations were real. He was still convinced that he had heard the voice of God.

"Did you do the right thing when you bled your mother?" I asked.

He looked me right in the face. "Yes, I did. Wouldn't you do that for your mother?" I stared at him, momentarily speechless, and he continued, "I think my mother's resting in peace now. If I hadn't stabbed her, I think she might have gone to hell. I couldn't let that happen to my mother."

"What do you think might happen if you were able to get a knife again?" I asked. In the same calm, resigned voice, he replied, "I'm still glad I can't get a knife because then I can't hurt nobody."

The attorney and I made brief eye contact. The attorney probably realized her client's chances of transferring were diminishing by the minute. After almost eight years of psychiatric treatment, Mr. Russo was still as delusional as the day he arrived. I was convinced that he would never be completely cured.

But was he still dangerous? He no longer heard voices and had not assaulted anyone in over a year. I went back and forth, mulling over the reasons for and against his transfer. I considered whether he could be safely cared for in a state hospital, closer to home. I realized that he could relapse and the voices could return at any time. If the voices returned, and he was able to get a weapon, he could, and probably would, attack again. But physically he was much weaker and he could no longer walk unassisted. Taking into account the arguments for and against his transfer, I concluded that he could be safely treated in a state hospital. In my final report to the court, I emphasized the importance of making sure he was closely supervised for the rest of his life.

When I called the assistant district attorney to discuss the interview, I could hear the anxiety in his voice. "Do you think he could stab someone again?" he asked.

I reassured him that the risk was low, relaying by way of evidence a conversation I'd had with David Kelly, an assistant district attorney who specialized in psychiatric cases. "He told me he could not remember an insanity acquittee from Brooklyn who'd been released to the community and committed another violent crime," I said.[3]

I pointed out to the assistant district attorney that Mr. Russo would need medical and psychiatric care for the rest of his life. I told him I wasn't worried about Mr. Russo's transfer to a state hospital so much as I was about the next step—I expected he would then be transferred to a nursing home. Mr. Russo could receive the physical care he required in a nursing home, but he wouldn't be supervised by forensic or psychiatric staff. Instead, he would be cared for primarily by hourly wage employees better trained in changing bedpans than in restraining violent patients and detecting emerging psychotic symptoms.

I told the assistant district attorney that I had no crystal ball to predict Mr. Russo's future. No psychological test could determine whether or not he would relapse and start hearing voices again. And it was impossible for me to know whether or not nursing staff would notice if he did.

The assistant district attorney interrupted to remind me that Mr. Russo had stabbed his mother while on a home visit *from* a nursing home. This fact had never been far from my mind during the entirety of my unfocused, unsatisfactory explanation of the limitations of the psychological research on risk prediction. I realized later that I was only making him more anxious, but I thought it worthwhile to point out that not even psychiatric hospitals are totally secure. I mentioned a defendant I had evaluated years earlier, a chronic schizophrenic who pushed a woman to her death onto the subway tracks. Days earlier he'd escaped from a state psychiatric hospital, and the staff didn't even notice until the police contacted them (see pp. 66–72).

The assistant district attorney was thinking out loud as well. "If my own expert doesn't think he's dangerous, I don't think I'd win in a retention hearing," he said. I wondered if he felt the self-protective urge to let the judge make the ultimate decision.

In the end, the assistant district attorney agreed to allow the transfer. Mr. Russo was admitted to the state hospital over a year ago and has not relapsed or hurt anyone since. Perhaps that should resolve some of my concerns. But Mr. Russo's brain will never be whole, and I can only hope that he will never hear God talking to him again. I still feel uneasy. Especially when I remember his smiling, unknowing face, as he confided before I left, "If God started talking to me, and told me not to tell the staff, I'd have to listen to God."

Chapter 12

THE LOST BOYS

"He Said I'd End Up Dead"

The photos from the crime scene revealed an apartment in disarray. Furniture and exercise equipment were pushed together to make room on the floor; clothing and bedding lay bunched up in the corners. Condom wrappers were strewn everywhere. The bedroom closet door was off its hinges and the contents spilled out onto the floor. In the bathroom, a pail was placed under the pipes to catch the dripping water. Blood was splattered and smeared across the floor, the walls, and the furniture. It pooled under the body of the victim, a young Hispanic man sprawled out naked between the cabinets and table in the kitchen alcove. He had been stabbed over twenty times. The knife, its blade broken, lay next to his body.

The doorman told police that 17-year-old Miguel had run up to him, shirtless and incoherent, crying for help. "I just stabbed some man," Miguel blurted out. The doorman called 911, and when the officers arrived, Miguel accompanied them up in the elevator. When they opened the door and saw the scene, they immediately took Miguel into custody. A few hours later he confessed and gave both a written and videotaped statement. He was charged with murder in the second degree, manslaughter in the first degree, and criminal possession of a weapon in the fourth degree.

The defense attorney hired me to evaluate his client. "Miguel may have stabbed the man in self-defense," he said. "But the number of times he stabbed him—well, I need you to assess him for a psychiatric defense." A few days later, he mailed me the legal documents, school records, and Miguel's videotaped statement.

I looked through the bloody crime scene pictures and tried to form a picture of Miguel in my head. What kind of teenager was capable of such brutality? Maybe I would find clues in his confession.

The video opens and I see the cinderblock wall typical of the rooms of a police precinct. The camera then pans around the room, focusing in turn on the assistant district attorney and the detectives. The suspect sits behind a heavy metal table in the small room.

I watched the video and let out an involuntary "Oh!" Miguel was the opposite of thuggish; instead, he was short and skinny. He wore jeans and a sleeveless T-shirt that made his thin arms seem thinner as they hung at his side. He was shoeless and his socks were dirty. A large fake diamond earring adorned his left ear. The camera zoomed in on the fresh cuts on his right hand and the white bandage wrapped around his left.

Miguel did not seem at all scared or anxious. Rather, he looked exhausted and a bit irritated as he responded to the Miranda warnings with a terse, "Yeah." The assistant district attorney asked him to explain what happened and Miguel launched into a ten-minute-long confession. He had met the victim at a porn shop in Times Square and agreed to go to his apartment and have sex with him in exchange for money.

I scrutinized Miguel's face for signs of remorse or embarrassment, but he did not appear at all distressed about engaging in sex with a man. Nor did he seem to feel guilty for having killed him. Without any prompting, he explained how he stabbed the victim to death.

I watched the video a few more times and then turned to Miguel's records. Born a month premature, he was a late talker, one of the many signs of his developmental delays. He repeated first grade and by the time he reached the second, was classified as learning disabled and emotionally disturbed. Now, at age seventeen, his reading ability was only at the fourth grade level.

Teachers described Miguel as silly and uncooperative in class. The school records contained detailed accounts of his poor attendance and even poorer grades. When present in class, he would leave his seat without permission, push peers, talk out of turn, and act disrespectfully toward teachers. He often refused to take off his head phones.

Miguel's problematic behavior was not limited to school. He smoked marijuana frequently and drank alcohol occasionally. He had been arrested four times for selling subway fare cards.

Miguel was never diagnosed with a severe mental illness, but he was referred to psychiatrists on more than one occasion. At age ten he was diagnosed with attention deficit/hyperactivity disorder (ADHD) and prescribed Ritalin. He stopped taking the medication four years later, even though he was still symptomatic. One psychiatric report indicated that Miguel's parents disapproved of medication. His father was particularly skeptical about the drug's effects and "did not see the need for it."

I finished reading through all the records and scheduled a time to evaluate him. He was housed at the Riker's Island jail.

A few days later, I took the bus to the Supreme Court building to meet with Miguel for the first time. I climbed the stairs to the attorneys' interview rooms and waited for him to be brought in. I expected him to be sullen and angry. Like many incarcerated teenagers, he would probably be acting the part of a hardened criminal to cover up his fear. Once again, Miguel surprised me. He walked slowly into the room, his arms handcuffed behind his back, and gave me a cheerful smile. Corrections Officer Royster caught my eye and I nodded okay. She uncuffed his hands and spoke kindly to him. Instinctively, we both knew he would not need to be hand-cuffed during the interview.

Officer Royster seemed especially warm toward him and I won-dered about their interactions in the elevator. Later, as I watched her speak with him over the course of several interviews, I realized that she was acting, the best term for it, "motherly." Officer Royster was always polite with defendants but she treated this young man with unusual tenderness. It was my first indication of how lost Miguel seemed, not just to me, but to every adult he interacted with. I met with him seven times and each time I found him more and more peculiar. It brought to mind Alice's classic line—"curiouser and cu-riouser."[1]

I warned Miguel that the interview was not confidential, but he seemed incapable of holding anything back. He seemed to trust that I would help him. During our first session, I asked about his child-hood, and the words rushed out of him.

Miguel told me that he was one of six children born and raised in Brooklyn. His devoutly Catholic parents valued obedience above all else in their children. "If I do something stupid, they beat me with a belt," Miguel said. "My mom would fold it and leave red marks. It didn't happen that often, only about once a month." He swore that he was never physically or sexually abused, and his candor made it impossible to disbelieve him.

"Tell me about school," I said.

"I was bad in school when I was little," Miguel admitted. "My teachers complained. I'd run around the school, have lots of fights. I failed eighth grade and had to do it over."

"Did you skip school?"

"I be absent a lot. My parents think I was going to school, but I was going to my cousin's house to play basketball or video games or to just hang out. I got caught and my parents ask me why I don't go to school. They were telling me to go; I wouldn't listen. They knew I didn't like school. I never liked school from the beginning."

His voice took on a whiny tone. "I got to wake up early; I be tired.

I got to do work in every class. The only thing I liked was gym and computers."

The more Miguel told me, the more I realized how sad and lonely he was. "I have lots of friends," he said at first, but when I asked for their names, he shrugged and admitted, "I just hang out with my brother, playing basketball and video games. I don't got no friends. Nobody but my brother."

Miguel told me that he was "straight." "I only like girls," he insisted. A few minutes later he told me that he had allowed a man to perform oral sex on him for twenty dollars when he was sixteen. He did not seem to appreciate the contradiction, and I decided not to push it just yet.

Miguel related stories in a silly, childlike manner and often blurted out strange things, unconscious of their effect. At one point in our interview, he complained that he wasn't "having any fun" at Riker's Island jail. I glanced at his face to see if he was kidding but he seemed serious. He actually thought he should be enjoying his stay at Riker's.

During the second interview Miguel made another unprompted comment which made me realize how truly lost he was. "Can I be housed with the women?" he asked, "I think I would like it better there." It was a strange, naïve request, but he really seemed to believe I could arrange a transfer for him. I assumed he wanted to find a new "mommy" at Riker's. I also sensed that he felt physically and sexually threatened by the more jail-savvy young men at the jail. Again, I was impressed with how he didn't really "get it." He did not understand that he would be imprisoned with men until he served out his time.

I administered a battery of psychological tests. Miguel concentrated hard and seemed to be trying his best on the I.Q. test. He scored within the low average range, an 82, which was consistent with his poor academic performance. Miguel's responses on the personality tests indicated that that he felt misunderstood and under-

---

appreciated. His strong need for approval conflicted with his longing for self-assertion. He tended to form self-destructive relationships and allowed others to exploit and abuse him.

I did not detect in him any signs of psychosis, depression, or severe mental illness. The only noticeable symptom of pathology was his lighthearted attitude, which was entirely incongruous with the seriousness of his legal charges.

After the second interview I called Miguel's parents, hoping they could shed light on some of his strange comments. When I spoke with his mother, she was painfully aware of her son's deficiencies.

"What's your son like?" I asked.

"He laughs a lot," his mother said. "I think because he's slow. He's a very giggly person, a very sweet kid. Not violent at all. No matter how big he is, he still acts like a kid."

"What do you mean, he acts like a kid?"

"He talks like a kid. He doesn't quite grasp what you say to him." I heard her sigh, "Miguel's been troubled all his life."

During the next few sessions with Miguel, I gently started asking about the weeks prior to his arrest.

"I know you left home," I said. "What happened?"

"It was Thanksgiving," he recalled, "and I got into an argument with Pop, for calling my sister names. I was real mad and left the house. It was cold and after a few hours I went to a shelter. I just wanted to get a job, so my parents could see a change in me before I go home. I wanted them to see that I could do something for myself, that I'm responsible and can be on my own.

"I wanted to get a job," he continued. "I went to a lot of places. I went to this office building, I asked for an application for a job. But they didn't call me."

Miguel's decision to leave home was impulsive. He had never held a job, had no marketable skills, and was unable to find work.

"So, how did you survive?" I asked him.

"My parents didn't give me money. I was on the streets for a few weeks. My grandmother sometimes gave me five dollars, my aunt give money for me to get pizza and Chinese food. I couldn't stay with nobody in my family. I really wanted to stay at my grandmother's but there was no room and I didn't think she wanted me to stay."

"Where did you sleep?"

"I went straight to the shelter," he said. "First one in Manhattan, then one in Brooklyn. I went back and forth for a few days. Then I find out about a place for kids, Covenant House. I only stayed there for one day. I didn't like it there. There were lots of people I didn't know and I couldn't make any friends there. I was lonely. When it was time to eat, I had no one to sit with, so I left."

I realized he must have been desperate for money and continued to press him for details.

"How did you support yourself?"

He looked sheepish. "I'd go to Forty-second Street to try to make money. Once I got a blow job for like thirty dollars."

This was the second time Miguel had exchanged money for sex. I did not need to be trained in Freudian theory to see that he may have had unrecognized homosexual feelings. I kept this issue in mind as I asked Miguel to tell me in detail about what led up to the killing. He told me that he met the victim in the Times Square area and asked him for a dollar.

"What happened next?" I asked.

"I told him I was starving," Miguel said. "He said, 'I'll get you something to eat.' We were talking for a while, about girls, then we start walking, to take the 2 train to his apartment in Brooklyn."

"What happened after you both got to the apartment?" I asked.

"We went to his house and he started making food. We were watching porn. He said, like, 'I'll give you a blow job.' I said, 'That's going to be thirty dollars.' He said all right, then he said, 'Can you spend the night?' I said, 'Yes, that's going to be fifty dollars.'"

"What happened next?"

"We smoked some crack," he said. "And had oral and anal sex a lot."

"Did you enjoy the sex?" I asked.

"No! No! Of course not. I'm straight. I just wanted the money."

Although Miguel described the sex in a matter-of-fact manner, performing anal and oral sex on a man probably was quite upsetting for a young man who consciously identified himself as heterosexual. Miguel insisted that the sex was unpleasant, but he admitted that he was able to perform well enough. He stayed at the apartment, smoking crack and having sex with the victim all night. The next morning, when Miguel said he had to leave, the man began to threaten him.

"When he wanted me to do it to him, when I said I wanted to leave, that's when he started threatening me," Miguel said. "He was too out of control. He said I'd end up dead. I was scared."

"Did you try to leave the apartment?" I asked.

"There were no phones in the apartment. And I had nowhere to go, the snow was coming up, and it was cold."

"What happened then?"

"I was trying to get hard and he was getting really angry," Miguel said. "I was so scared. When he went in the bathroom, I went to the kitchen to get two knives and hid them on the floor, under the blanket. The man felt the knives on his knee when we were having sex. He tried to reach for one knife and I snatched it from him before he got it. I thought he was so strong that if he got the knife he would have had the upper hand, so I guess I caught him while he was on his knees. I think I caught him on the chest."

"Why didn't you run away after you stabbed him once?" I pressed.

Miguel started to cry, and I waited for him to collect himself a little. "The man was fighting me back," he explained in a shaky voice. "He was trying to hold my wrist. I was just trying to survive, trying not to get killed. The first knife broke, so I dropped the knife on the floor and grabbed the other one. I didn't use it though. I threw the knife down, grabbed my jeans and ran. I went straight down the lobby and found the doorman. I told him what I done and asked can he help me."

Miguel's story was consistent with that which he had related to the assistant district attorney and detectives. I was convinced that Miguel was telling the truth. I believed that a series of increasingly traumatic events had caused Miguel to feel desperate and panicked. After leaving his parents' home precipitously and spending two weeks alone and destitute for the first time in his life, he had placed himself in a situation he was emotionally and developmentally unable to handle.

When he accompanied the victim to his apartment, he used crack cocaine for the first time in his life, which certainly heightened his already intense emotions. He hid the kitchen knives as a precautionary measure and only used it when the victim tried to grab one, convinced that he would be killed otherwise.

He stabbed the victim many times, more than was necessary, if self-defense was the only motivation. Yet he grabbed the knife in a state of high emotional arousal. His ambivalence about participating in homosexual acts, in addition to his fear for his life, caused him to act quickly, without taking time to cool off or deliberate.

I prepared a report concluding that Miguel had acted in a state of extreme emotional disturbance. I described him as a boy faced with an adult crisis. Physically, he was a typical adolescent, but emotionally he was, as his mother said, just a kid. I quoted a few of the stranger things he said to me, the questions that a boy a third his age would have asked.

I sent my report to the defense attorney. A week later I called him to make sure my report had arrived and to ask about the progress of the case. I knew the prosecutor would probably hire his own expert to give a second opinion. If that psychologist or psychiatrist reached different conclusions, the case would most likely go to trial. If the prosecution-retained expert agreed with the findings in my report, however, the ADA might offer Miguel a plea of man-slaughter.

The defense attorney called me about six months later.

"Your report made a big difference," he said. "The assistant dis-trict attorney made a good offer. He's willing to drop the murder charge and let Miguel plead to manslaughter in the first degree."

"What's the sentence?" I asked.

"He is offering ten years and my client wants to accept."

I was quiet, not sure how to respond.

"I sort of wanted to try this case," the defense attorney added. "I thought we had a good chance of winning. But the neighbors didn't want to testify about the victim's character, and the crime scene was so ugly. We might have lost."

Miguel would probably serve two thirds of his time and be re-leased when he was in his mid or late twenties. I knew that man-slaughter was the best he could have hoped for, even if the jury believed he had acted in a state of extreme emotional disturbance. I had very mixed feelings about his decision to accept this plea. I just could not imagine him serving time upstate with adult prisoners. I tried to picture him as an adult, and couldn't. Would prison make him finally grow up?

An Elaborate Ruse

When she didn't answer the bell, the neighbors broke in and found the eighty-three-year-old woman dead on the floor of her Staten Island apartment. Her body lay between the couch and coffee table, as if she had rolled off the couch. The authorities concluded that she had died of cardiac arrest. Her daughter began funeral preparations, but her son became suspicious and insisted that an autopsy be performed. Unexpectedly, the autopsy showed that the woman had three broken ribs. The coroner concluded that her death was caused by injuries sustained in a beating and declared her death a homicide. Four days later the police brought the victim's daughter and her fifteen-year-old son Anthony into the precinct for questioning. The teenager had been living with the victim at the time of her death. Since there was no evidence of forced entry, he was the primary suspect.

Anthony initially told the detectives that he had no idea what had happened to his grandmother and was not even in the house when she died. He insisted that he had nothing to do with her death. Under the pressure of repeated questions, however, he changed his story. In written and videotaped statements, he confessed to punching her a few times in the chest after she hit him with a belt. He explained that they had been arguing and she accused him of selling her jewelry to buy marijuana.

The assistant district attorney called me to discuss the case. It was not clear to me why Anthony was being charged as an adult in criminal court. I knew that adolescents are often afforded more leniency in the criminal justice system. Some may have their cases transferred to family court.

The assistant district attorney explained that he did consider recommending that Anthony's case be sent to family court, but decided to charge Anthony, as an adult, with murder in the second degree and manslaughter in the first degree. The prosecutor had a reputation as an aggressive ADA and I was not surprised by his decision.

The prosecutor told me that Anthony's attorney had already retained a psychologist who believed that Anthony was intellectually limited and emotionally disturbed. She concluded that Anthony was not competent to waive his Miranda rights when he gave the confession.

The defense attorney had requested a Huntley hearing to determine whether his client knowingly, intelligently, and voluntarily waived his rights.[2] During this pretrial hearing the judge would examine all the circumstances surrounding the interrogation. He or she would hear evidence about any coercive police conduct and factor in Anthony's particular vulnerabilities to interrogation pressure, which could include his immaturity, limited education, low intelligence, emotional problems, and lack of prior legal experience.

Research has shown that adolescents are easily intimidated by police, vulnerable to suggestion, and more likely to confess than adults.[3] It is widely known that adolescents are at greater risk of giving false confessions, as exemplified by the widely publicized case of the Central Park jogger. On April 19, 1989, a 28-year-old woman was viciously raped and beaten while jogging in New York City's Central Park. Five black teenagers were brought in for questioning; four gave confessions implicating each other. Within a few weeks they retracted their confessions and accused the police of improper coercive interrogation tactics. In a preliminary hearing about the admissibility of their statements, the judge ruled that they had waived their Miranda rights knowingly, intelligently, and voluntarily. Although no DNA evidence tied the five teens to the assault, the confessions were introduced at their trials and all were convicted.

In 2002, convicted rapist and murderer Matias Reyes confessed to the crime. His DNA was a match. The five young men, now in their late twenties, were released. They had already served prison sentences ranging from five to thirteen years.

The prosecutor hired me to give a second opinion about whether Anthony was competent to waive his Miranda rights. He sent me a package of documents containing the police records, videotaped statement, autopsy report, crime scene photos, school and foster care records, and the defense psychologist's report and notes.

I made myself a cup of tea and put the video into the VCR. It began by slowly panning across the room. Seated on one side of the table was a small white boy who looked much younger than his fifteen years. He was dressed casually in the baggy clothes popular with teens, which swam on him, making his small frame look even smaller.

The video camera zoomed in on Anthony's face. He was very cute, with long curly brown hair framing his childlike face. The camera then focused on Anthony's mother who sat next to him, slumped down in her seat, staring vacantly off into space. She did not move or look at her son once.

The police detectives had followed the letter of the law pertaining to the questioning of their young suspect: detained teenagers under sixteen are not permitted to be questioned without a guardian present. Anthony's mother was there during the interrogation as well as during her son's confession.

In years past, juveniles were afforded few legal protections. All this changed in 1967, when 15-year-old Gerald Francis Gault was arrested for making lewd phone calls. If he had been a few years older, the most he could have been sentenced to was two months in jail. Gault's parents were not present when he was being questioned and no one advised him of his right to remain silent or his right to an attorney. He was convicted and committed to a state industrial school for six years.

Gault's case was appealed to the Supreme Court and his conviction was overturned. Justice Abe Fortas wrote the majority decision and included this:

> The child receives the worst of both worlds; he gets neither the protections accorded to adults nor the solicitous care and regenerative treatment postulated for children.[4]

Since that key Supreme Court decision, juveniles are granted most of the same procedural rights as adults, including the right to an attorney and protection against self-incrimination.

I had expected the video to portray Anthony as a distraught, frightened, and intellectually limited teenager. He was, however, preternaturally composed and unrepentant. He answered questions without pausing or searching for answers. He spoke directly to the assistant district attorney and never turned to his mother for support or guidance.

The Miranda rights were read to him, and Anthony calmly answered "yes" to each. There was no indication that he did not understand them. When the assistant district attorney asked Anthony's mother directly whether she also understood each of the rights, she stirred herself long enough to mumble "yes" before drifting back into her own private world.

The mother's only spontaneous comment during the entire video was a gruff, "Tell the truth." After that, she sat mute, staring at the floor. I was not sure if she was in shock, or depressed, or in any condition to effectively protect her son's rights. I felt torn as I watched her. She seemed overwhelmed with the fact that her son was suspected of killing her mother.

The assistant district attorney began the interrogation by reviewing the facts of the crime, posing questions in a polite, measured way. He was neither antagonistic nor overly friendly. I thought his approach was quite effective. It set Anthony at ease and encouraged him to tell all.

Anthony explained matter-of-factly that he and his grandmother had been arguing. She hit him with a belt and he became so angry that he punched her a few times in the chest until they both fell to the floor. After a few minutes he calmed down, apologized, and helped her onto the couch. He claimed to be unaware that she was badly injured. She lay on the couch, quiet and uncomplaining, while he went into his room to watch TV. When he woke the next morning, he found her dead body. He tried to revive her with CPR to no avail.

I was taken aback when Anthony recounted the ruse he concocted next. He slipped out of the apartment through a window, leaving her keys inside and the front door locked. Then he alerted family members that he could not reach his grandmother, leading to the "accidental" discovery of her body.

Anthony was poised and polite throughout the interview. There were no signs that he was confused or intimidated. He also did not seem intellectually slow. His face was glum, but his eyes never teared up and his voice never became choked with emotion.

His sweet appearance and cool tone were in such stark contrast to the crime he had committed. He sounded mildly chagrined, as though he was being called into the principal's office for a minor school infraction. It was possible that he did not understand how much trouble he was in.

I watched the videotaped confession again and then started reading through the packet of records. The police reports revealed that Anthony had been in trouble before. His grandmother had called the police three times to complain that he was stealing money from her.

I looked through Anthony's school and foster care records for evidence of intellectual limitations but found nothing. The records did not mention mental retardation or even borderline intellectual functioning. He had never been placed in special education classes and had never even been *referred* for an educational evaluation.

Mentally retarded children typically demonstrate serious academic problems from the day they enter kindergarten. Anthony's most recent grades were all D's and F's, but his attendance record indicated that this was largely a result of his chronic truancy. When he was younger and attended school regularly, his grades were mostly B's.

Anthony's school and foster care records from the past few years contained detailed notes about his problematic behavior. He skipped classes, disobeyed rules, was rude to teachers, argued and fought with peers, and performed poorly academically. He was once suspended for carrying a box cutter to school.

I finished reading through Anthony's records, then turned to the defense psychologist's report. Anthony scored a 68 on the intelligence test she administered. She concluded that Anthony's immaturity and low I.Q. rendered him incompetent to waive his Miranda rights when he made his confession.

A score of 69 or less is a sign of mental retardation but is not a definitive diagnosis. In order to diagnose an individual with mental retardation, his intellectual deficits must be accompanied by an inability to function in the real world, to adapt to situations as they arise, and respond appropriately.

I was surprised to see that the psychologist had not written anything about Anthony's real life functioning. Her evaluation and report seemed to me incomplete and sloppy. She did not review Anthony's past school records, foster care records, or interview family members or teachers. She concluded that Anthony had no diagnosable mental disease but was, nonetheless, intellectually impaired and emotionally disturbed.

I was even more puzzled when I realized that the psychologist made no mention of Anthony's written or videotaped confessions in her report. Did she even see them? I could not understand how she could have reached a conclusion about Anthony's ability to waive his Miranda rights without having watched his confession.

I met Anthony a few days later. He was engaging and friendly, quite unlike the boy who had so coolly described his grandmother's death on the videotape. I felt sorry for him when he told me about the numerous upheavals and the emotional deprivation he went through as a child. His mother was a crack cocaine addict and his father was murdered when Anthony was only seven years old. Within a year of his father's death, child protective services removed him from his mother's care due to allegations of physical abuse and neglect.

"Tell me about when you were first placed in foster care," I said.

"My mother wanted us to be a singing group. She'd hit us if we sang off-key," he replied. "People complained they heard stuff, screaming and crying. My older sister told her teacher that my mother threw hot water on us. That's when they put us in foster care."

"And what about the foster homes?"

A wistful expression crossed his face as he replied, "They were nice. They took me places. They treated me like I was their son."

Anthony told me how he was shuffled back and forth between four different foster families during the next three years. He never remained in one stable family situation for more than a year at a time. Eventually, when he turned eleven, his mother remarried and regained custody.

Anthony said he found it difficult to live with his mother and new stepfather. He admitted to acting out "a bit" in school and at home. He resisted his stepfather's rules, was truant, disobeyed curfew, and smoked marijuana almost every day. Three years later, Anthony moved in with his grandmother.

"Why did you leave your mom's home?" I asked.

"She sent me to my grandma's," he said with a shrug.

"Tell me what your grandmother was like."

His voice took on a sheepish, childlike tone as he told me how his grandmother gave him a room of his own and money for allowance "all the time." But then his tone changed abruptly.

"She called the cops four times!" he said.

"Why?"

"She was always accusing me of stealing money. She did it two or three times a week, but she forgets stuff. Once she told me to get out of the house, told me she'd call the cops, then she found her jewelry under her pillow." Anthony sounded bitter.

I listened quietly to his story, but I was skeptical. I suspected he had been stealing from his grandmother.

I left this first interview wondering why no one had ever taken this obviously troubled teen to psychotherapy. He seemed to be another "lost boy" who had slipped through the cracks, abandoned by his mother, teachers, and foster parents. Yet, I could not forget his apparent lack of remorse during his confession.

I gave Anthony an I.Q. test during the second interview. He worked slowly and unenthusiastically, which lowered his score on some of the timed items. He scored a 75 on the I.Q. test I administered. This score was not much higher than the score he received from the defense psychologist. I was convinced that his lackadaisical approach had lowered his score on both tests.

I did not believe that Anthony was mentally retarded. His school records and ability to function in everyday life pointed to average intellectual abilities. The elaborate steps he took to hide his crime showed that he was certainly not without resources.

I believed Anthony had normal intelligence, but I was not yet convinced that he understood all the terms and concepts of the Miranda warnings. The fact that Anthony was only 15 years old at the time of the offense was another important factor for me to consider. I was familiar with the research which found that adolescents need extra safeguards because they are more likely to misunderstand the words used in the warnings. Most adolescents do not possess a full understanding of the ramifications of waiving their rights.

I questioned Anthony extensively about the Miranda warnings. He gave all the right answers and seemed to understand all the terms and concepts. But had he voluntarily waived his rights?

For someone as young as Anthony, any degree of police coercion or intimidation could be deemed unduly forceful. Did his age and emotional problems make him especially vulnerable to pressure?

Anthony had no history of psychiatric treatment and had never been referred to counseling. He denied ever having serious symptoms of depression or anxiety. When I asked him about the traumas he'd experienced in his life, he seemed unconcerned, as if he held no grudges. I wondered if he was minimizing the impact of the abuse and neglect, but no matter how much I probed, he insisted that he had always been "a pretty happy kid."

I concluded that Anthony did not have any diagnosable mental illness or mental retardation that would make him more susceptible than other juveniles to pressure during questioning. I saw no evidence that his waiver of his Miranda rights was not voluntary.

A few months after I had submitted my report, the Huntley hearing took place. Anthony's lawyer argued that his videotaped and written statements should be excluded for two reasons: Anthony's low I.Q. and emotional problems rendered him incompetent to waive his Miranda rights, and his mother had not provided adequate guidance during the interrogation and confession.

The defense psychologist testified about her evaluation and her conclusions, and then I took the stand. I told the judge that, in my opinion, Anthony had been competent to waive his rights. Anthony lost the Huntley hearing. The judge ruled that his confession could be presented at trial. When the prosecutor called to tell me the news, I wondered how a jury would react to the videotape that I found so chilling.

The prosecutor then asked me to meet with Anthony again to assess his mental state at the time of the offense. He expected Anthony's attorney to offer some type of psychiatric defense at trial. The defense psychologist would likely testify that Anthony was emotionally disturbed when he killed his grandmother.

When I met with Anthony for our third and last interview, I asked him about his mental state in the hours before and after he beat his grandmother.

Anthony described his often tense relationship with his grandmother in the same detached manner I had seen on the videotape. His story never altered.

"Why did you hit your grandmother?" I asked.

"We were watching TV," he said. "Then she said I had her money, forty dollars. We started arguing and she grabbed a belt and hit me with it. She called me a thief. She said I was a son of a bitch."

"What happened next?"

"I started punching her, I hit her in her face, her chest, I was feeling like everybody was always picking on me. I felt ticked off in my head, like I was about to explode. I was swinging, then I came to my senses. I helped her up to the couch and said I'm sorry. I told her I was sorry and I loved her."

"What were you feeling when you hit your grandmother?" I asked.

"I was so angry. I felt like I was fighting off evil."

"What happened next?"

"She forgave me," he answered. "She said 'Okay, darling.' I sat down on the other couch and started thinking. What did I do? I couldn't believe what happened. I started cleaning the place."

"Were you worried that she was injured?"

"Yes, I was worried she was hurt bad," he replied. "I was hoping she didn't catch a heart attack. I was hoping she'd be all right."

"Why not call the police?"

"I was afraid I'd get in trouble for that. They'd probably think I did it on purpose."

"Did you see she was hurt?"

"I didn't see bruises then."

"Didn't you hear her ribs cracking?" I persisted.

"No."

My questions about his grandmother's broken ribs seemed to make him anxious. He abruptly veered off topic, volunteering the fact that he tried giving her CPR for ten minutes. He insisted that her ribs must have broken while he was performing CPR.

"What did you do after you realized she was dead?" I asked.

"I fixed her up on the couch like she died of natural causes," he replied. "I put her head on a pillow. I put a hat on her to cover her eyes." Anthony probably covered his grandmother's face because he could not bear to see her lifeless eyes.

Anthony had a moral dilemma and many hours to resolve it, but did nothing to save his grandmother's life. While she lay dying, he watched television and then went to sleep. He chose not to call for help. He chose not to risk getting in trouble. At no point in the interview did Anthony take responsibility for his actions. The closest he came was a half-pleading appeal for my sympathy: "It wasn't my intention to hurt her."

Anthony said so many of the right things, but I was not convinced that he actually felt remorse. Was it possible, though, that he was emotionally disturbed?

There is a relatively new psychiatric disorder called reactive attachment disorder which commonly affects children living in orphanages or raised in a series of foster homes. Unable to form secure attachments during the critical early years of life, these children are later incapable of developing normal relationships with caregivers. Some of the children become emotionally withdrawn and inhibited, while others are overly and indiscriminately friendly. Some display sociopathic behavior.[5] Anthony's early childhood certainly fit the typical pattern of a child with reactive attachment disorder. And he certainly showed worrisome sociopathic tendencies.

In the end, I concluded that Anthony, while emotionally troubled, did not fit the legal criteria for the insanity defense. I called the assistant district attorney to discuss my findings. The assistant district attorney paused and then told me he would offer a plea of manslaughter.

Months passed while the Anthony and his attorney discussed the manslaughter plea. Finally, they rejected the offer, perhaps believing it to be too severe, or confident that Anthony would do better going to trial.

The defense psychologist was called to the stand to testify about her conclusions that Anthony was mentally retarded and emotionally disturbed. Then the assistant district attorney called me to the stand. He asked me to explain to the jury why I did not believe

Anthony was mentally retarded and did not fulfill criteria for the insanity defense. In response to his questions, I readily agreed that Anthony was a troubled adolescent who was not insane, but merely enraged when he hit his grandmother.

The jury did not find Anthony guilty of murder or manslaughter. He was instead found guilty of criminally negligent homicide and sentenced to eighteen months to two years in a juvenile facility.

In the end, the jury's decision may have come down to the powerful effect of the defendant's appearance. Anthony never took the witness stand. But, as he sat at the defense table in his oversize shirt, his tie knotted too big for his thin neck, he made for a sympathetic defendant. Maybe the jury was convinced that such a young, vulnerable-looking, lost boy was redeemable.

Even though I had been retained by the prosecution, I was actually a bit relieved by the verdict. The thought of such a young teenager in prison troubled me.

Almost ten years later I called the assistant district attorney to discuss a different case. "What ever happened to Anthony?" I asked.

"I'll look him up on the computer," he said, and I heard the faint clicking of the keyboard.

Within a few minutes he was back on the line. "Anthony didn't learn his lesson," he grimly informed me. "He was just recently released after serving six years for robbery."

I was not surprised. Although years had passed since I evaluated Anthony, I still could not get the image of his chilling composure during his video confession out of my mind.

Chapter 13

FAKERS?

Most of the defendants I examine are not totally honest with me. Many exaggerate or fake symptoms of depression or psychosis. Some hide their native intelligence and feign mental retardation.

My job as a forensic examiner is not only to spot the malingerers, as they are called in the field, but to understand why they are faking in the first place. Malingering does not, in and of itself, mean that a defendant has no psychiatric illness. Sometimes a defendant will exaggerate his symptoms to make sure I do not miss them. Others, of course, are just lying to get out of trouble.

One of the most difficult questions for me to answer is whether or not a defendant is faking. These next four cases demonstrate some of the difficulties I have had answering these questions.

"Who Did What?"
Neighbors called 911 to report a loud argument. When the police entered the apartment, they found the body of the strangled tenant. Skin samples taken from under the woman's fingernails matched her ex-boyfriend's DNA. He did not have an alibi.

Mr. Allen claimed to have no memory of killing his ex-girlfriend. Yet, since she had recently ended their relationship and kicked him out of their shared apartment, he was the primary suspect. Mr. Allen gave a series of increasingly self-incriminating written confessions and there was no question of his guilt. "I didn't do it," became "I have no explanation," which was in turn amended to "I need help, I killed her. I want a lawyer."

"I didn't know what I was doing," he told the police. "I put a block in one of my minds." This, it seemed, was Mr. Allen's first mention of another "mind." Later, he told his lawyer about "Tom," his other personality. That's when the lawyer contacted me to evaluate him. He told me about his client's story. The sudden appearance of this Tom character set off alarm bells in my head. It looked as though the case would hinge upon whether or not he had multiple personality disorder.

I reviewed the defendant's foster care and police records before scheduling the first appointment. He was physically abused by his mother and at age twelve, was placed in the first of a series of foster homes. At age sixteen, he was moved to a group home and for the next few years was shuttled through a series of ever-changing group homes. His police records indicated that he was arrested a few times for minor offenses, including possession of marijuana and stolen property.

The documents included numerous psychiatric and psychological evaluations that described him as "troubled" and "needy," but no clinician ever diagnosed him with a mental illness. It was clear that Mr. Allen had grown up abused and troubled, but there was no hint of multiple personality disorder.

Multiple personality disorder is now categorized in the field as dissociative identity disorder. The symptoms include the presence of two or more distinctive personality states and an inability to recall important events and personal information. These personality states are called "identities" or "alters" and are thought to take control of the individual's behavior.

The alters have distinct biographical histories and self-image and typically vary in gender, age, vocabulary, and mood state. They have different voice qualities and physical postures. The primary identity, or host, uses the individual's given name while the alters use different names. An alter may be aware of all, none, or some of the other alters. The host is typically dependent, depressed, and submissive, and the alters may be belligerent and emerge in situations that the primary identity finds particularly stressful. The emergence of an alter is called the "switch" and it can occur suddenly in a matter of seconds, or minutes or gradually over hours. The switch is usually precipitated by eye blinking, yawning, or another physical tic.

Many clinicians doubt that dissociative identity disorder is a valid psychiatric illness and believe it is merely symptomatic of highly-suggestible individuals. I studied dissociative identity disorder in graduate school but had never evaluated anyone diagnosed with the disorder. Watching popular movies about the disorder, such as *The Three Faces of Eve* and *Sybil*, hardly qualified as clinical experience.[1] As I prepared for my first interview with Mr. Allen, I reread some of the clinical literature so I could look out for the classic signs of dissociative identity disorder. If Mr. Allen actually had this rare psychological disorder, he should describe episodes of amnesia. If he were to transition between personalities during our sessions, the switch should be triggered by a stressful situation.

The Diagnostic and Statistical Manual–IV cautions that dissociative identity disorder "must be distinguished from *Malingering* in situations in which there may be financial or forensic gain."[2] Mr. Allen's circumstances certainly fit that warning. I would have to watch him closely.

I arrived at the Supreme Court building in the early afternoon. After being cleared to enter by the Corrections Department personnel, I passed through a series of locked gates into the counsel area. The windowless space was subdivided into four separate interview areas.

I watched the officer take off Mr. Allen's handcuffs. He was a small, weathered, white man who looked older than his 28 years. He was missing some teeth and, by the look of his remaining teeth, had not been to a dentist in quite a while. His handshake was peculiar and unpleasant. He held his hand in a curved, almost claw-like position, the fingers totally limp. His handshake had no power in it, no grip and, to make it even creepier (if that was even possible at this point), his palm was moist and clammy.

Mr. Allen spoke so softly that it was difficult to catch what he said. I had to lean in to hear, which brought our bodies uncomfortably close. It felt too intimate. I started by asking about his upbringing and history and Mr. Allen easily confided details about his sad and troubled life. Too easily, I thought.

He described the type of early abuse and neglect typical of patients with dissociative identity disorder. His mother, he said, was mentally ill, used drugs, and physically abused him as a child.

"Can you give me a specific example of abuse?" I asked, careful to record his words verbatim.

"She slammed me against walls and burned me with cigarettes and hot water," he said calmly. "She even whipped me with an electrical cord."

I asked Mr. Allen about the past few years of his life, and he described an aimless, unfulfilling existence. He typically drank two six-packs of beer each day, and a few years before his arrest, had started smoking crack cocaine. He never worked consistently, was frequently homeless, and slept in parks.

After a while, I asked him about his ex-girlfriend. He knew that he was the prime suspect in her murder.

"How was she killed?" I asked.

"Someone can make somebody else get angry," he cryptically said, making a vague gesture with his hands. "Maybe I didn't do it, maybe another identity did it."

"What identity?" I asked.

"Tom," he said without hesitation. "Maybe Tom wasn't angry; maybe he was trying to protect me. That's his personality. Or he was trying to take over."

"Tell me about Tom."

"He tries to keep everything under control. Tom goes to church and is a God-fearing, respectful person. He's trying to protect me."

We talked a bit more about Tom until Mr. Allen spontaneously changed the subject.

"Mike's there too," he said, pausing for effect. "He's not good."

"What do you mean?" I asked, careful to keep my voice even.

"Mike's a vulture," he replied. "He preys on the weak. He's very controlling. He's not me. He's the opposite of me."

"How do you know about Tom and Mike?"

"I'll be at a place and I don't know how I got there," he said. "I'd be going somewhere and all of a sudden I'd be somewhere else."

"When does this happen?"

"Off and on. Mostly when I'm stressed. And I'm stressed a lot."

"How old were you when it started?"

"It's been going on my whole life," he replied, sighing dramatically.

We were only about an hour into the first session and I was already confused. As we talked about "Tom" and "Mike," it became clear to me that Mr. Allen was laying a foundation for an insanity defense. I was sure that he was going to claim that one of his alters had murdered his ex-girlfriend. Yet I had no idea whether he was placing the blame on Tom or Mike.

When I asked for more details about his alters, his answer surprised me. He started to describe paranoid delusions, or what he thought delusions should sound like.

"I'm schizophrenic," he volunteered authoritatively. "A counselor said I'm different people at different times."

"Can I see this counselor's records?" I asked, keeping my tone neutral. I was careful not to slip and reveal my suspicions.

"The government took them and hid them," he replied. "They have been watching me for years."

Then came the best part of the session (at least for me). He looked intently up at the water-stained ceiling tiles and lowered his voice. "They're probably looking at me right now," he whispered conspiratorially, subtly inviting me to follow his gaze upward to the ceiling which held, for him at least, such interest.

"Why?" I asked, involuntarily following his gaze upward.

"They know all about me. They know I'm different," he explained. "They know I have powers. I can tell when things will happen; I have dreams that tell the future. That's why I don't sleep at night."

I forced myself to appear concerned, all the while stifling a laugh at his over-the-top theatrics. I felt fairly certain that he was faking, but couldn't decide whether he also, in fact, had a serious mental illness. We had been talking for an hour and so far he had reported paranoid and grandiose delusions and symptoms of dissociative identity disorder. I decided that I needed to switch gears, so I pulled the psychological tests out of my briefcase.

I asked Mr. Allen to fill out the 567-item True-False personality test called the Minnesota Multiphasic Personality Inventory-2.[3] The MMPI-2 is a widely used personality assessment test that includes nine clinical scales including depression, mania, paranoia, schizophrenia, and others. It is particularly useful in a forensic setting because it includes questions to detect malingering and exaggeration.

Mr. Allen worked on this test alone for over an hour, which gave me time to try to sort out his story in my mind. Afterward, I asked him to draw pictures of a house, a tree, a man, and a woman.[4] His tree looked more like an underwater hydra plant than a tree. The house was a barren box with two empty windows and a tiny knobless door. But it was his drawing of a woman that I found the most disturbing. She was naked and her arms were stumps that cut off at the elbow joints. Her hair radiated out in all directions as though she had been electrocuted. He had drawn only some dots for her eyes and nose and a curved line for her mouth. Her breasts, belly button, and pubic hair, in contrast, were drawn with exacting detail.

Mr. Allen's responses on the Rorschach were equally peculiar. Psychologically healthy people typically see animals, people, and nature in the inkblots.[5] Mr. Allen told me he saw a demon, an alien space ship, a dead lamb, spots in the shape of "666," a dead cat slit open, a vagina, a penis, and a skeleton with an alien head. I leaned over the metal table between us, looking closely at the blots. I was unable to see most of the images he so vividly described.

His responses were more pathological than those I had heard from severely ill schizophrenics. Yet his responses were not consistent with his biographical information. He had never been diagnosed with a mental illness or admitted to a psychiatric hospital. This inconsistency added to my suspicion that he was malingering.

It was enough for the first meeting. I was exhausted. Stifling a yawn, I told him I would see him next week and stood up to leave. Whether or not Mr. Allen had multiple personalities, it certainly felt as if I had been interviewing more than one person.

Before the second session I scored his MMPI-2. Mr. Allen's test was invalid because his answers were too extreme to be believable. Once again, it looked as if he was faking.

A week later, the corrections officer escorted Mr. Allen into the interview office for our second session. Physically, he looked alert and relaxed. His gait and movements were normal, but he wore a baffled expression on his face. Before I could say hello, he announced, "I don't remember meeting you. My lawyer asked if I met you. I don't remember you."

As usual, Mr. Allen was not one to disappoint; the session had certainly started off on an exciting note. I decided to play along and, doing my best to keep my face expressionless, I asked him about the first session. I showed him the MMPI-2 booklet of questions, and he told me he did not remember taking the test. I pulled out the pictures he had sketched and he professed to have no memory of drawing them, either.

Mr. Allen claimed to have absolutely no knowledge of our first session. Apparently, he was assuming the role of a different alter from the one I had interviewed the week before. Yet, he just didn't *seem* any different. He spoke in the same tone of voice and used identical mannerisms; even his mood was unchanged. The man talking with me that day *seemed* to be the same one I had visited the week before.

Knowing that the alters should describe different biographical histories, I devised a quick test to see if I could beat him at his own game.

"How old are you?" I asked. I had asked the same simple question the previous week.

He stared at me blankly, shaking his head to indicate he didn't know.

I tried again. "What is your date of birth?"

"I don't know," he said.

I played along and, oh-so-helpfully, told him his correct age and date of birth.

"How far did you go in school?" I asked.

"I left after elementary school," he replied.

We chatted for a few minutes. Then I said, as if posing the question for the first time, "What is your date of birth?"

"I don't know."

"But I just told you," I pointed out with my poker face.

"No, you didn't, not today," he claimed, his face equally blank.

"Yes," I mildly protested. "Yes, I did. I just told you your date of birth a few minutes ago."

"No, you didn't," he insisted.

I let it drop. "How far did you go in school?"

"I left in high school," he replied.

"Don't you remember telling me a few minutes ago that you left after elementary school?"

"No, why would I do that?" he answered, with a blameless expression on his face.

Feeling like I was in the middle of Abbott and Costello's classic "Who's on first?" routine, I forged on.

"Do you have any sense of missing time today?"

"Not to my knowledge."

The session felt like it was spinning out of control and I was no longer sure which alter I was supposedly speaking with. Then, I realized I had made a critical slip-up: I should have asked him to identify himself by name at different junctures throughout the interview.

I was convinced that he was pretending to have switched alters during the session. His contradictory answers were a ruse to trick me into believing the alter I was speaking with *now* was different than the alter who had walked into the room only a few minutes earlier. He was pretending that one alter had started the interview, then, without any physical sign, another alter emerged. Neither alter, of course, was the man I interviewed a week ago.

There were many indications that his was all an Academy Award performance. But there were several big flaws in his act. If he had done much research on dissociative identity disorder, he would have realized that one alter shouldn't change seamlessly into another without any changes in mood, attitude, speech style, or mannerisms. The shift does not occur out of the blue without any obvious provocation or telltale physical signs. These inconsistencies, in combination with his invalid score on the MMPI-2, pointed to malingering.

I concluded that he did not have dissociative identity disorder. That question was resolved in my mind, but my work was not over. I still needed to understand why he killed his girlfriend.

"What do you remember about the evening your ex-girlfriend

was killed?" I asked, with no real hope of receiving a straight answer.

"I have no memory of it," he said after a long pause.

"Do Tom or Mike remember?"

"No!"

At this point in the interview, I was feeling frustrated and unsympathetic.

"How do you feel about killing your ex-girlfriend?" I asked.

"I can't feel anything because I don't remember it."

"Do any of the other personalities feel remorse?" I said, somewhat provocatively.

"Not that I'm aware of," he coolly replied, sitting back in his
chair.

It was time to end the session. I felt a growing dislike for Mr.
Allen, but I had to give him this much: it certainly had not been a
boring session.

Altogether I met with Mr. Allen four times. At one point, I told him
that I did not believe his stories about Tom and Mike. I was not sure
how he would react. He seemed disappointed, but not surprised.
Again and again I encouraged him to drop the pretense and tell me
what really happened, with no success. My straightforward appeal
was futile. He kept up his act and never told me why he killed his
ex-girlfriend.

Mr. Allen told me that since he (the host) had not committed any
crime, he should be found not guilty by reason of insanity. He never
quit trying to con me into signing off on his insanity defense.

As the metal gate clanged shut after our last session and I walked
down the hall to the elevator, I let my mind wander. Mr. Allen's
performance reminded me of the most famous criminal to claim
multiple personalities—Kenneth Bianchi. From 1977 to 1978, ten
women were murdered in the hills above Los Angeles and the press
dubbed the killer "the Hillside Strangler." In 1979, Bianchi was ar-

rested for committing two additional murders and implicated his cousin, Angelo Buono, Jr., in the first ten.

Psychiatrist John Watkins hypnotized Bianchi and uncovered an alter named "Steve Walker," who allegedly was the one responsible for the killings. There were many indications that Bianchi was faking dissociative identity disorder. Detectives searched his home and found books on psychology. Additionally, Bianchi had stolen a college transcript from another student and set up a fake psychotherapy practice.

A prosecution psychiatrist, Martin T. Orne, purposefully suggested the existence of a third alter. Bianchi fell into his trap. Before long, "Billy," a previously unmentioned alter, emerged. Bianchi put forth a not guilty by reason of insanity defense at his trial, but was found guilty and sentenced to life. Eventually, he admitted to faking dissociative identity disorder.[6]

Despite their obvious similarities, Mr. Allen seemed less sophisticated than the famous Mr. Bianchi. I concluded that there was no evidence that Mr. Allen suffered from dissociative identity disorder. He impressed me as a big faker. While making new personalities out of whole cloth is rare in clinical practice, it was not so unusual in the criminal world.

Since Mr. Allen never dropped the charade, there wasn't much I could do for him. If he had been honest, I might have found mitigating factors to lessen the severity of his sentence. I did believe he had serious emotional problems. The psychological tests showed him to be, at best, a very strange guy. It was even possible that he had killed his ex-girlfriend in a state of extreme emotional disturbance.

Mr. Allen decided not to put forth any psychiatric defense. Without a psychologist to testify that he suffered dissociative identity disorder, he and his attorney must have concluded that he had little chance of being found not guilty by reason of insanity. He accepted a plea and was sentenced to twenty years.

"They Were Going to Let Me Die!"

A group of armed teenagers robbed a store while one waited outside as a lookout. A few hours later, Mathew, the eighteen-year-old lookout, was brought into the precinct as a suspect. He confessed to the robbery after a three-hour interrogation. His written and videotaped statements included many specific details about the crime which only the guilty party or the police would know. Later, he retracted his statement, claiming that he had been coerced into making the confession.

Months later, I was hired by the assistant district attorney who was prosecuting the case. "The defense attorney retained a psychologist," she explained. "The doctor concluded that the defendant was unable to voluntarily waive his Miranda rights."

"Why is that?" I asked.

"The defendant is diabetic and takes medication to control his insulin level. His attorney is asserting that his client told the detectives about his diabetes but didn't get his medication."

"So what happened?"

"The defendant claims that an ambulance was called, but when EMS workers arrived, he was denied medical care. He insists that the detectives told him he could not go to the hospital until he confessed."

I knew that the great majority of adolescents are terrified when brought into the precinct to be questioned by police. Even those who are innocent are often intimidated or coerced into confessing. The tragic case of the adolescents falsely convicted for the Central Park Jogger crime illustrates how critical it is to determine whether an adolescent is legally competent to waive his Miranda rights before he makes a confession.

"If the story about the ambulance is true, the confession will probably be thrown out," I said. "Why don't you contact all the hospitals in the area to see if an ambulance was ever dispatched?"

As we talked, I glanced through the defense psychologist's report. The psychologist had given Mathew personality and intelligence tests, and reported that Mathew was particularly vulnerable to pressure and intimidation. He concluded with Mathew's assertion that he was factually innocent and had confessed out of fear for his life.

I paged back to the beginning of the report to see what materials the psychologist had reviewed during the evaluation. Something crucial was missing: the psychologist had not reviewed Anthony's written or videotaped statements.

Was I mistaken? I checked again. No, there was no mention of the confession anywhere in the report. Looking up from the papers, I pointed out this lapse to the assistant district attorney. She was as surprised as I was by this obvious mistake. I did not understand how a forensic psychologist could be so careless. How could he conclude that Mathew was not competent to waive his Miranda rights without having seen the confession?

When I went home, I read the written statement and watched the videotape a few times. Mathew, a thin, gangly, white teenager, showed no signs of being confused or disoriented. In the video, he did not complain about feeling ill. He was not sweating or in obvious need of medical attention.

I returned to the assistant district attorney's office the next week to meet Mathew. His attorney was there to observe the interview. Mathew told me the same story he had told the defense psychologist: he was innocent and had falsely confessed out of fear.

His confession included many accurate details of the crime.

"How did you know about all the facts of the robbery?" I asked.

"The detectives told me about what happened and told me what to write," he answered after a long pause.

"Why did you agree to confess?"

Mathew then told me in detail how EMS had been called to examine him, and had attempted to take him to the hospital, only to be turned away by the police. His face twisted and his voice choked up as he described how he begged for medical attention during the interrogation.

Either he was telling the truth or he was a great actor. I had nothing more to ask him about the ambulance visit; I would have to confirm his story later with the detectives.

Not surprisingly, the detectives gave me a different account. They admitted to being aware of Mathew's medical condition but insisted that he never asked for medical attention. They were very firm about this. They never threatened the defendant or told him what to write in his statement. They never called an ambulance, but they did take him to the hospital to receive his scheduled dose of insulin.

"When did you take him to the hospital?" I asked, carefully watching their faces.

"After he made the videotaped confession."

"After? Did he seem sick during the interrogation?"

"Not at all," they said quickly, almost in unison.

I decided not to press them any further, but I was far from convinced. In the end, it was a relatively simple case. When the assistant district attorney contacted EMS of the nearby hospitals, Mathew's ruse became clear. No ambulance had ever been dispatched to the precinct; no EMS workers had examined him.

After the prosecutor told me this, I reread the defense psychologist's report more carefully. The psychologist had seemed to believe Mathew's story, but he was very careful with his wording. The psychologist concluded that Mathew was unable to voluntarily waive his Miranda rights "if he was, in fact" refused medical treatment.

It seemed that the defense psychologist was hedging his bets. The psychologist had never investigated Mathew's claims of mistreatment or asked the defense attorney to subpoena the EMS records. It was a lapse that could easily discredit him on the witness stand.

I watched Mathew's videotaped statement a few more times before I prepared my report. I saw no signs that he was in any physical distress. He seemed tired, but he spoke clearly and effortlessly. There was no evidence that he did not understand his legal situation or the words used in the Miranda warnings.

I believed that Mathew had voluntarily waived his rights. He had created a very detailed and plausible story which turned out to be a lie. His ability to create such a false story told a great deal about his intelligence and resourcefulness. Only an individual of average intelligence and fortitude could make up and stick to such a detailed and plausible story.

The defense attorney requested a Huntley hearing to determine whether Mathew knowingly, intelligently, and voluntarily waived his Miranda rights. If the judge ruled in favor of the defense, Mathew's confessions would not be admitted in court.

On the morning of the hearing, I took the subway to the courthouse. It was one of the old marble buildings I like so much, complete with a sweeping staircase up to the entrance. I showed my court identification and passed quickly inside, avoiding the long line of people waiting to go through security.

The defense psychologist was sitting on the bench outside the courtroom. I had never met him before, so I walked over to introduce myself. He was relaxed and friendly and he greeted me cheerfully. He was significantly older than me, a full professor of forensic psychology at a prestigious university with a long list of publications. Yet since he had neglected to review the defendant's confession, I was convinced that he did not have much clinical experience. I had to resist the urge to tell him so, especially when he started giving me advice about my résumé, recommending a few specific changes to make. His suggestions were good, but I was annoyed. He was treating me like one of his graduate students, despite my years of clinical experience conducting thousands of interviews.

Finally, the courtroom door was unlocked. Without a word, we both walked in and took a seat on opposite sides of the aisle.

It was a short hearing. We both testified, and I left in the middle of the afternoon. The next week, the assistant district attorney called to tell me that the judge had ruled that Mathew voluntarily waived his Miranda rights. If Mathew decided to go to trial, his written and videotaped statement would be allowed as evidence. The judge did not specifically mention the defense psychologist's failure to review Mathew's statements, but the assistant district attorney was convinced that this lapse factored heavily into the judge's decision.

After he lost the Huntley hearing, Mathew and his attorney decided to accept a plea of one to three years in prison. And I decided to make the defense psychologist's recommended changes to my résumé.

"I Can't Remember"

Mr. D'Martino was arrested for racketeering and suspected of Mafia connections. He claimed to have little memory of important events and facts related to his legal charges. He was referred to the inpatient forensic psychiatry ward of a New York City hospital to complete an evaluation of his competency to stand trial.

Mr. D'Martino's attorney had requested a competency to stand trial evaluation because his client claimed to have memory problems. The attorney told the hospital staff that he believed his client had suffered a stroke. Although the doctors suspected their patient was malingering, a CT scan, neurological evaluation, and blood tests were ordered to rule out a medical or neurological condition.

There are many advantages in hospitalizing a suspected malingerer. The forensic staff is comprised of psychiatrists, psychologists, social workers, and nurses who are all trained to detect inconsistencies in the patient's behaviors. These inconsistencies point to exaggeration of genuine symptoms or outright faking. It is almost impossible to fake symptoms twenty-four hours a day. Not with so many staff watching.

I was asked by the judge to conduct a competency to stand trial evaluation. I went to the hospital and took the elevator to the forensic service. The corrections officer on duty unlocked the heavy gate to allow me onto the psychiatry ward. Most of the patients were either in bed or watching television in the day room.

First, I headed over to the nurses' station. They pointed out the defendant and clued me in to the patient's ruse. I watched, partially hidden behind a screen, and observed how Mr. D'Martino dragged his left leg as he slowly, so painfully, hobbled across the day room to sit at the table for lunch. I saw him grimace in agony and noticed that no one rushed to help him.

Approximately twenty minutes later, Mr. D'Martino struggled to his feet to walk back to the dorm. This time, he dragged his *right* leg. Oops, I guess he forgot which side was "affected" by the stroke. The nurses and I looked at each other. We tried to look busy with our paperwork, stifling giggles as Mr. D'Martino hobbled by, an exaggerated expression of pain on his face. I scribbled some observation notes, picked up his file, and went out to the day room for the formal interview.

My conclusion: Mr. D'Martino was faking. Genuine muscle paralysis or weakness doesn't change sides. I confronted him with this and other inconsistencies in his behavior. I also broke the news—all his medical tests were negative and his CT scan did not show any evidence of a stroke or brain damage.

Although Mr. D'Martino never "fessed up," there was enough evidence for me to confidently conclude he was malingering and competent to stand trial. The presiding judge agreed and, shortly after it began, my role in the case ended. I wondered whether he would try the same ruse at trial and whether the jurors would catch on. Months later, I heard that he was convicted.

"I Didn't Understand"

Michael and his friends were out late one evening on a quiet street in Brooklyn. Seeing a middle-aged man walking alone, they surrounded him and stole his money and watch. The police brought Michael in for questioning. The youngest of the group and the only one without a criminal record, he confessed and was charged with armed robbery. Later, Michael retracted his confession. He was mentally retarded, his lawyers said, and therefore was unable to intelligently and knowingly waive his Miranda rights.

There is little advantage to waiving your right to counsel and confessing to a crime, yet suspects do so every day—especially young suspects. Adolescents are more vulnerable to coercion and lack the legal experience to understand the necessity of refusing to speak with detectives until they have an opportunity to consult with an attorney. Many, particularly those with low I.Q.'s, do not fully understand the meaning of the Miranda warnings.[7]

The assistant district attorney called to ask if I would be interested in seeing the defendant. I knew the ADA from a previous case as a gregarious, generously proportioned man in his forties. When I met him at his office, he told me bluntly that he did not believe Michael's story.

"I know he's not mentally retarded. He's faking," he said.

"What makes you so sure?"

He looked embarrassed, "He delivered fried chicken wings to my house."

"What?"

"I ordered fried chicken take-out from a local restaurant," he said. "When I answered the doorbell, the defendant was standing there. He worked for the restaurant, and had driven to my house to deliver the chicken. He didn't recognize me, so I paid fast and shut the door."

I struggled to kept a straight face, knowing that the prosecutor was sensitive about his weight and had probably suffered some ribbing when he told everyone at work about the fried chicken delivery.

But he was right: the defendant's behavior that evening provided important forensic clues. The assistant district attorney had already verified that the defendant did, indeed, have a driver's license. He also obtained a copy of the defendant's permit test, which Michael had passed, indicating that he could read. He was also capable of driving a car and locating an address.

The prosecutor did not end his investigation there. When he learned that Michael worked part-time in a small grocery store, he arranged for an undercover detective with a hidden camera to enter the store and ask Michael to help him find an item.

The assistant district attorney showed me the tape. Michael had no difficulty remembering where things were stocked and easily found the item on the shelf. When the undercover cop went to pay, Michael went behind the counter to ring it up on the cash register.

I had not even met with Michael and already I knew he was capable of operating a car, reading, and holding down a job with complex responsibilities. This was not what I would expect in a person with mental retardation.

The assistant district attorney gave me a packet of legal papers and the defense psychologist's report which I sat down to read later that day. The psychologist administered an I.Q. test and a reading exam. She scored his I.Q. at 68, his reading ability at the third-grade level, and concluded that Michael was mildly mentally retarded. She seemed to accept Michael's I.Q. score as a true reflection of his ability without considering the possibility that he was malingering.

A defendant can lower his or her score on an intelligence test by purposely answering questions incorrectly. It is easy to detect malingerers when they get very easy questions wrong, such as "What is the shape of a ball?" The difficulty arises, however, when they answer "I don't know" to the more difficult questions. It is also harder to tell when defendants are faking the perceptual motor tasks, like puzzles or block assembly, which they can complete slowly to lose points.

The defense psychologist administered a specialized psychological test called the Grisso Test[8] to measure Michael's understanding of the Miranda warnings. Test-takers must explain and define the words used in the Miranda warnings such as "attorney" and "right." They also have to answer questions about their understanding of the legal issues portrayed in vignettes of suspects and defendants.[9]

The biggest problem I find with both the I.Q. and Grisso tests is how easy they are to beat. I find it absolutely essential to administer a malingering test along with the other psychological tests. These specialized tests determine whether test-takers are really putting forth their best effort. It is the best way to ensure that the I.Q. score is accurate.

I wondered if the defense psychologist did not know that malingering tests existed, or if she did not even consider the possibility that Michael was malingering.

I reviewed Michael's school records. His B's and C's in elementary school were neither great nor terrible. At age thirteen, he was placed in special education classes and categorized as learning disabled. By tenth grade, he was skipping class frequently.

Michael's school records did not appear to belong to a mentally retarded adolescent. Mild mental retardation sometimes goes unidentified until the child is placed in a school setting, where he will take special classes or receive extra services. But most mentally retarded defendants usually appear disabled even before they enter school.

* * *

I finished reading through the records and scheduled a date to meet Michael. A few days later, I packed my bag with every test I thought I might need—including the bulky I.Q. test and three different malingering tests—and then headed to the subway. I arrived at the Supreme Court building and headed toward the holding area.

Michael's lawyer, whom I contacted ahead of time, met me at the holding area, and we walked together to the interview room. A corrections officer brought Michael in a few minutes later.

He was a thin, short, African American teenager. With a baby face, he did not seem intimidating enough to commit a robbery. He was polite, but formal, and kept his distance throughout the interview. I did not tell Michael that I already knew quite a bit about him. Having this clear advantage made me a little uncomfortable, but I reassured myself I was not doing anything unethical, since I had told him upfront that I was retained by the assistant district attorney. I was very clear that I was not there to help him and told him he should direct any questions he had to his lawyer.

I asked Michael how he spent his days and he told me he could not complete even the simplest task. He said he could not take the subway alone, cook or clean his own room or shop for a carton of milk. I strongly suspected that he was lying to me.

I asked Michael what happened during the police interrogation. He told me they had not threatened him, but he confessed because he thought they would let him go if he told them what they wanted to hear. I asked him to explain the Miranda warnings in his own words and his definitions were adequate. When I pointed this out, he said, "I didn't understand anything when the police questioned me. I only learned my rights when my lawyer told me."

I re-administered the I.Q. test. As I expected, he performed poorly, scoring within the mild mentally retarded range. Yet he also flunked the malingering tests. He answered very simple questions incorrectly. These results indicated that he was either being uncooperative or deliberately attempting to perform poorly.

When I integrated my findings with my knowledge of his adequate functioning in real life, I was confident that he was not mentally deficient. His low I.Q. score could not be an accurate reflection of his true abilities. I prepared and submitted my report, concluding that Michael was able to intelligently and knowingly waive his Miranda rights when he gave his confession.

Michael and his attorney decided to request a Huntley hearing to determine whether Michael was competent to waive his Miranda rights. The defense psychologist and I testified and the judge ruled that Michael was, in fact, competent. His confession would therefore be admissible at trial.

The assistant district attorney called me the next week to tell me that Michael decided to accept the plea offer of one to three years. He had already served over a year, and would be released soon.

"Who's My Lawyer? He's Dead"

A month after Mr. Gates was fired from his job at an insurance company, he returned with a handgun and killed two co-workers. He fled the scene, but there were many witnesses to the crime, and he was captured within a few hours. His case was hopeless: there was no question that he would be sentenced to many years, if not life, in prison. Unfortunately, Mr. Gates refused to talk about his case with his defense attorney.

Mr. Gates' attorney called to ask if I would see his client.

"Was he insane when he shot those workers?" the attorney asked me. "Perhaps he acted under extreme emotional disturbance. If nothing else, perhaps there might be some mitigating factors I could show to get him a better plea offer."

"What makes you think he was insane?" I asked.

"Well, to begin with, I'm his third attorney. My client spit at his first attorney and threatened his second." He laughed as he added, "Both, understandably, requested to be relieved."

"Why do you think you were asked to take the case?" I asked.

"Maybe the judge didn't think I would be threatened by my client's antics."

I smiled. At almost six-foot-two and about two hundred twenty pounds, the attorney was an imposing figure.

"People know I don't take crap and I have a specialty dealing with mentally ill clients," he continued. "The judges know to send me defendants that are hard to get along with."

The attorney mailed me a pile of documents. His client had a long history of psychiatric illness and treatment and had been hospitalized many times, diagnosed with severe depression, and treated with ECT (Electroconvulsive Therapy), also known as "shock therapy."

Three weeks before the crime he had been admitted to a psychiatric hospital, "weeping profusely," threatening suicide, and appearing paranoid. During the course of his stay, he vacillated between severe depression and euphoria. At one point, he told a staff member that he "loved life." Symptoms of mania were observed. He was sexually provocative with female staff and other patients and was seen frequently singing to himself.

Although Mr. Gates was diagnosed with a severe depression, he was discharged after only seven days. Only two days earlier, he had complained of patients looking at him and people trying to hypnotize him. He was released with a prescription for antidepressant medication but refused a referral for follow-up psychiatric care.

Two weeks later, Mr. Gates returned to his old job and shot his two co-workers. After his arrest, he was admitted to a short-term forensic psychiatric unit of a New York City hospital. He told the staff that he was hearing voices and wanted to kill himself. His first attorney requested a competency evaluation, whereupon Mr. Gates was found not competent to stand trial and was transferred to a long-term forensic hospital for treatment.

Within a few months he was returned to court, only to be found incompetent again and returned to the hospital. He went back and forth between Riker's Island jail and the forensic hospital a few more times.

The forensic hospital staff eventually concluded he was faking his illness in order to avoid a near certain conviction at trial. They observed a pattern of behavior that was not consistent with acute mental illness. Each time he was admitted to the hospital he appeared depressed, but in the weeks before returning to Riker's Island to face his charges, he was calm and cheerful. He slept well and had a good appetite. He would eat extra food if it were available. Only when he was returned to Riker's Island and scheduled for a court appearance did he start acting depressed and psychotic.

Aware of the inconsistencies in Mr. Gates' behavior, the court-appointed competency doctors concluded that he was malingering. After a few years of shuttling between the hospital and the court, he was declared competent to stand trial.

Knowing Mr. Gates' history of violence, I decided to speak to him from a safe distance. I asked the corrections officer to keep him in the cell during our interview. When I approached the bars, he wore a sour expression on his face.

A stocky, surly-looking white man in his fifties, he looked like he had not paid any attention to his appearance in weeks. His gray hair was long and uncombed, his face covered in stubble, his clothes dirty.

I pulled up a chair about three feet from the bars, which seemed to me safe spitting distance. Then I tried to engage him in a conversation. When I attempted to explain who I was, he thrust out his left arm to show me a few superficial cuts on his wrist. "See? Do you see this?" he shouted, as if that was all he needed to say. I pressed him to explain the cuts and he barked, "Talk to yourself, Miss! Stupid!" He turned away and walked to the corner of the cell, refusing to talk with me any further.

That was the end of our first session.

I tried again the next week. This time I started by explaining why his attorney had sent me. He cut me off, "Who's my lawyer? He's dead," he said. As patiently as I could, I explained my role in his case and he again interrupted. "Stupid bitch! There's a nuclear bomb in this place. Go away!"

Struggling to keep my voice calm, I asked him about his charges. His face turned red and he shrieked, "If you come back, I'll punch you in the nose!"

That was the end of our second session.

I was convinced that Mr. Gates was malingering and pretending to be suicidal and paranoid during these interviews. He did not say much, and what he did say made very little sense, but it was apparent that he had an objective in mind—to be returned to the psychiatric hospital.

Mr. Gates never spoke with me again. I asked to see him on two more occasions, but he refused to leave Riker's Island to meet with me. I agreed with the competency evaluators. Mr. Gates was not cooperating with his attorney, but he was doing so willfully and was, therefore, competent to stand trial.

Mr. Gates decided to go to trial, pleading not guilty by reason of insanity. Without a forensic expert to testify that he was insane when he killed his co-workers, he had virtually no chance of being found not responsible for his crimes.

I did testify at his trial, but my testimony was limited. Standing in the witness box, with my right arm raised, waiting to be sworn in, I looked out to the courtroom and noticed something amiss. Mr. Gates was sitting at the defense table, looking both irate and glum. But his lawyer was not sitting next to him—where he was supposed to be. Instead, the defense attorney was sitting at the other table, next to the prosecutor, smiling broadly. Apparently, this strange game of musical chairs had not dampened his typical cheery mood.

My testimony focused primarily on the defendant's psychiatric records. I described his long history of depression and psychiatric treatment and explained to the jury that Mr. Gates had been discharged from the psychiatric hospital only weeks before the offense. I did not testify about his mental state at the time he killed his co-workers. Since he never told me what happened, I could not form an opinion with, as is said in court, "a reasonable degree of psychological certainty."

I left the witness box and the court recessed.

"Why were you sitting with the prosecutor?" I asked the defense attorney as we walked out of the courthouse.

"I had to move," he said nonchalantly. "I thought my client would sock me during the trial. He probably wanted a mistrial."

A few days after I testified, the defense attorney called to tell me about the rest of the trial. "It was a circus," he said. His client started "acting up" in court, yelling at inappropriate times and refusing to follow the court rules of decorum. Eventually, he was suspended from the trial. He was removed from the courtroom and spent the remaining trial days in a back room, watching the proceedings by video monitor.

"We piped the trial to him," his lawyer told me. "The jury wasn't out very long. Mr. Gates was found guilty and sentenced to twenty-five years to life."

"Now that it's over," I said, "tell me, honestly. What did you think of your client?"

"I think he was strange as hell. He showed me the notebook he was writing in. It was filled with designs for extraterrestrial communication devices."

"So you *did* think he was crazy."

"I did, but we just couldn't make the case for insanity. He refused to talk to me about the case, even though I think he came to like me."

"What gave you that impression?" I asked.

The attorney chuckled. "Each day before the hearings began, he called out to me, 'Go forth, black panther.'"

NOTES

PART 1: EVALUATIONS OF MENTAL STATE AT THE TIME OF THE OFFENSE

1. New York State Penal Law.
2. Eric Silver, Carmen Cirincione, and Henry J. Steadman, "Demythologizing Inaccurate Perceptions of the Insanity Defense," *Law and Human Behavior* (1994): 63–70; Henry J. Steadman et al., *Before and After Hinckley: Evaluating Insanity Defense Reform* (New York: Guilford Press, 1993); Gary Melton et al. *Psychological Evaluations for the Courts* (New York: Guilford Press, 1997).
3. New York State Penal Law.

Chapter 1: The Widower Walks Away

1. Joseph Tiffin, *Purdue Pegboard: Examiner Manual* (Chicago: Science Research Associates, 1968).
2. Marshall F. Folstein, Susan E. Folstein, and Paul R. McHugh, "Mini-Mental State: A Practical Method for Grading the Cognitive State of Patients for the Clinician," *Journal of Psychiatric Research* (1975): 189–98.
3. *Wechsler Adult Intelligence Scales-III*, The Psychological Corporation (New York: Harcourt Brace, 1997); Hermann Rorschach, *Psychodiagnostics* (New York: Grune and Stratton, 1921, 1951); Paul Kline, *The Handbook of Psychological Testing* (New York: Routledge, 1999).
4. Ibid.
5. Daniel Schwartz, MD, psychiatric report.
6. *Frye v. United States*, 293 F. 1013 (D.C. Cir 1923).

Chapter 2: A Botched Suicide

1. Marvin E. Wolfgang, "Suicide by Means of Victim-Precipitated Homicide," *Journal of Clinical and Experimental Psychopathology* 20 (Oct.–Dec. 1959): 335–49.

2. Daniel B. Kennedy, Robert J. Homant, and R. Thomas Hupp, "Suicide by Cop," *FBI Law Enforcement Bulletin* (August 1998): 21–27.
3. Mark Lindsay and David Lester, *Suicide by Cop: Committing Suicide by Provoking Police to Shoot You* (Amityville, NY: Baywood, 2004); Harold V. Lord, *Suicide by Cop—Inducing Officers to Shoot: Practical Direction for Recognition, Resolution and Recovery* (Flushing, NY: Looseleaf Law, 2004).
4. Robert D. Miller, *Suicide by Cop and Criminal Responsibility* (Washington, DC: Federal Legal Publications, 2002).
5. Grand jury testimony.
6. Ibid.
7. *Wechsler Adult Intelligence Scales-III*, The Psychological Corporation (New York: Harcourt Brace, 1997).
8. Assistant District Attorney David Kelly, personal communication.

Chapter 3: The Butcher of Tompkins Square Park

1. Paul Kline, *The Handbook of Psychological Testing* (New York: Routledge, 1999); Hermann Rorschach, *Psychodiagnostics* (New York: Grune and Stratton, 1921, 1951); Henry A. Murray, *Thematic Apperception Test*, manual (Cambridge: Harvard University Press, 1943).
2. Transcript, trial testimony of Cheryl Paradis, PsyD, *People v. Rakowitz*, indictment no. 11664/89, New York State Supreme Court, New York County.
3. Ibid.
4. Ibid.
5. Ibid.
6. Ibid.
7. Ibid.
8. Ibid.
9. Ronald Sullivan, "Man Acquitted of Killing and Boiling Roommate," *New York Times*, February 23, 1991, A29.

Chapter 4: The Alien Invasion and Other Delusions

1. Kevin J. Weiss, "'Wet' and Wild: PCP and Criminal Responsibility," *Journal of Psychiatry & Law* 32 (Fall 2004): 361–84.
2. Rita Chi-Ying Chung and Keh-Ming Lin, "Help-Seeking Behavior Among Southeast Asian Refugees," *Journal of Community Psychology* 22 (1994): 109–20.
3. Daniel A. Martell and Park E. Dietz, "Mentally Disordered Offenders Who Push or Attempt to Push Victims onto Subway Tracks in New York City," *Archives of General Psychiatry* 49 (6) (June 1992): 472–75.
4. Henry A. Murray, *Thematic Apperception Test*, manual (Cambridge: Harvard University Press, 1943).

5. Assistant District Attorney David Kelly, personal communication.
6. Ibid.
7. *In the Matter of K.L.*, 1 NY3d 362 (2004).

Chapter 5: The Women Who Wept
1. American Psychiatric Association, *Diagnostic and Statistical Manual of Mental Disorders*, 4th Edition (*DSM–IV*) (Washington, DC: American Psychiatric Association, 1994).
2. Martin E. P. Seligman, *Helplessness: On Depression, Development and Death* (San Francisco: W.H. Freeman/Times Books/Henry Holt, 1975); Martin E. P. Seligman, *Learned Optimism* (New York: Knopf, 1991).
3. Jayne Mooney, *The North London Domestic Violence Survey, Final Report* (Middlesex, UK: Center for Criminology, 1999).
4. Bureau of Justice Statistics, www.ojp.usdoj.gov/bjs (last revised July 11, 2007).
5. *The Burning Bed*, directed by Robert Greenwald, Tisch/Avnet Productions Inc., 1984.
6. Lenore E. Walker, *The Battered Woman* (New York: Harper & Row, 1979).
7. Allan M. Dershowitz, *The Abuse Excuse: And Other Cop-Outs, Sob Stories, and Evasions of Responsibility* (Boston: Little, Brown, 1994).
8. Celia Wells, "Battered Woman Syndrome and Defenses to Homicide: Where Now?" *Legal Studies* 14 (1994): 266–76.
9. Theodore Millon, Roger Davis, and Carrie Millon, *Millon Clinical Multiaxial Inventory–II (MCMI–II)*, manual (Bloomington: Pearson Assessments, 1997).

Chapter 6: The Man Who Knew Too Little
1. *One Flew Over the Cuckoo's Nest*, directed by Milos Forman, Fantasy Films, 1975.
2. Naomi Breslau et al., "Sleep Disturbance and Psychiatric Disorders: A Longitudinal Epidemiological Study of Young Adults," *Biological Psychiatry* March 39 (6) (1996): 411–18; Daniel E. Ford and Douglas B. Kamerow, "Epidemiologic Study of Sleep Disturbances and Psychiatric Disorders. An Opportunity for Prevention?" *Journal of the American Medical Association* 262 (11) (1989): 1479–84.
3. Sanford Drob, H. Weinstein, and Robert Berger, "The Determination of Malingering: A Comprehensive Clinical-Forensic Approach," *Journal of Psychiatry and Law* (1987): 519–38.
4. Chiung-Lei Huang et al., "Zolpidem-Induced Distortion in Visual Perception," *Annals of Pharmacotherapy* 37 (5) (May 2003): 683–86.

5. John S. Markowitz and Timothy D. Brewerton, "Zolpidem-Induced Psychosis," *Annals of Clinical Psychiatry* 8 (2) (1996): 89–91.
6. Sanofi Aventis, *Letter to Healthcare Professionals* (March, 2007).
7. Court transcript.
8. Ibid.
9. Ibid.

PART 2: EVALUATIONS OF COMPETENCY TO STAND TRIAL AND WAIVE MIRANDA RIGHTS

1. *Dusky v. United States*, 362 U.S. 402 (1960).
2. *Miranda v. Arizona*, 384 U.S. 436 (1966).
3. Ibid.

Chapter 7: The Brain Chip

1. *The Manchurian Candidate*, directed by Jonathan Demme, Paramount Pictures, 2004.
2. *The Matrix*, directed by Andy Wachowski and Lana Wachowski, Groucho II Film Parnership, 1999.
3. *Tarasoff v. Regents of the University of California*, 551 P2d 334 (Cal 1976); Simone Simone and Solomon M. Fulero, "Tarasoff and the Duty to Protect," *Journal of Aggression, Maltreatment & Trauma* 11 (2005): 145–68; Michael L. Perlin, "Tarasoff and the Dilemma of the Dangerous Patient: New Directions for the 1990's," *Law and Psychology Review* (1992): 16–29.
4. *People v. Tortorici*, 709 N.E. 2d 87, 91 (NY 1999).
5. Charles Patrick Ewing and Joseph T. McCann, *Minds on Trial: Great Cases in Law and Psychology* (Oxford: Oxford University Press, 2006).
6. American Psychiatric Association, *Diagnostic and Statistical Manual of Mental Disorders*, 4th Edition (Washington, DC: American Psychiatric Association, 1994).
7. Ibid.

Chapter 8: The Good Samaritan

1. *Dusky v. United States*, 362 U.S. 402 (1960).
2. American Psychiatric Association, *Diagnostic and Statistical Manual of Mental Disorders*, 4th Edition. (Washington, DC: American Psychiatric Association, 1994).

Chapter 9: A Descendant of British Royalty

1. Mark C. Bardwell and Bruce A. Arrigo, *Criminal Competence on Trial: The Case of Colin Ferguson* (Durham, SC: Carolina Academic Press, 2002).

Chapter 10: The Arsonist

1. American Psychiatric Association, *Diagnostic and Statistical Manual of Mental Disorders*, 4th Edition (Washington, DC: American Psychiatric Association, 1994).
2. Gisli H. Gudjonsson, *The Psychology of Interrogations, Confessions and Testimony* (New York: John Wiley, 1992).
3. Dean Koontz, *The Book of Counted Sorrows* (Newport Beach, CA: Dogged Press, 2008).
4. Hermann Rorschach, *Psychodiagnostics* (New York: Grune and Stratton, 1921, 1951).
5. Paul Kline, *The Handbook of Psychological Testing* (New York: Routledge, 1999).
6. *People v. Huntley*, 15 N.Y. 2d 72, 255 N.Y.S. 2d 838, 204 N.E. 2d 179 (1965).
7. Joseph A. Davis and Kelli M. Lauber, "Criminal Behavioral Assessment of Arsonists, Pyromaniacs and Multiple Firesetters," *Journal of Contemporary Criminal Justice* 15 (1999): 273–90; Rebekah Doley, "Making Sense of Arson Through Classification," *Psychiatry, Psychology and Law* 10 (2) (2003): 346–52; Richard N. Kocsis and Ray W. Cooksey, "Criminal Psychological Profiling of Serial Arson Crimes," *International Journal of Offender Therapy and Comparative Criminology* 46 (6) (2002): 631–56; Herschel Prins, "Adult Fire-Raising: Law and Psychology," *Psychology, Crime & Law*, 1 (4) (1995): 271–81; United States Department of Justice, *Uniform Crime Report for the United States* (Federal Bureau of Investigation, United States Department of Justice, 1982).
8. New York State Penal Law.

PART 3: EVALUATIONS OF JUVENILES AND ASSESSMENTS OF DANGEROUSNESS AND MALINGERING

Chapter 11: The Dutiful Son

1. Kieran O'Driscoll and John Paul Leach, "'No Longer Gage': An Iron Bar Through the Head: Early Observations of Personality Change After Injury to the Prefrontal Cortex," *The British Medical Journal* (December, 1998):1673–74.
2. *Criminal Law Handbook of New York* (Charlottesville: Mathew Bender and Company, 2008).
3. Assistant District Attorney David Kelly, personal communication.

Chapter 12: The Lost Boys

1. Lewis Caroll, *Alice's Adventures in Wonderland* and *Through the Looking-Glass* (1865) (London: Penguin, 2003).
2. *People v. Huntley*, 15 N.Y. 2d 72, 255 N.Y.S. 2d 838, 204 N.E. 2d 179 (1965).

3. Thomas Grisso, *Evaluating Juveniles' Adjudicative Competence: A Guide for Clinical Practice* (Sarasota: Professional Resource Press, 2005).

4. *Re Gault*, 387 U.S. 1 (1967).

5. American Psychiatric Association, *Diagnostic and Statistical Manual of Mental Disorders*, 4th Edition (Washington, DC: American Psychiatric Association, 1994).

Chapter 13: Fakers?

1. *The Three Faces of Eve*, directed by Nunnally Johnson, Twentieth Century-Fox Film Corp., 1957; *Sybil*, directed by Daniel Petrie, Lorimar Productions, 1976.

2. American Psychiatric Association, *Diagnostic and Statistical Manual of Mental Disorders*, 4th Edition (Washington, DC: American Psychiatric Association, 1994).

3. James N. Butcher et al., *Minnesota Multiphasic Personality Inventory 2: Manual for Administration and Scoring* (Minneapolis: University of Minnesota Press, 1989).

4. Paul Kline, *The Handbook of Psychological Testing* (New York: Routledge, 1999).

5. Hermann Rorschach, *Psychodiagnostics* (New York: Grune and Stratton, 1921, 1951).

6. Ray Aldridge-Morris, *Multiple Personality: An Exercise in Deception* (East Sussex, UK: Lawrence Erlbaum Associates, 1989); Martin T. Orne, David F. Dinges, and Emily C. Orne, "On the Differential Diagnosis of Multiple Personality in the Forensic Context," *International Journal of Clinical Experimental Hypnosis* 32 (2) (April 1984): 118–69; John G. Watkins, "The Bianchi (L.A. Hillside Strangler) Case: Sociopath or Multiple Personality?" *International Journal of Clinical Experimental Hypnosis* 32 (2) (April 1984): 67–101.

7. Thomas Grisso, *Evaluating Competencies: Forensic Assessments and Instruments, Second Edition* (New York: Kluwer Academic/Plenum, 2003); Thomas Grisso, *Evaluating Juveniles' Adjudicative Competence: A Guide for Clinical Practice* (Sarasota: Professional Resource Press, 2005).

8. Thomas Grisso, *Instruments for Assessing Understanding and Appreciation of Miranda Rights* (Sarasota: Professional Resource Press, 1998).

9. Ibid.

BIBLIOGRAPHY

Aldridge-Morris, Ray. *Multiple Personality: An Exercise in Deception.* East Sussex, UK: Lawrence Erlbaum Associates, 1989.

American Psychiatric Association, *Diagnostic and Statistical Manual of Mental Disorders*, 4th Edition (*DSM–IV*). Washington, DC: American Psychiatric Association, 1994.

Bardwell, Mark C., and Bruce A. Arrigo, *Criminal Competency on Trial: The Case of Colin Ferguson.* Durham, SC: Carolina Academic Press, 2002.

Breslau, Naomi, Thomas Roth, Leon Rosenthal, and Patricia Andreski. "Sleep Disturbance and Psychiatric Disorders: A Longitudinal Epidemiological Study of Young Adults." *Biological Psychiatry* March 39(6) (1996): 411–18.

Bureau of Justice Statistics. www.ojp.usdoj.gov/bjs (last revised July 11, 2007).

Butcher, James N., W. Grant Dahlstrom, John R. Graham, Auke Tellegen, and Beverly Kaemmer. *Minnesota Multiphasic Personality Inventory 2: Manual for Administration and Scoring.* Minneapolis: University of Minnesota Press, 1989.

Caroll, Lewis (1865). *Alice's Adventures in Wonderland* and *Through the Looking-Glass.* London: Penguin, 2003.

Chung, Rita Chi-Ying, and Keh-Ming Lin. "Help-Seeking Behavior Among Southeast Asian Refugees." *Journal of Community Psychology* 22 (2) (1994):109–20.

Criminal Law Handbook of New York. Charlottesville: Mathew Bender and Company, 2008.

Davis, Joseph A., and Kelli M. Lauber. "Criminal Behavioral Assessment of Arsonists, Pyromaniacs and Multiple Firesetters." *Journal of Contemporary Criminal Justice* 15 (1999): 273–90.

Demme, Jonathan. *The Manchurian Candidate.* Paramount Pictures, 2004.

Dershowitz, Allen M. *The Abuse Excuse: And Other Cop-Outs, Sob Stories, and Evasions of Responsibility.* Boston: Little, Brown, 1994.

Doley, Rebekah. "Making Sense of Arson Through Classification." *Psychiatry, Psychology and Law* 10 (2) (2003): 346–52.

Drob, Sanford, and Robert Berger. "The Determination of Malingering: A Comprehensive Clinical-Forensic Approach." *Journal of Psychiatry and Law* (1987): 519–38.

Dusky v. United States, 362 U.S. 402, 1960.

Ewing, Charles Patrick, and Joseph T. McCann. *Minds on Trial: Great Cases in Law and Psychology.* Oxford: Oxford University Press, 2006.

Folstein, Marshall F., Susan E. Folstein, and Paul R. McHugh. "Mini-Mental State: A Practical Method for Grading the Cognitive State of Patients for the Clinician." *Journal of Psychiatric Research* (1975): 189–98.

Ford, Daniel E., and Douglas B. Kamerow. "Epidemiologic Study of Sleep Disturbances and Psychiatric Disorders. An Opportunity for Prevention?" *Journal of the American Medical Association* 262 (11) (1989): 1479–84.

Forman, Milos. *One Flew Over the Cuckoo's Nest.* Fantasy Films, 1975.

Frye v. United States, 293 F. 1013 (D.C. Cir 1923).

Greene, Douglas. Ambien and Ambien CR, "Dear Healthcare Professional," letter Sanofi-Aventis U.S. (March 2007).

Grisso, Thomas. *Instruments for Assessing Understanding and Appreciation of Miranda Rights*. Sarasota: Professional Resource Press, 1998.

——. *Evaluating Competencies: Forensic Assessments and Instruments, Second Edition*. New York: Kluwer Academic/Plenum, 2003.

——. *Evaluating Juveniles' Adjudicative Competence: A Guide for Clinical Practice*. Sarasota: Professional Resource Press, 2005.

Gudjonsson, Gisli H. *The Psychology of Interrogations, Confessions and Testimony*. New York: John Wiley, 1992.

Huang, Chiung-Lei, Ching-Jui Chang, Chi-Feng Hung, and His-Yen Lin. "Zolpidem-Induced Distortion in Visual Perception." *The Annals of Pharmacotherapy* 37 (5) (May 2003): 683–86.

In the Matter of K.L., 1 NY3d 362 (2004).

Johnson, Nunnally. *The Three Faces of Eve*. Twentieth Century-Fox Film Corp, 1957.

Kennedy, Daniel B., Robert J. Homant, and R. Thomas Hupp. "Suicide by Cop." *FBI Law Enforcement Bulletin* (August 1998) 21–27.

Kline, Paul. *The Handbook of Psychological Testing*. New York: Routledge, 1999.

Kocsis, Richard N., and Ray W. Cooksey. "Criminal Psychological Profiling of Serial Arson Crimes." *International Journal of Offender Therapy and Comparative Criminology* 46 (6) (2002): 631–56.

Lindsay, Mark, and David Lester. *Suicide by Cop: Committing Suicide by Provoking Police to Shoot You*. Amityville, NY: Baywood, 2004.

Lord, Harold V. *Suicide by Cop—Inducing Officers to Shoot: Practical Direction for Recognition, Resolution and Recovery*. Flushing, NY: Looseleaf Law, 2004.

Markowitz, John S., and Timothy D. Brewerton. "Zolpidem-Induced Psychosis." *Annals of Clinical Psychiatry* 8 (2) (1996): 89–91.

Martell, Daniel A., and Park E. Dietz. "Mentally Disordered Offenders Who Push or Attempt to Push Victims onto Subway Tracks in New York City." *Archives of General Psychiatry*, 49 (6) (June 1992): 472–75.

McKinney's Consolidated Laws of New York—Annotated: Book 11A of the Criminal Procedure Law. St. Paul: West, 1995.

Melton, Gary B., John Petrila, Norman G. Polythress, and Christopher Slobogan. *Psychological Evaluations for the Courts.* New York: Guilford Press, 1997.

Miller, Robert D. *Suicide by Cop and Criminal Responsibility.* Washington, DC: Federal Legal Publications, 2002.

Millon, Theodore, Roger Davis, and Carrie Millon. *Millon Clinical Multiaxial Inventory–II (MCMI-II).* Manual. Bloomington: Pearson Assessments, 1997.

Miranda v. Arizona, 384 U.S. 436 (1966).

Mooney, Jayne. *The North London Domestic Violence Survey: Final Report.* Middlesex, UK: Center for Criminology, 1999.

Murray, Henry A. *Thematic Apperception Test.* Manual. Cambridge: Harvard University Press, 1943.

O'Driscoll, Kieran, and John Paul Leach. "'No Longer Gage' an Iron Bar Through the Head. Early Observations of Personality Change After Injury to the Prefrontal Cortex." *British Medical Journal* (December 1998): 1673–74.

Orne, Martin T., David F. Dinges, and Emily C. Orne. "On the Differential Diagnosis of Multiple Personality in the Forensic Context." *International Journal of Clinical Experimental Hypnosis* 32 (2) (April 1984): 118–69.

People v. Huntley, 15 N.Y. 2d 72, 255 N.Y.S. 2d 838, 204 N.E. 2d 179 (1965).

People v. Tortorici, 709 N.E. 2d 87, 91 (NY 1999).

Perlin, Michael L. "Tarasoff and the Dilemma of the Dangerous Patient: New Directions for the 1990's." *Law and Psychology Review* (1992): 16–29.

Petrie, Daniel. *Sybil.* Lorimar Productions, 1976.

Prins, Herschel. "Adult Fire-Raising: Law and Psychology." *Psychology, Crime & Law,* l(4)(1995): 271–81.

Re Gault, 387 U.S. 1 (1967).

Rorschach, Hermann. *Psychodiagnostics*. New York: Grune and Stratton, 1921, 1951.

Simone, Simone, and Solomon M. Fulero. "Tarasoff and the Duty to Protect." *Journal of Aggression, Maltreatment & Trauma* 11 (2005): 145–68.

Seligman, Martin E. P. *Helplessness: On Depression, Development and Death*. San Francisco: W.H. Freeman/Times Books/Henry Holt, 1975.

———. *Learned Optimism*. New York: Knopf, 1991.

Silver, Eric, Carmen Cirincione, and Henry J. Steadman. "Demythologizing Inaccurate Perceptions of the Insanity Defense." *Law and Human Behavior* (1994): 63–70.

Steadman, Henry J., Margaret A. McGreevy, Joseph P. Morrissey, Lisa A. Callahan, Pamela Clark Robbins, and Carmen Cirincione. *Before and After Hinckley: Evaluating Insanity Defense Reform*. New York: Guilford Press, 1993.

Sullivan, Ronald. "Man Acquitted of Killing and Boiling Roommate." *New York Times*, February 23, 1991, A29.

Tarasoff v. Regents of the University of California, 551 P2d 334 (Cal 1976).

Tiffin, Joseph. *Purdue Pegboard: Examiner Manual*. Chicago: Science Research Associates, 1968.

United States Department of Justice. *Uniform Crime Report for the United States*. Washington, DC: Federal Bureau of Investigation, United States Department of Justice, 1982.

Wachowski, Andy, and Lana Wachowski. *The Matrix*. Groucho II Film Partnership, 1999.

Walker, Lenore E. *The Battered Woman*. New York: Harper & Row, 1979.

Watkins, John G. "The Bianchi (L.A. Hillside Strangler) Case: Sociopath or Multiple Personality?" *International Journal of Clinical Experimental Hypnosis* 32 (2) April (1984): 67–101.

Wechsler Adult Intelligence Scales-III. The Psychological Corporation. New York: Harcourt Brace, 1997.

Weiss, Kevin J. "'Wet' and Wild: PCP and Criminal Responsibility." *Journal of Psychiatry & Law* (Fall 2004): 361–84.

Wells, Celia. "Battered Woman Syndrome and Defenses to Homicide: Where Now?" *Legal Studies* 14 (1994): 266–76.

Wolfgang, Marvin E. "Suicide by Means of Victim-Precipitated Homicide." *Journal of Clinical and Experimental Psychopathology* 20 (Oct.–Dec. 1959): 335–49.

ACKNOWLEDGMENTS

There are so many people that I want to thank for their help with this book. Special thanks go to Steven Friedman, my friend and mentor, who first suggested that I write this book. I am especially grateful to Bob Peck of the Brooklyn Legal Aid Society for his input and support. He always made time to answer my legal questions and point me in the right direction.

It is a pleasure to recognize my colleagues from Kings County Hospital, Marymount Manhattan College, and the Brooklyn District Attorney's office: Daniel Schwartz, Lucille Horne, Richard Weidenbacher, Thomas O'Rourke, Alan Perry, Elizabeth Owen, David Kelly, Linda Solomon, Lewis Frumkes, Claire Owen, Sue Beherens, Roy Tietze, Ann Jablon, and too many others to name. They gave generously of their time and guidance.

I am indebted to Hana Silverstein, Rusty Fischer, Claire McCullough and Baruch Wolhendler, who read through early drafts of the book and made excellent suggestions. Thanks to my editor Michaela Hamilton for her vision and enthusiasm. I was so lucky to find her.

I am deeply grateful to my husband, Gene. Without his patience and humor, I would never have started, or finished, *The Measure of Madness.*

INDEX